The
North
Sea

Also by Alistair Moffat

The Sea Kingdoms: The History of Celtic Britain and Ireland
The Borders: A History of the Borders from Earliest Times
Before Scotland: The Story of Scotland Before History
Tyneside: A History of Newcastle and Gateshead
from Earliest Times
The Reivers: The Story of the Border Reivers
The Wall: Rome's Greatest Frontier
Tuscany: A History
The Highland Clans
The Faded Map: The Lost Kingdoms of Scotland
The Scots: A Genetic Journey
Britain's Last Frontier: A Journey Along the Highland Line
The British: A Genetic Journey
Hawick: A History from Earliest Times
Bannockburn: The Battle for a Nation
Scotland: A History from Earliest Times
The Hidden Ways: Scotland's Forgotten Roads
To the Island of Tides: A Journey to Lindisfarne
The Secret History of Here: A Year in the Valley
Between Britain: Walking the History of England and Scotland

The
North
Sea

Along the Edge
of Britain

ALISTAIR MOFFAT

CANONGATE

First published in Great Britain in 2025
by Canongate Books Ltd, 14 High Street, Edinburgh EH1 1TE

canongate.co.uk

1

British Library Cataloguing-in-Publication Data
A catalogue record for this book is available on
request from the British Library

ISBN 978 1 83726 122 2

Typeset in Dante MT by Palimpsest Book Production Ltd,
Falkirk, Stirlingshire

Printed and bound by CPI Group (UK) Ltd, Croydon CR0 4YY

The manufacturer's authorised representative in the EU for product safety is
Authorised Rep Compliance Ltd, 71 Lower Baggot Street, Dublin D02 P593 Ireland
(arccompliance.com)

MIX
Paper | Supporting
responsible forestry
FSC
www.fsc.org FSC® C013604

For the woman who wept at the memory of the men who flew the night sea.

Contents

Introduction   I

I.   THAMES

   1. The Beginning of History   II

   2. Beside the Seaside, Beside the Sea   29

   3. The Sea and the City   49

II.   HUMBER

   1. Waterworld   77

   2. Billy Butlin   104

   3. Over the Night Sea   III

III. TYNE

   1. The Holy Coast   129

   2. Fish and Chips   144

   3. The Edge of Beyond   151

   4. The Salt Sea   165

IV. FORTH

    1. The Links   179

    2. The Invention of Time   191

    3. Peril Under the Sea   208

    4. Blood on the Ice   235

V. CROMARTY

    1. Yonder   251

    2. German Bight   262

    3. The Last of the Hunters   273

    4. Beyond the Forest   290

VI. FAIR ISLE

    1. Across the Sea of Orcs   311

    2. Local Heroes   326

    3. Envoi: Stories of the Sea   335

Acknowledgements   341

Introduction

Viking, North Utsire, South Utsire, Forties, northwesterly 5 to 7, occasionally gale 8, backing southwesterly and decreasing 4 or 5 for a time, wintry showers, rain and snow later, good, becoming moderate or poor. Cromarty, Forth, Tyne, northwesterly backing southwesterly for a time, 4 or 5, occasionally 6, rain later, moderate or good. Dogger, northwesterly 5 to 7, occasionally gale 8, decreasing 4 or 5 and backing southwesterly for a time, wintry showers, rain later, good, becoming moderate. Fisher, German Bight, northwesterly 6 to gale 8, decreasing 4 or 5 and backing southwesterly later, wintry showers, good. Humber, Thames, Dover, north or northwest 5 or 7, backing southwesterly for a time, wintry showers, good, becoming moderate or poor . . .

The *Shipping Forecast* is a national lullaby. Snug in their beds at the end of another day, hundreds of thousands listen to the hypnotic language of the sea, poetic and mysterious, its rhythms beating out steadily, the announcer's voice even, a little monotonous, almost chanting. Always broadcast at 00.48 precisely, always 350 to 380 words, it begins with a litany, the names of places far beyond the curtains of the night bedroom, out in the dangerous darkness of the North Sea. Few know where Viking, North Utsire, South Utsire or Forties lie, or understand what a backing wind might be. But none of that matters as the bedclothes are pulled close and the announcer talks of gales and winter rain as swelling waves beat on fishing boats and oil tankers as they plough up and down through the watery wastes, worlds away from the safe and sleepy warmth of the day's end.

It seems that those listening late at night on land need the *Shipping Forecast* more than those in peril on the sea. When these broadcasts began in their current form in 1949, captains and their navigators paid close attention, and if bad weather was imminent, that is, arriving in six hours or less, they might not set sail or decide to run for safety to the nearest harbour. But now even small vessels are equipped with sophisticated, satellite-based forecasting. Mike Cohen of the National Federation of Fishermen's Organisations recently commented that 'even the small 15 metre boats in Bridlington have satellite internet . . . I've had video calls from people in the middle of the North Sea.' He went on, 'Fishermen want detail for exactly the spot they're in – not just a summary for the nation.' When Cohen's members were asked about the value of the *Shipping Forecast*, their replies were surprising, nothing to do with meteorology: '[it] acted as a link across communities, a link across time' or 'a reassuring connection to the past'. Cohen himself believed that listening to it was like 'going to the edge of the nation and looking off'.

Immediately before the announcer reads the forecast, the BBC plays 'Sailing By', a popular and pleasant piece of light music composed by Ronald Binge. Its use of woodwind, flute, harp and xylophone with swelling strings makes it sound appropriately watery, and its slow-waltz time feels wave-like, and soporific. After the forecast has finished the national anthem lulls listeners to sleep and Radio 4 closes down for the night.

The place of the *Shipping Forecast* in the nation's sense of itself was heavily underlined in 1995. After the BBC published plans to move the time of the broadcast from 00.48 to 01.00, only twelve minutes later, there was an immediate outcry. The BBC was besieged by a huge and negative public reaction; from all over Britain an avalanche of letters was sent and the switchboards were jammed. Encouraged by their furious constituents, MPs made outraged speeches at Westminster, and there were angry editorials. The proposed schedule change was quietly dropped.

What this furious reaction – to a very minor change – showed was something unexpected, and elusive. Even though the forecast is of little practical use to shipping, it appears to be a rare example of undisputed Britishness, cross-border, something precious and not to be tampered with. Zeb Soanes began reading the forecast in 2001. He was born and raised on the shores of the North Sea, in the old fishing port of Lowestoft. He wrote that '[the forecast] reinforces a sense of being islanders with a proud sea-faring past'. Later, he added:

The forecast gives the wind direction and force, atmospheric pressure, visibility and the state of the sea . . . [it is] popular with millions of people who never have cause to put to sea and have little idea of what it actually means . . . far out over the waves it's a wilder and dangerous picture, one that captures the imagination and leads it into uncharted waters whilst you sleep. Dependable, reassuring and never hurried, in these uncertain times, the *Shipping Forecast* is a still, small voice of calm across the airwaves.

It is also a distillation of memory, an ancestral memory of a time when the North Sea was not a formless, wind-swept, perilous, precarious blank, a space to be crossed. The sea was once central to the lives of all the islanders of Britain. Until the Atlantic began to be crossed regularly in the seventeenth century, it was our sea, *Mare Nostrum,* a maritime highway, a vital source of food. Its dangerous moods, its near land-locked shape, its violence, fauna and flora helped form our idea of ourselves, all of us, and not only the communities who lived on or near its edges. Now, twenty-six million Britons live by the North Sea, but they rarely see it as more than a distant, grey horizon, and much of its story has long been submerged or lost amongst the wrack and tang along its shoreline.

⋆ ⋆ ⋆

Living almost exactly halfway up, or down, the length of Britain, close to the border between England and Scotland, to tell the story of the North Sea I had to make a funda-mental, defining decision. It seemed that much the best way was to get as close to it as possible, to make a journey up, or down, its long coastline. I'd stop at places that punctuate the narrative and occasionally get into a boat to understand how the land looked from the sea and what it felt like to be on it. But where to start? North or south? Distance made no difference. I live almost exactly 650 kilometres south of Shetland and 650 kilometres north of Kent.

In 1959 my mum gave me a copy of *Philip's Modern School Atlas* for my birthday. In her neat copperplate she wrote on the title page: Alistair M. Moffat, 42 Inchmead Drive, Kelso, 16-6-59. I covered the atlas with brown paper neatly folded on the inside of the boards and stuck down with red tape, wrote my name on the front and drew a compass under it. More than sixty years later I still look at its maps and graphs. It is a magnificent compendium of comprehensive, clear and attractively drawn and coloured maps of everything that mattered, from world rainfall, isobars and winds to Asia's population, languages and religions. From a precocious age I knew that over much of Siberia the indigenous population spoke not Russian but Ostyak, Yakut and Tungus. My mum knew how to get value for her 17/6d.

Page 11, Europe Physical (as opposed to Europe Political), not only shows the whole of the North Sea but also, in faint red lines, it marks off the areas of the *Shipping Forecast*, naming each one. These supply a handy definition of where the North Sea begins and ends. The northern boundary of Viking runs straight from the Norwegian coast near Bergen to the tip of Unst, the northernmost island in the Shetland archipelago. The southernmost area is Thames, and the straight red line marking it off from Dover (where the English Channel meets the North Sea at the Straits of Dover) runs from the Rhine Estuary near Zeebrugge to North Foreland at the easternmost tip of Kent.

Most persuasive is the fact that page 11 clearly shows the shape of the North Sea. It is like a funnel with the narrowest part in the south and the widest where the sea meets the North Atlantic between Shetland and Norway. Where Europe was closest, it seemed obvious that contact would be greatest, and history would happen. North Foreland was clearly the place to begin.

Passengers on trains that trundle south out of the station at Berwick-upon-Tweed immediately see a spectacular view of the North Sea coast. Instead of a tunnel or the back gardens of endless suburban terraces, they look out from the Royal Border Bridge towards the distant outlines of the Holy Island of Lindisfarne and of Bamburgh Castle. It is magnificent, and when I began my journey to Kent on a bright spring morning, the view stirred an ancient memory. The same year as my mum gave me the precious gift of the *Philip's Modern School Atlas* we went on a first seaside holiday, thirty kilometres from landlocked 42 Inchmead Drive, Kelso.

After crossing the great bridge, the train had begun to pick up speed as we passed the caravan park at Spittal, a modest resort to the south of the Tweed Estuary. My dad had borrowed a caravan from a friend, and we all crammed into it after days on the beach, when it wasn't raining. On a dark night we went down into the little town for a treat, a fish and chip supper – or rather two fish and chip suppers shared between the five of us and bulked out by extra bags of chips and essential pickled onions.

On the way back up the hill to the caravan park the sky seemed to darken even more, and suddenly it poured with torrential rain. At the top of the steps leading from the road I turned to look out to sea, already drenched and not hurrying. Just at that moment thunder roared and sheet lightning crackled across the sky. For a moment it lit the North Sea so brightly that I could see the silhouette of a large ship on the furthest horizon. It's an image I've never forgotten, one of drama, danger and a sense of beyond.

On pages 26 and 27 of the *Philip's Modern School Atlas* are maps of the old counties of England and Wales, and Scotland and Ireland. A comparison with page 19, British Isles – Population and Industries, is telling. My family for many generations worked as farm servants and ploughmen in Berwickshire, which now has a population of only 19,000. Only Sutherland is smaller. In Kent, the density is a hundred times greater with a population today of 1.88 million over broadly the same area, and the southeast of England is by far the most heavily populated part of Britain. As my train trundled south, I was moving from one world into another.

Having lived on a farm for more than twenty-five years, where our nearest neighbours are a kilometre or so away, I find myself unused to crowded pavements, packed transport and the length of time it takes to do almost everything. Highlanders travelling south often feel the same way and talk eloquently of 'Abhainn an t'Sluaigh', 'the River of People'. Would it wash away attempts to make connections with the past, to discern patterns, to see if there were cultural links between the communities strung out along the 1,300 kilometres and more of the North Sea coastline? Would I be able to *see* anything? Older places are often palimpsests, pages where recent events have overwritten earlier texts, but the metaphor of layers of stories and meanings seemed too fixed, too static as the River of People flowed, tumbling all the debris of history in its currents. Perhaps much had been washed away.

As the train rattled on southwards, crossing the Tyne Bridge at Newcastle, passing the grandeur of Durham Cathedral, it felt as though I was on an expedition. The day before, I had decided to take only a small backpack with clean pants, shirts, socks and a toothbrush. Spare items like specs and a second mobile phone (to use as a camera) that I had habitually taken when walking in the wilds of the Highlands or the Cheviot Hills were discarded after I reminded myself that I would be visiting terra incognita not terra barbarica. If I needed something, there were shops. But travelling light, with only the backpack, makes for easy movement and easy changes of plan. And it forces a focus on what I'd come to see and not the business of getting there or moving around.

I
Thames

The Beginning of History

Perfectly horizontal where it met the sky, steel-grey and on a windless day, undisturbed, with no whitecaps and only the most sluggish of waves on the foreshore below the cliffs, the North Sea seemed peaceful, almost pond-like. A dozen long tankers lay at anchor, and just visible, far out towards the straight horizon, the sails of scores of wind turbines were motionless. I was walking uphill, not a common direction on the flat landscape of the Isle of Thanet, the easternmost part of Kent. Rising white and somehow monumental, the North Foreland light-house was my destination, the place where the red line in my *Philip's Modern School Atlas* made landfall. It was the beginning of the North Sea, the beginning of a 1,300-kilometre journey and the beginning of many stories.

Freshly and brightly painted so that in daylight it would act as a very visible seamark, and flanked by two tidy and identical houses, the lighthouse seemed the antithesis of the remote, wave-lashed towers manned by teams of keepers working in shifts around the clock. North Foreland stands in a manicured garden, its lush lawns freshly cut and shrubs trimmed. Outside one of the houses was a picnic table surrounded by four chairs. Whoever lives in the houses and likes to dine alfresco has nothing to do with maintaining the light. In 1998 North Foreland was the last lighthouse in Britain to become fully automatic when Prince Philip presided at the ceremonial switchover from manual operation.

Appearances were, as usual, deceptive. The lighthouse may stand more than 300 metres from the edge of the sea cliffs, but it has been carefully placed to have maximum effect. Its light rises fifty-seven metres above mean high water, and in clear weather it can be seen out to sea from a distance of thirty kilometres. Vessels are advised by Trinity House – the authority that manages lighthouses for England, Wales, the Channel Islands and, surprisingly, Gibraltar – to stand well offshore 'because confused seas build up inshore'.

On the fresh spring morning when I walked up the little hill to North Foreland to look out over a calm sea, it was in fact nothing of the kind. Below the pond-like surface, immensely powerful elemental forces were at work, forces that would shape history and form cultures. It was high tide, a moment of intense daily drama, when the sea became confused.

The twice-daily tides may helpfully be thought of as the effects of a single, gigantic wave that approaches the shores of Britain from the west. As the earth turns and aligns with the moon, its gravitational pull creates a huge blob in the ocean as it tugs the water towards it. This creates a high tidal wave that travels across the Atlantic, and at Land's End it divides. One wave goes north, passing the Irish and Welsh coasts before rounding the northern shores of Scotland and turning south into the North Sea. The second wave flows up the English Channel. As the peak of each one passes a stretch of coastline, that time is high tide, and when the trough following it arrives, about six hours later, that is low tide. The two high tidal waves that flow around Britain meet where the Thames Estuary becomes the North Sea, offshore from North Foreland. As these powerful currents collide, the sea becomes 'confused', ships' captains become wary and history happens.

When the moon tugs at the waters of the Atlantic Ocean it also creates an equally enormous blob in the Pacific, on the diametrically opposite side of the globe, to create its tides. This may seem counterintuitive, but in fact it is logical. The gravity of the moon is strong enough not only to pull the waters of the Atlantic towards it, it can also pull the mass of the earth away from the Pacific Ocean to create a second blob. And the same thing happens when the positions of the oceans relative to the moon is reversed. This is why there are two high tides each day in the world's seas.

Because of the meeting of the two great waves at the mouth of the Thames Estuary, the tidal range is high, averaging 7.5 metres, or four tall men standing on each other's heads. The Romans and the Greeks called the North Sea 'the Ocean'. Some time around 325 BC a Greek explorer, Pytheas of Massalia (the name of the colony at Marseilles), circumnavigated the British Isles. His account was entitled *On the Ocean*, and while the original manuscript has not survived, it was so widely plagiarised and quoted by other classical authors that some of it can be reconstructed. Pytheas certainly saw North Foreland from the sea and may have come ashore near where the lighthouse now stands, for he described the headland as one of the 'corners' of Britain, calling it 'Kantion', or Kent, no doubt repeating his transliteration of a native place name. It looks Old Welsh in origin, and may mean something like 'corner land' or 'land on the edge'.

The Roman historian and politician Pliny the Elder, writing around 70 AD, quotes the Greek explorer: 'Pytheas of Massalia informs us that in Britain the tide rises 80 cubits.' Since that ancient unit of measurement is roughly half a metre, giving a tidal of range of thirty-seven metres, it must be either a great miscalculation or an exaggeration. But it nevertheless makes the point that in contrast to the normally calm waters of the Mediterranean, where the range is only half a metre, or one cubit, the tides of the North Sea were seen by the Greeks and the Romans as enormous – and terrifying. Pytheas was also the first to associate the phases of the moon with the tidal cycle and was therefore able to predict the times of low and high tide.

In 54 BC the great orator, lawyer and politician Cicero was anxious about his brother Quintus. He was an officer in Julius Caesar's invasion force when it crossed the Channel to Britain. Here is part of Cicero's reply to his brother:

How glad I was to get your letter from Britain! I was afraid of the Ocean, afraid of the coast of the island. The other parts of the enterprise I do not underrate; but yet they inspire more hope than fear.

Both of Caesar's attempts to invade were failures but not, as Cicero guessed, because of the inability of the Roman army to defeat the native kings. The Greek geographer Strabo was clear about why the expeditions were aborted:

The Deified Caesar crossed over to the island twice, although he came back in haste, without accomplishing anything great or proceeding far into the island, not only on account of the quarrels that took place in the land of the Celti, among the barbarians and his own soldiers as well, but also on account of the fact that many of his ships had been lost at the time of the full moon, since the ebb-tides and the flood-tides got their increase at that time.

From North Foreland I walked downhill through some well-set suburbs and eventually found the England Coast Path. It threaded its way around the eastern edges of Broadstairs and Ramsgate along sheer chalk cliffs above a rocky foreshore. The only major break in these white ramparts was Ramsgate Harbour. Hundreds of pleasure craft of various sizes and sorts were moored at its jetties.

The sight of them stirred a memory. I had read about the improvised fleet of 'little ships' that sailed across the Channel to the rescue of 330,000 British, French and Allied soldiers stranded on the beaches at Dunkirk in the early summer of 1940. They had sailed from Ramsgate. Private yachts, pleasure boats and launches were requested by the Admiralty because their shallow draught would allow them to get much closer to the beaches than any destroyers or cruisers. Most of the fleet of little ships had come from the banks of the Thames or the harbours of the south coast. The Royal Navy checked each one for seaworthiness and made sure they were properly fuelled before they mustered at Ramsgate Harbour.

Most of the ships were crewed by naval ratings and officers, but some owners insisted they sailed their own vessels. *Sundowner* was a motor yacht owned by Charles Lightoller, a man who knew something about the dangers of sea travel. He had been a second officer on board the *Titanic*. Lightoller needed no naval help, and he crewed his boat with his son Roger and a sea scout, Gerald Ashcroft. They picked up 127 soldiers from Dunkirk while under heavy fire from the Luftwaffe and packed the men so closely together that when they manoeuvred into Ramsgate Harbour the yacht almost capsized because of the numbers clinging on to its narrow decks. But Lightoller and many of the other skippers were familiar with the tides and currents off the Kent coast. The most experienced will have timed their run for the safety of Ramsgate with the tide surging up the Channel from the southwest. Two thousand years before the evacuation from Dunkirk another military expedition almost came to grief because its sailors lacked such essential local knowledge.

Ramsgate seemed to stop very suddenly, and according to my map the England Coastal Path dived off a street and into bushy woodland. It became a narrow, beaten earth track rather than tarmac, and I found myself passing a row of coastguard cottages on my right and then fields grazed by horses. To the left was the sea, but the budding hawthorns, wind-bent trees and high fencing hid it from view. After a kilometre or so of ducking under branches and squelching through muddy puddles, the view at last opened up. The chalk cliffs dipped down to a wide, low bay fringed by what looked like marram grass, and beyond it a beach not of sand but of brown mud.

After more altercations with overgrown bushes, I emerged to find a wide, grassy area with a road above it and terraces of houses on the other side. A sign announced a 'picnic area', and there was a welcome bench that allowed a view over Pegwell Bay. Almost featureless, even unremarkable, it was nevertheless what I had come a long way to see.

With Cicero's brother as one of his staff officers, Julius Caesar launched his first expedition to Britain in 55 BC. And, as the great orator had feared, it turned out to be a near-disaster. Merchants who knew the waters of the Channel and the southern North Sea had been summoned to brief Roman sea captains, but, for whatever reason, they had supplied little information about good harbours or the nature of the feared tides and currents. Caesar took only two legions and carried them across the narrow sea in eighty transports escorted by several warships. Recent archaeology has discovered Roman fortifications at Ebbsfleet on Pegwell Bay, a kilometre or so from where I was sitting. The bay was a wide and inviting break in the high chalk cliffs that guard much of the Kent coast.

After Julius Caesar ordered his transports to sail as close to the muddy beach as possible, the North Sea became a determinant factor in what happened next. The ships carrying the legions were too low in the water to get close to the shore, and soldiers were forced to jump into the deeps. Many were reluctant, and it was later said that a standard bearer took the initiative and plunged into the sea, daring his comrades to follow and protect their sacred eagle. Even though the tale is almost certainly apocryphal, part of Caesar's highly effective output of propaganda, the Romans did manage to establish a beachhead and quickly dug the defensive ditches of a fort, the remains of which the archaeologists of Leicester University uncovered in 2017.

That turned out to be the extent of Caesar's attempt to conquer Britain. For it was defended not so much by its native kings and their warriors but by the nature of the sea. The transports carrying the Roman cavalry Caesar needed in order to make inroads into Kent had sailed into Pegwell Bay but had been turned back by storms and the tides of a confused sea, where the great tidal waves that circled Britain met. The warships that had been dragged ashore and beached on the mudflats were inundated by unusually high tides, and the transports riding at anchor in the bay were smashed against each other by the heaving seas. Some were wrecked, others lost their masts. But even though the beleaguered Romans were attacked several times, they managed to repair their badly damaged fleet and get away back to Gaul and safety.

A year later some lessons had been learned. Caesar led a much larger force across the Channel, with 800 ships mooring in Pegwell Bay. For the native British watching from the clifftops, the arrival of this huge armada must have been an astonishing, belly-hollowing sight, more ships and more soldiers than anyone had ever seen. Advised by Gaulish shipwrights, the new transports had a shallower draught to allow them to approach closer to the shore. And Roman navigation had also improved. The anchorage in the bay was protected by long sandbanks to the east. Known as the Downs, it was used for millennia as a refuge in bad weather. It was the daily collisions of the two tidal waves that had created the shifting sandbanks, the swirling currents sufficiently powerful to move great tonnages of sand. Almost sixteen kilometres long and about half a metre above the surface at low tide, the best known of the banks is the Goodwin Sands. But the anchorage is unprotected in the south and it may be that a particularly high tide surged up the Channel towards the Roman fleet. As Caesar advanced inland from Ebbsfleet, he received news that forty of his ships lying at anchor had been badly damaged. A legion had to march back to Pegwell Bay to repair them. Unwilling to spend a winter in Britain at the end of an unreliable supply chain, Caesar embarked his army and returned to Gaul.

For two millennia the North Sea was a watery rampart, but it also acted as a link that brought more than war. Until the coming of the railways in the middle of the nineteenth century, travel on land was always slower and arguably more dangerous than moving across the water or along the coastlines of the seas and the oceans. Peaceful cultural links with Western Europe and further afield were constantly being forged through trade and migration, but invasions and raids were more dramatic, more memorable, more of a story. And as I stood up and stretched my stiff legs (it had been a longer walk from North Foreland than it looked on the map), I decided to move further round Pegwell Bay in search of a more recent landing.

And in moments I found it. Off to my left a remarkable object seemed to hove into view. It was a large replica of a Viking dreki, a dragon-ship, cradled on a long wooden rack and covered with a tight tarpaulin. The carved head on the prow, no doubt designed to strike fear, looked oddly clown-like, something from a fairground, despite its fangs and pointy ears. A sign explained:

The replica Viking ship 'Hugin' was sailed from Denmark in 1949 by 53 Danes to commemorate the 1,500th anniversary of the arrival of the legendary Hengist and Horsa, two Saxon chieftains, who landed at nearby Ebbsfleet. Hengist became the first Saxon King of Kent.

Well, why not? And to add to the fun, a signpost nearby pointed directly out to sea, and on it was one word: Rome. The significance seemed clear. Saxons 1: Romans 0. Caesar failed precisely where the Saxons had succeeded. This, of course, ignores the four centuries of the Roman province of Britannia, but, to use an Anglo-Saxon term, it seemed churlish even to remember that. The point was a simple one. The Romans were a bunch of foreigners, maybe even Italians for goodness' sake, but when our lads, Hengist and Horsa, arrived, well that was that. The English had come home. I'm certain that interpretation is not entirely fanciful.

Another inscription close by was even more emphatic. On a chunky, much-weathered stone that looked as though it belonged in a graveyard were these words:

This stone set down and inscribed by the Corporation of Ramsgate was unveiled by HH Prince George of Denmark on 29th July, 1949, and commemorates the beginning of English history with the landing at Ebbsfleet in this vicinity of Hengist and Horsa in AD 449.

The beginning of English history? I suppose it had to start somewhere – and helpfully, Ramsgate Corporation knew exactly where. And presumably Prince George of Denmark agreed, his ancestors having had a hand in it. But rather than smirking at the ironies swirling around this lump of historical certainty, it is worth unravelling it a little. Origin stories or legends still matter in a nation's sense of itself, and fiction can be as powerful as historical fact in the formation of identity.

The date of 449 and the arrival of the brothers Hengist and Horsa first appear in the work of Bede of Jarrow, a monastic historian of the early eighth century. His magisterial work, *The Ecclesiastical History of the English People* noted that the brothers were Jutes (and not Saxons) from Jutland, part of northern Denmark. That was the reason why Ramsgate Corporation invited Prince Georg (he gained a second 'e' thanks to the English stone carver) of Denmark – a member of the royal family and a cousin of King George VI of Great Britain as well as a career diplomat – to unveil the stone. And it was why the crew of fifty-three Danes sailed the North Sea in their replica dragon-ship, even though these ships did not exist in the fifth century. The title of Bede's great work also allowed Ramsgate Corporation to claim that English history began on their doorstep at Pegwell Bay because that was where the first of the English landed. In a tidy summary of events and processes that were undoubtedly much more complicated and messy, Bede explained that England was the product of the coming of the Saxons, the Jutes and the Angles, the latter giving the nation its name. This neat account was still clearly believed and accepted in 1949, and to some extent it is still a powerful component of many people's sense of Englishness. No amount of historical nit-picking will alter England's notion of itself as basically Anglo-Saxon.

The sign by the replica ship is younger than the inscribed stone, and it talks of Hengist and Horsa as 'legendary'. The names mean Stallion and Horse, but that is not to say that such people did not exist. Warriors in history often took the names of animals. But rather than indulge in a spasm of pseudo-academic debunking of myths, two much more important aspects of these stories are worth emphasising. The North Sea certainly brought the English to England, and, as invaders or settlers, they came, like the Romans, to Pegwell Bay in Kent, to the place where the story of the sea begins. And it turned out that the England Coast Path led me to one of the places where England began.

It also, eventually, led me to another beginning, the first stirrings of what turned out to be another quintessential component of Englishness. On a zig-zag railing designed to force a slight diversion off the Coast Path, I noticed a small sticker. Around a drawing of a winding path that led to a monumental crucifix were the words 'Augustine Camino'. It looked like a borrowing from the Camino de Santiago, the Way of St James, the pilgrim route to Santiago de Compostela, the shrine of the Apostle James in northern Spain. This camino was dedicated to the life and achievements of the apostle of the English, the first bishop of Canterbury and the founder of the Church in England. Few may now attend church every Sunday, but recent surveys show almost half of the population still identify as C of E, Church of England.

In 597 Augustine landed at Pegwell Bay with forty companions. He had been sent to Britain on a mission of conversion by Pope Gregory I. Here is the relevant passage from Bede's *Ecclesiastical History of the English People*:

At this time the most powerful king there [in Britain] was Ethelbert, who reigned in Kent and whose domains extended northwards to the River Humber, which forms the boundary between the North and South Angles. To the east of Kent lies the large island of Thanet, which by English reckoning is six hundred hides [small farms] in extent; it is separated from the mainland by a waterway about three furlongs [600 metres] broad called the Wantsum, which joins the sea at either end and is fordable in only two places. It was here that God's servant Augustine landed with companions, who are said to have been forty in number . . . the king ordered them to remain on the island where they had landed, and gave directions that they were to be provided for with all necessaries until he should decide what action to take.

When I left the stranded Viking ship to walk down to where Augustine probably came ashore, there was a noticeable dip where the Wantsum Channel had once been. By the end of the Middle Ages, it had silted up and is now marked by the meander of the River Stour before it falls into Pegwell Bay. It lay on an east-facing spur of the island.

Judging by the speed and relative ease with which Ethelbert (and his people, who followed the example of their king) was converted, it very much sounds as though diplomacy had reached the bay before Augustine and his companions had splashed ashore. The queen of Kent, Bertha, was a Gaulish princess whose father had made it a condition of her marriage contract that she was allowed to practise her faith amongst her pagan subjects. There was also the issue of prestige. Ethelbert called himself *Bretwalda*, Britain-Ruler, and Bede noted that he held *imperium* south of the River Humber. A powerful sense of borrowed glory was in the air, of the Kentish king and others who followed him wishing to bask in the afterglow of the Roman Empire, an aura that would confer the legitimacy that incomers craved. Christianity was the imperial religion, and its pontiff ruled from Rome.

Augustine's *camino* runs in the opposite direction to the route taken by its hero. The pilgrim way begins in Rochester, its cathedral founded by the saint, and then goes to Canterbury, Ethelbert's capital place, where the great cathedral eventually rose. The landing in Kent also meant that the primate of the Church in England would become the archbishop not of London but of Canterbury. From there pilgrims walk the route of the *camino* across country to Pegwell Bay where the original mission made landfall. In Ramsgate there is a shrine at the Church of St Augustine that has perhaps more presence and colour than the windblown mudflats beyond the fringe of marram grass. But it was built in the nineteenth century and was not a place where history happened.

I saw only one more slightly tattered sticker for the *camino* and met no pilgrims, but on my map was St Augustine's Cross. It seemed to stand not far from the shore, somewhere amongst the fairways and greens of St Augustine's Golf Club. I worried that since I wasn't a member I might not be allowed to look at it. But in fact I found the monument very quickly in a fenced enclosure off Cottington Road – or rather I found a late-nineteenth-century replica of an original Anglo-Saxon cross that stands in the market square of Sandbach in Cheshire. Apparently the landowner who had the modern version of St Augustine's Cross carved liked the design. It had another very informative inscription, this time in Latin. Here is a translation:

> After many dangers and difficulties by land and sea Augustine landed at last on the shores of Richborough [close to Pegwell Bay] in the Isle of Thanet. On this spot he met King Ethelbert, and preached his first sermon to our own countrymen. Thus he happily

planted the Christian Faith, which spread with marvellous speed throughout the whole of England. That the memory of these events may be preserved among the English, G G L-G [Granville George Leveson-Gower], Earl Granville, Lord Warden of the Cinque Ports has erected this monument, AD 1884.

Pegwell Bay seemed an uncommonly rich source of historical hyperbole, to say nothing of a misplaced nationalism. Just as English history apparently began with Hengist and Horsa about 400 metres from the replica cross, so Christianity was planted in England by Augustine in 597. The reality is that it wasn't. There had been many congregations of Christians in the later period of the Roman province of Britannia, and the martyr, St Alban, who gave his name to the town, was a Roman soldier who died in 305. Three British bishops attended the church council at Arles in the south of France in 314, and there are many other references to Christians and Christianity in the Roman period and in the fifth century after the province was abandoned.

Britain's sole surviving work of history before Bede was written by Gildas, a priest. He compiled *De Excidio et Conquestu Britanniae, On the Ruin and Conquest of Britain*. According to Gildas, Britain was being ruined by its hopeless, squabbling, immoral native kings who could not unite to keep the pagan English – the Angles, Saxons, Jutes and others – at bay. As with the stone commemorating Hengist and Horsa, definitions are at once sloppy and unintentionally precise. Augustine may be seen as the apostle of the English but not of the British. Many were already Christians, even in Kent. When the native kings did occasionally unite to fight the Anglo-Saxons, they called themselves *Y Bedydd,* the Baptised, and their enemies were *Y Gynt,* the Heathens. And Augustine's mission was most certainly not the stimulus for the spread of Christianity over the whole of England. Not only were many natives already baptised, such missions of conversion as were needed came from a quite different direction. St Columba sailed from Ireland to found his monastery on Iona in 563, and in 634 Aidan travelled from there to Lindisfarne to begin the conversion of Northumbria, a large Anglian kingdom whose aggressive and expansionist rulers became *Bretwaldas.*

What to make of all these collisions and coincidences, of matters of a dubious but enduring sense of English national identity so confidently asserted in one tiny corner of the Kent coastline? A vast armada of 800 Roman warships and troop transports riding at anchor in the Downs, the arrival, if not of Hengist and Horsa, then certainly the establishment of the first powerful dynasty of Danish / Germanic incomers in Kent, the coming of a version of Christianity with Augustine, to say nothing, or very little, of Viking raiders in the early ninth century – all of these epoch-making events took place along a few hundred metres of shoreline. Pegwell Bay's deceptive anonymity turns out to be a cradle of Englishness, and it was one rocked by the waters of the North Sea.

It was the sea that shaped – and continues to shape – the coastline, sculpting the chalk cliffs, breaking through to the mouth of the Thames Estuary to create the Wantsum Channel and make Thanet an island, piling up the sandbanks to supply the shelter of the Downs and, most determinant of all, it was the sea that created the confusion off North Foreland, where the great tidal waves and currents that wash around Britain meet. The closeness of Kent to the coast of Western Europe was of course also determinant, but the concentration of events and meetings at Pegwell Bay is remarkable. It was a good place to begin and to see how the North Sea shaped history.

2

Beside the Seaside, Beside the Sea

Everyone delights to spend their summer
   holiday
Down beside the side of the silvery sea
I'm no exception to the rule
In fact, if I'd my way
I'd reside by the side of the silvery sea.

But when you're just the common or garden
Smith, Jones or Brown
At business up in town
You've got to settle down
You save up all the money you can till summer
   comes around
Then away you go
To a spot you know
Where the cockle shells are found.

Oh! I do like to be beside the seaside
I do like to be beside the sea!
I do like to be upon the Prom, Prom, Prom!
Where the brass bands play

'Tiddley-om-pom-pom-pom!'
So just let me be beside the seaside
I'll be beside myself with glee
And there's lots of girls besides
I should like to be beside
Beside the seaside!
Beside the sea!

Written by John A. Glover-Kind and sung by the popular music-hall singer Florrie Forde, 'I Do Like to Be Beside the Seaside' became and has remained an anthem and a celebration of a cultural love affair. I first heard its catchy, earworm chorus on a train in the 1950s. It wasn't a normal passenger service but a transport to a different and wonderful world, one that lay beside the seaside, beside the sea.

Each summer, in the school holidays, the churches of Kelso organised what was known as Spittal Trip. A special train was chartered from British Rail, and before boarding it schoolchildren gathered in church halls and each one was given a label with a number on it to thread through their lapels, like evacuees in the Second World War. Some parents came along as helpers. Led by the local minister in his dog collar and black coat (probably not humming the chorus of Florrie Forde's anthem under his breath), the children marched through the town to the railway station where the older ones were given small rolls of coloured streamers. By the time the guard had blown his whistle and the driver had hooted his horn several times, the steam hissed and the train clanked into life, the streamers had been unrolled and wedged into the sliding windows of the carriages so that they flew behind us as we were transported in all senses.

We were all off to the seaside, and amongst other songs we sang 'I Do Like to Be Beside the Seaside'. I can still recall its jaunty chorus, word for word. There was no brass band on the promenade at Spittal, a very small and modest sort of resort, but the whole trip was magical – and free, and much anticipated by excited, landlocked children who lived sixty-five kilometres from the sea. Once we alighted from the train at Tweedmouth we marched in double file down to another church hall where each of us was given a brown paper bag filled with a sandwich, a Scotch pie and an iced bun. There were wooden crates of splits – small bottles of lemonade with straws poking out of their necks – for us to drink before we set off for the beach to build sandcastles and splash around in the waves. There exists a photograph of me with my sisters (Barbara has the label in her lapel) sitting on the sand with the wall of the prom behind us. Beside us on deckchairs are Ronnie and Suzie Taylor, who lived at 39 Inchmead Drive. Spittal Trip was a relic, a cheerful example of Victorian charity, one that survived into the middle of the twentieth century and an annual wonder for us as we counted off the days. And it was also something steeped in tradition, a sandy, sticky, gaudy tradition that was the sole experience of the North Sea for many millions of day-trippers, caravan renters and holidaymakers. It was another world but one that most could afford to visit.

A lifetime later I found myself in St Pancras station,

London, looking for a train that would take me back to the seaside, beside the sea. Behind the soaring magnificence of its façade, rescued from the threat of demolition by the poet John Betjeman and others in the 1960s, is a vast new concourse of shops, cafés and restaurants all sympathetically integrated. I'd never used the station before and spent so much time looking around and also up at the monumental bronze sculpture 'The Meeting Place' and the superb statue of Betjeman – hanging on to his hat, glancing up at the sky or, more likely, the splendid architecture of what he had helped preserve – that I had to hurry to catch my train to Margate.

Once through the anonymous eastern sprawl of London and its many suburban stops, the train began to slide quietly through the Kentish countryside. The spring sunshine lit the lush landscape as we passed undulating, well-drained pasture bordered by hedges new and fresh into leaf. As the train slowed on the approach to Canterbury I watched a groundsman mow and roll a cricket pitch, its grass as smooth as billiard-table baize. When we drew into the station I could make out the spikey spires of the cathedral, its pale stone luminous. Moored on the banks of the River Stour were many boats, the sort of pleasure craft summoned to Ramsgate Harbour in the summer of 1940. And then, when the train slowed once more, I watched a few preliminary moments of an English idyll: two ladies unfolding chairs on the veranda of a wooden cricket pavilion. It looked out over a manicured ground bounded by a wide loop of the Stour and fringed by willows, whose leaves would soon weep over its banks. It struck me that I was travelling through *Angleterre profonde,* the most English part of England – perhaps it could be seen as the ancient legacy of Angles, Saxons and the Jutes who landed their ships on the mud of Pegwell Bay and founded Ethelbert's Kingdom of Kent.

In the 1960s John Betjeman seemed often to be on TV, chuckling and musing about the detail of (middle-class) life in England and bemoaning modernism in most of its forms, particularly architectural. As I gazed at the contented Kent countryside I understood that the Poet Laureate not only wrote to order when national events needed versifying but was also the bard of *Angleterre profonde.* I remembered him reading 'The Village Inn' on TV and looked it up on my phone. Here is the first verse:

> The village inn, the dear old inn,
> So ancient, clean and free from sin,
> True centre of our rural life,
> Where Hodge sits down beside his wife.

It was mostly bogus, of course, a poetic pining after a past that probably never existed and was certainly alien to most of England's population, the inhabitants not of villages but large towns and cities. But the sentiments were popular, bathed in a drowsy nostalgia, scenes from an English version of Brigadoon. When Betjeman was first proposed as Poet Laureate in 1967, after the death of John Masefield, Lord Goodman, Harold Wilson's lugubrious advisor, was chairman of the Arts Council. He wrote to the Labour prime minister's appointments secretary:

The songster of tennis lawns and cathedral cloisters does not, it seems to me, make a very suitable incumbent for the poet laureateship of a new and vital world in which we hope we are living. An aroma of lavender and faint musk is not right for an appointment of this kind at this moment. It is much too nostalgic and backward looking.

That seemed to me to sum up precisely the attraction of Betjeman for most people. His work was often sticky with nostalgia, but it could also be very funny – and very English. His dislike of modern architecture was very widely shared, as it harked back to an impossible idea of a bucolic present that might involve cattle:

> Come friendly bombs and fall on Slough!
> It isn't fit for humans now,
> There isn't grass to graze a cow.
> Swarm over, Death!

On the train from London to Margate I was following not only John Betjeman but also many millions of others who had come in search of another aspect of Englishness. To be beside the seaside, beside the sea was an aspiration for many, many more than might have had access to tennis lawns or the pony club or any of the other tropes of Betjeman's beloved but irredeemably middle-class England. From the middle of the nineteenth century trains from London brought vast numbers east to the Kentish coast on day trips or for longer visits, and even before then thousands would sail down the Thames on large passenger ferries. Margate station is built like a grand gateway to the sea. When trippers like me emerged from under its arch the vista over the beach and out to the blue yonder was immediate and unimpeded, the sands only two hundred metres away. I was drawn to the windy promenade as though it was a magnet.

Margate beach is remarkable. At low tide when I arrived, it stretched a long way before it met the lapping waves of a calm North Sea, and the sand was so fine that it looked like it had been sieved and then swept clean. It was flawless, strangely uniform, as though a vast fleet of trucks had unloaded it the day before and smoothed it out. No seaweed, wrack or any sort of irregularity disturbed its perfect surface. There were no crumbling breakwaters, no rocks or clumps of marram grass, nothing to interfere with its perfection.

Perhaps it was the beach and its flawless sand that sparked the cultural revolution that eventually brought about Britain's full-blown love affair with the seaside. Coastal towns and villages, whose people were fisherfolk or worked in harbours or ports, had traditionally turned their backs to the sea. Often with their gable ends facing it, houses had sought protection from the wind and weather, and they rarely had sea views. Their occupants saw enough of it every day. The oldest part of Margate is set back from the seafront, its streets narrow, its houses huddled close.

Attitudes began to change in the early eighteenth century as seaside places slowly began to turn their faces towards the North Sea and become resorts. On the Yorkshire coast Scarborough developed as a spa where illness might be cured or eased by the iron-rich waters of its springs. Doctors also began to preach the virtues of sea bathing, something no one had done willingly in the past, to alleviate gout. Others might benefit from walks on the beach, breathing in the clear, bracing sea air. The medical benefits of bathing in the brine were not related to exercise, a crawl or a backstroke through the waves. Total, and sometimes forcible, immersion was recommended. For example, young girls suffering from all sorts of complaints related to age and a growing maturity as much as any illness, were shoved under the surface of the sea by attendants known as 'dippers' and often held down until the recommended time had expired, no matter how much they struggled. It must have been terrifying.

Sea bathing could also lead to displays of immodesty. These chilly, spartan therapies involved the female patients wearing early versions of swimsuits. These were ankle-length, loose with long sleeves and made from wool or flannel. The problems arose when these voluminous garments got wet – and clinging. Bathing machines were the answer and first used on Margate beach around 1750. Women would enter them in their normal clothes by a door on the end facing the shore before shedding their corsets and changing into swimwear. The Irish writer, Wally Chamberlain Oulton, described what happened next:

> Four wheeled carriages, covered with canvas, and having at one end of them an umbrella of the same materials which is let down to the surface of the

water, so that the bather descending from the machine by a few steps is concealed from the public view, whereby the most refined female is enabled to enjoy the advantages of the sea with the strictest delicacy.

Sea bathing for men and women was strictly segregated at first. Not only did the ladies wish to preserve their modesty, men were at that time in the habit of bathing in the nude, all of which proved very tempting for those with excellent eyesight or those in possession of a telescope, binoculars or opera glasses. Men enjoyed the sight of ladies lying in the lapping waves of the foreshore where an incoming tide might lift up their long bathing suits a little to reveal a few inches of pearly white leg. And women were similarly uninhibited as they wandered closer to where naked men were bathing so that they could shamelessly admire such manhood as was on display. By the time Florrie Forde sang about 'lots of girls besides I should like to be beside', the beach had become morally as well as geographically liminal. Even in Victorian Britain there was a slackening, if not a suspension, of famously strict codes.

As Margate turned to face and embrace the sea, the town took all sorts of cultural initiatives in the eighteenth century as more and more trippers boarded the ferries from London. In 1730 commercial sea bathing was on offer when, for a fee, the dippers would take people out into the cold waves and immerse them. By the 1770s there were boarding houses in the town and the first seaside hotel opened its doors. In 1790 that wonderful and eccentric staple of a British beach holiday clopped down to the sands, and donkey rides began. I remember three placid, bored donkeys at Spittal in the late 1950s. When I was plonked on the back of one of them, it was the warm, hairy flanks of another living creature moving beneath me that has stayed in my memory as it plodded a hundred metres along the beach, turned and plodded all the way back to where it had started.

At Margate and all of the other seaside resorts that developed in the nineteenth and early twentieth centuries, it was the beach that formed the focus for visitors. Between the land, which was owned by private individuals or corporations, and the sea, which belonged to no one, the sands seemed to belong to everyone, at least for a few hours. Despite the fact that in most of Britain the Crown owns the foreshore, they were seen as a public space where families might choose a space to pitch windbreaks, unfold deckchairs or simply lay down a towel where they might sunbathe. There was no formal regulation or even much of a presence of any sort of authority beyond the occasional lifeguard. And yet people appeared to respect each other's spaces, avoid trampling on sandcastles or straying over impromptu football or cricket pitches. On sunny, warm days a wide and long beach like Margate's would be swarming with people all co-existing without fuss or friction. And when the tide came in the crowds retreated, and the North Sea washed away all trace of their few hours on the perfect sand. And when the tide went out the following day the cycle of cheerful occupation repeated itself.

On the promenade and behind it there were other

attractions for holidaymakers when the beach was restricted. As I made my way along the seafront, breathing the bracing air of an east wind, I came across a tall tower with 'Dreamland' emblazoned on it. There was a poster advertising a concert with Status Quo on 15 August 2024. From the photograph, I could see that it was not a tribute band but the real thing. The Dreamland website told me, to my amazement, that the band first performed in Margate in 1968, no fewer than fifty-six years before. By the time he took the stage at Dreamland in 2024, the lead singer, Francis Rossi, was seventy-five years old. He and his fellow band members are a musical phenomenon with more than sixty chart hits in Britain, more than any other band.

They may have enjoyed a consistent run of success, but the venue they played in Margate has had a much more chequered history. Dreamland began life in the late nineteenth century as a pleasure garden, a menagerie and a dance hall behind the promenade. In 1920 its signature attraction opened. Now a listed historic structure, the Scenic Railway is a wooden rollercoaster that rattles passengers up and down a short, looping railway track before climbing up to several high points and then descending at speed, accompanied by squeals and shouts, before returning safely to the start. It is an original version of a thrill ride, and so far as I could see built almost entirely out of wood. It is also the only scenic ride in Britain that carries a brake-man on every trip. Mercifully, when I visited the old railway, it was closed.

As was much of Margate seafront. I had come to

the Kent coast on a sunny April day, but almost all of the attractions were closed. Life's a Beach, Beach Treats, Tivoli Amusements and the Flamingo were all shuttered, their colourful, gaudy frontages more than a little forlorn. On the beach there were a few dog walkers, and under the arches of an arcade I could see three tents pitched by people I assumed were homeless. Next to a very brightly painted façade, with little indication of what was behind it, was a blue door with 'Bleak House' inscribed over the lintel.

The heyday of Dreamland, Margate and all of the seaside resorts around Britain lasted from the 1950s to the early 1960s. Giving workers a week's paid leave every year, the Holiday Pay Act was passed into law in 1938. The hiatus of the Second World War and the austerity immediately following it delayed any impact, but as the post-war economy recovered the British began to pack their buckets and spades and head for the beach and all the attractions behind it. Crazy golf, the one-armed bandits of the amusement arcades, Punch and Judy and all the traditional pastimes were accompanied by candy floss, ice cream and, of course, fish and chips. Longer holidays began to supplement weekend or bank holiday outings, and the effect on the economies of resorts like Margate was profound.

But it turned out to be a brief heyday. By the middle of the 1960s and accelerating into the 1970s package tours to Spain and elsewhere were offering guaranteed sunshine and cheap beer and wine. Bracing afternoons in the east wind that blows off the North Sea, clutching Thermos flasks and huddling together on the hard benches of open-fronted shelters, were exchanged for the baking-hot temperatures of Benidorm, Malaga and, later, the Algarve and Tenerife. Margate and the other British resorts such as Blackpool and Bognor Regis still saw a high volume of day-trippers coming at the weekend or on bank holidays, but the overall volume of business was insufficient to sustain the infrastructure of attractions that had built up since the early 1950s. People still came to Margate, but few stayed longer than a day. After decades struggling to compete not only with holidays in the Mediterranean but also with new theme parks in England, Dreamland closed in 2002.

Beyond Bleak House, the clifftop path widened into a tarmacked surface, broader than some Scottish trunk roads, and the suburbs of Cliftonville, eastern Margate, retreated beyond what looked like parkland, unloved grassy areas criss-crossed by muddy tracks. It felt like another liminal space, one large enough to accommodate many strolling holidaymakers, but I found myself walking alone in the sunshine, passed and nodded to by only the occasional dog walker. Weeds grew on the verges, and at intervals old-fashioned cannons of the sort that might have fired broadsides from Horatio Nelson's *Victory* were emplaced. They all pointed out to sea – defending what? History? Heritage? England? Brexit? There were no explanatory information boards.

More could be gleaned from the empty benches strung out between the cannon that also looked out to sea. Many had become informal memorials, a brass plate remembering 'Karen Taylor, 1973–2023, an amazing and loving mother, daughter and friend'. Just as would be found leaning against tombstones in cemeteries, there were withered floral tributes attached to the benches with several cable ties to prevent the sea breeze from blowing them away. Others had laminated cards 'In Loving Memory of a Dear Friend at Christmas'. On a bench with a carved inscription – 'Our Dad loved magic & our Dad was magic! Good night. God Bless' – there was what I at first took to be a pot of fresh roses that on closer inspection turned out to be plastic.

I found these benches very moving, even though I knew nothing of the people they commemorate. What touched me was the trouble those who loved them took, and also the sense that their departed spirits linger on those places that look out over the North Sea. Far more than in the regimented rows of a graveyard full of headstones, there was a sense of the living person. They clearly came to the clifftop to gaze at the long view, and the withered flowers remembered them doing something they loved, something that perhaps gave them peace, and their spirits and memories of them were still to be found in the land of the living and not hidden away behind the walls and railings of grave-yards.

Further along the clifftop tarmac, blocks of new flats crowd closer to the shore. I sat down in the corner of one of the benches and looking up to my right noticed an old man sitting in a glass-fronted balcony. He seemed completely still, his hands folded in his lap, staring fixedly out to sea. I wondered at his thoughts. He sat on the edge of the land, perhaps on the edge of life, looking out over a version of eternity, the edge of beyond. All of the elements of the turning world were around him – the land, the sea and the vastness of the sky. Perhaps he was coming to terms with that version of eternity. Perhaps Margate was a good place to spend the evening of a life. Immediately below the old man's balcony the past will have walked and talked as the summer trippers came; young people chatting, maybe flirting, almost certainly using their smartphones for even more contact. Young couples, some pushing a buggy or shepherding toddlers, may have been followed by older visitors with their dogs sniffing along behind them. For the man on the balcony, looking down at memories of good times, it might have been warming as he stared hypnotically at the grey horizon.

The shade of John Betjeman flitted around the balcony, the old man, his reverie, and perhaps his past life. Having visited the town several times, Betjeman wrote 'Margate 1940'. As Britain looked across the Channel at the looming threat of Nazi invasion, Betjeman offered his summary of what deserved to be defended. It was not only the lofty ideals of parliamentary democracy or the rule of law but also the everyday, the unremarkable rhythms of life, a version of Englishness most people would recognise. Betjeman wrote lovingly and lyrically about privet hedges, bandstands, bottles of sauce and squash, walks on the promenade and the familiar, faded comforts of Margate's seaside hotels. The last verse remembers the rhythms of the end of a bucket-and-spade day beside the sea.

From third floor and fourth floor the children
    looked down
Upon ribbons of light in the salt-scented town;
And drowning the trams roared the sound of
    the sea
As it washed in the shingle the scraps of their
    tea.

The 2021 Census showed that the population of the Isle of Thanet had grown significantly older. Almost 25 per cent are over sixty-five and the overwhelming majority of them are retired. The internet carries long listings of retirement accommodation. There is a new retirement village in Margate with 444 cottages and flats and a population of 630. At the ready are 'a sizable frail-care and dementia-care facility' and accommodation is sold by 'life right', the payment of a lump sum in return for occupation until death or formal relinquishment. All sorts of clumsy metaphors rumble around these arrangements, and no doubt a great deal of dark humour circulates in these communities of the ancient and failing, those who can afford the cost of 'life right'. There is another similar village in Ramsgate and many other varieties of accommodation for retirees.

The sea wind was freshening, and over the horizon leaden-grey clouds were massing. I turned back towards the promenade and headed for a striking modern building that seemed to have its back to the land and its face to the sea. The Turner Contemporary Art Gallery was named for the greatest of English painters, J.M.W. Turner. He had been a schoolboy in Margate in 1786, and the gallery was built on the site of the boarding house where he stayed on his frequent visits to the town. It represents a bold, and very successful, attempt at regeneration, bringing a very different sort of promenade attraction to revive Margate's fortunes, similar to initiatives in Dundee with the V&A on the shores of the Firth of Tay and Titanic Belfast in Northern Ireland. The Turner opened in 2011, and more than 500,000 visitors came in its first year, and by August 2013 a million had visited.

Almost all my life, from my time at university, I have enjoyed looking at paintings, and especially the work of J.M.W. Turner. As part of my degree in medieval history I spent six weeks at the British School in Florence, where I studied Italian in the mornings and for the rest of the day devoured the art of the Renaissance: architecture, sculpture and painting. Access to the Uffizi and all the other galleries was free for students. Looking back, it seems remarkable that a young person with no money and from a background that could never have afforded it could experience all that enrichment. The state paid for everything, for it was a time, all too brief, when education was thought to be so valuable and potentially life-changing that it should cost nothing and be linked only to ability and not money. Since that golden time I've come to enjoy all sorts of figurative art, especially painting.

The Turner Contemporary lived up to its name. *Beyond Form: Lines of Abstraction, 1950–1970,* an exhibition of radical abstract works by fifty women artists, had opened in February 2024. A great deal was lost in translation for, sadly, I could make little of it. With vast windows looking over the North Sea and very pleasingly proportioned spaces, the gallery was magnificent, but the sculptures and paintings didn't speak to me, not one of them.

I retreated to the shop, hoping to buy a monograph, perhaps a catalogue, a book or even a pamphlet that would tell me something of J.M.W. Turner's association with Margate. But there was nothing about the artist who had given his name to the gallery, only postcards of two of his paintings: *A Distant View of Margate after Sunset* and *Sun-Rise, Whiting Fishing at Margate*.

Since my visit I've become even more interested in Turner's links to the Isle of Thanet and the sea that surrounds it on three sides, and it turned out that one of the most powerful links had little to do with painting. The boarding house that stood on the site of the Turner Contemporary was run by Mrs Sophia Booth and her husband, Mr Booth, thirty-seven years her senior. In 1827, on most Saturdays, Turner boarded the passenger ferry at Tower Bridge in London and came down the Thames to Margate to paint and to visit the woman he had fallen in love with. Sophia was twenty-nine when the great painter first set eyes on her, and on the death of her husband they became constant companions. Turner took to calling himself Mr Booth or Admiral Booth. Even though he was twenty-three years older the relationship appears not to have been platonic. There exist about a hundred erotic drawings and watercolours, many of them of the same female nude, almost certainly Sophia, and none of them intended for public display.

However, it is clear that she was not the only seaside attraction. Margate seemed to fascinate Turner, and views from the harbour and the town feature in more than a hundred of his paintings. 'The skies over Thanet are the loveliest in Europe,' he said to the art critic and writer John Ruskin. The sea and the ships also fascinated Turner, and his handling of colours and moods is masterly. Intense, introverted, eccentric and reputedly antisocial, he seemed always to be striving, painting similar scenes over and over again in a relentless effort to get it right, to catch the fleeting moment. Unlike his contemporary John Constable, whose landscapes seemed settled, often domestic and often with a summer warmth about them, Turner painted movement. The tides, and especially those that churned the sea off Thanet, were constantly shifting, covering and then revealing the foreshore. The wind moved clouds and also filled the billowing sails of ships and boats. It beat up storms and could bring darkness to a daytime sky. But it seems that more than anything Turner was fascinated by how the light changed on the edge of the land – and how far he could see it changing out over the North Sea. His painting of light was what so profoundly influenced the early French impressionists, Claude Monet in particular, and John Ruskin hailed Turner as the father of modern painting.

The threadbare cliché of an artist's muse seems not quite to fit. Sophia Booth did not inspire J.M.W. Turner to become a great painter – he was that before he came to Margate – but she brought him back often and made him look more often and more intently at the same place as he strove to catch its drifting moods, its atmosphere and its particular light. *Sun-Rise: Whiting Fishing at Margate* is breath-catching as the low morning sun throws a glistening shaft across the surface of the sea between fishing boats and what seems to be a much larger sailing ship anchored in the bay.

In 1846 Sophia came to live with Turner in Chelsea, and when he died five years later she inherited several sketchbooks. Her son Daniel had some of the drawings and watercolours in them put up for sale separately. They realised a sum large enough for him to buy a country house, and it seems that his mother lived there until her death in 1875. Margate has not forgotten Sophia Booth, and on the Harbour Arm there is a bronze sculpture of a shell lady that has been named after her. As Turner did, she looks out to sea. Perhaps she is waiting for the arrival of the ferry from Tower Bridge.

3

The Sea and the City

During the night, screams of 'Daddy, Daddy!' woke
Geoff and I. We saw Jean falling into the water. Our
mattress was floating, and as Geoff jumped off the
bed, I was thrown against the wall. Jean was floating
very close to the chimney and could have been drawn
up it if Geoff had not been so quick! She was floppy
and listless, and I grabbed her from Geoff and started
patting her back. Suddenly, she came round and was
sick. I stood her on the bed and wrapped her in
blankets.

But, I was waist-deep in water. Geoff managed to
grab a couple of jackets that were on hooks, so we
were still dry, and some of Jean's clothes that were
airing on a line in the kitchen. He then pushed the
table to the corner of the room, put a chair on top,
knocked a hole in the ceiling, got the clothes he had
gathered and climbed into the loft saying, 'Give me
the baby.' I was crying and saying, 'I can't, she's too
heavy.' He shouted at me, 'Drop the bloody blanket
and give her to me or I will hit you.' This is something
he would never do, but it brought me to my senses.

I jumped on the table then on the chair, holding this nude, wriggling, crying baby. As he took her, he fell backwards through the ceiling, ending up with one arm over a rafter and Jean in the other. He had fallen into Jean's bedroom, and as he fell, he felt the feather bed under his feet. By this time I was somehow in the loft. I do not know how I got up there! I took Jean, and Geoff pulled the dry feather bed from the top of the piano, and in doing so the piano slid down [under the water]. As Jean's bed came [floating] towards him, he grabbed the coat I had left there the night before . . .

There was a big blue flash as the water reached the electrics and everything went dark, but the moonlight was very bright, and I was sitting next to a hole in the ceiling. I could see the water getting higher and higher, it had covered our windows, leaving another eighteen inches before it was in the loft. I kept saying to Geoff, 'Break a hole in the roof, break a hole!' Then suddenly the water started to drop. The water eventually went down to the bottom of the window where we could see it was the same level as the top of Central Wall Road . . . some time later we heard voices. Geoff called them, there were policemen and firemen in a boat with no oars. They were pulling it along on a rope. Geoff managed to get the clothesline from the kitchen and the aerial wire that was in the loft. Between them they managed to pull the boat to our window and rescue us . . .

Joan Lythgoe never forgot the events of the night of Saturday 31 January 1953. She and her husband, Geoff, lived on Canvey Island on the north bank of the Thames Estuary, directly in the path of a massive storm surge that drowned more than 300 people on the eastern coasts of Scotland and England and destroyed thousands of homes. It was the shape and nature of the North Sea that created and intensified what became a fatal tide, one that arrived with no warning and caused the worst peace-time disaster in Britain.

When the great tidal wave that had divided at Land's End earlier on that terrible day travelled up the western coasts before turning east and then south, it was driven by a gale force wind between Scotland and Norway. An area of low pressure lay over the North Sea, and that allowed the waves to rise higher. And because the sea is shallow, a greater volume of water built up. Approximately 15 billion cubic metres was added to a gigantic standing wave more than a 160 kilometres across. And the full moon Joan Lythgoe saw through the hole in her roof meant that the gravitational pull on the huge tide was even greater.

On the Lincolnshire coast people noticed a strange yellow tinge in the sky at twilight in the late afternoon. High winds started to blow, and the temperature suddenly dropped. It was dark when the giant wave smashed through the sea defences at Mablethorpe and the other small towns and villages to the south. The sea ran between the dunes. and the flat hinterland was quickly inundated. It was the beginning of great slaughter, because when the storm finally abated the corpses of more than 46,000 animals were found in the fields close to the coast. At about 5 p.m. a policeman reported that there was no ebb tide because 'the wind seemed to be holding the water'. And the low pressure had become trapped over the North Sea in the narrowing funnel between the East Anglian and Dutch coasts.

By 6.30 p.m. the giant wave was breaking into King's Lynn, turning the streets into rushing rivers. Nine people were drowned and hundreds forced to flee their homes. At 7.27 p.m., unaware of what was happening up the coast, a train left Hunstanton for King's Lynn. It was met with a wall of water and forced to a juddering stop. Moments later a complete bungalow was driven against the carriages of the train. Neil Quincy recalled that minutes later in Hunstanton, 'It wasn't like a river overflowing, it was like a raging sea. The first bungalow in our road, it went in through the front door and took the whole back wall out, everything.' At that time there was a substantial American airbase nearby, and thirty-seven bungalows occupied by service personnel were swept away.

As it surged southwards, the deadly wave was gathering strength. A policeman in Harwich watched the sea rising and the high wind howl into a gale. But when he walked down a street near the flood defences, knocking on doors to warn people, he suddenly had to run. The sea had broken through, and a metre-high wave chased him, racing into the heart of the town.

On Canvey Island Andrew Manser was woken by a dog barking incessantly, very agitated. Roused by the wind rattling his rafters, a local resident, Mr Lynch walked up to the sea wall on the south of the island and was appalled to see that the water level on the other side had reached its top. When the sea broke through, houses were suddenly flooded, and like the Lythgoes, the Manser family were forced into the loft. But they were tragically less fortunate. Three out of seven children were drowned, two of them babies. Even though the storm surge had hit King's Lynn eight hours before, no warnings were sent down the coast. It was the weekend, so services such as weather forecasting were not operating and radio stations closed down in the late evening. It was a time when telephones were rare and communication was difficult. Fifty-nine people were drowned on Canvey Island, and all 13,000 inhabitants were evacuated as the North Sea crashed into the town.

★   ★   ★

Famous as a square on the Monopoly board, Fenchurch Street station was not easy to find, tucked away in a corner of the City of London. Not linked to the Tube network, it felt like a relic of a bygone age rather than an integral part of Transport for London. But it was a gateway that would take me back to the terrible and terrifying events of January 1953, its trains serving the eastern suburbs of London and, beyond them, the coastal towns of the northern shore of the Thames Estuary. Hemmed in by high-rise buildings, there were few views from the line, and it was the names of the stations that told me we were getting closer to the North Sea: Pitsea, Leigh-on-Sea and the terminus at Southend-on-Sea. Only when I alighted at Benfleet was the fatal geography of Canvey Island revealed. The station stands at the foot of a ridge and looks out over a perfectly flat and almost featureless landscape. The taxi took me across Benfleet Creek where an old barge rotted on its banks, and in the west a wide area of what looked like marshland bordered the western end of the ridge.

It was early morning, and a watery sun warmed the land and glinted off the grey Thames Estuary. The driver dropped me at Thorney Bay, one of the many places where the great storm surge broke through the sea defences. It was low tide in the bay, little more than an inlet, and several dog walkers threw balls for their pets on the sandy foreshore. I followed the path eastwards behind the massive concrete sea wall but could get no further than where the bay ended and the coastline ran in a more or less straight line. Cranes, dumper trucks and a bulldozer were working on building up the defences and stripy barriers forbade access.

I'd left London very early and only managed a cup of terrible coffee at Fenchurch Street station. Breakfast beckoned. Below the sea wall the Bay Café was opening up and a cheerful lady was putting out a sign and arranging outdoor tables and seating. 'Nine o'clock we open,' she said, 'but you go on in. We'll do something for you.' And they did. The Big Bay Breakfast was splendid, the classic full English, the toast perfect and the piping-hot coffee very welcome. As I spread the last shred of marmalade the café began quickly to fill up. Local people, by their accent, and regulars, for they all greeted each other by name, sat down on the tables around me and ordered similar hearty fare. All of them nodded to me, a complete stranger at what felt like a daily social ritual, and they smiled. And then the daughter of Joan and Geoff Lythgoe sat down at the table next to me.

Judging that almost all of the early-morning clientele were in their seventies, I started to ask questions, and that was when Jean Blackwell told me that her mother had written down what she remembered of the night of 31 January 1953. Jean's husband Roger was four and a half at that time, and he recalled the shock of seeing deep water in the garden of his parents' house. The morning after, from an upstairs window, he saw black lumps of coke from the bunkers behind his and his neighbours' houses floating in the street. 'Mud,' he said, 'that was all the sea wall was, mud and some timber. Built by the Dutch, it was.' Mixed with the wistful but not distant recollection of tragedy, there were touches of black humour. Roger and Jean told me that the pub formerly known as the Red Cow was renamed the King Canute because that was as far as the sea water reached. When I asked if people now felt safe from the sea behind the massive sea wall, given what had happened, they all nodded. But then Roger smiled and said, 'Until the next time.'

When the taxi picked me up to take me back to Benfleet station we passed a surprising sign. VOTE CANVEY was a message from the Canvey Independence Party. It struck me that the island was, of course, a place apart, but also how tragedy can pull people together and galvanise identity. The people who came most mornings to order breakfast in the Bay Café had voted for Canvey, because they had come back and remade a community and a place that had been all but destroyed.

★   ★   ★

It felt like travelling through Megalopolis. I had taken the Docklands Light Railway and spent much of the journey craning my neck, looking upwards from the carriage window. I'd never seen Canary Wharf before. Its soaring skyscrapers were at once immensely impressive and saddening. As a sporadic visitor to London over the last twenty-five years, I had noticed the process of change, how the city's very particular identity was being submerged, physically belittled. These mighty structures might have some whiffs of character, or at least distinguishing features, something different from the rectilinear, blocky stacks that punctuate the horizon, like the Shard and others, but they made the city look like every other major world city. Looking down I noticed that there were very few people about. Maybe they were all crammed into dealing floors, their sleeves up, betting vast sums on the flickering numbers of the twenty-four-hour stocks-and-bond markets – or, more likely, in the baleful aftermath of the Covid pandemic, some of these gigantic buildings were half empty as more and more people stayed at home to work.

When I emerged at Greenwich station I found myself in a place with a clear and distinct identity, a place closely linked with not only the mighty River Thames but also with the North Sea. Later that day I planned to visit the Maritime Museum, the splendour of old Royal Naval

College and, most importantly, the Royal Observatory in Greenwich Park. But first, I wanted to walk the Thames Path to go and see London's answer to the 1953 storm surge, the Thames Barrier.

No one could tell me how far it was from Greenwich to the barrier, or how long it would take to walk there. I wish they had. After I passed the *Cutty Sark*, beached for ever and for some reason next to a merry-go-round, its wooden horses bobbing up and down in time with oompah music as little ones clung on to stripy poles, the Thames opened up before me. Having seen the river only in central London, girded by the Embankment, I was taken aback at its scale, how wide it was, and also how flat the land on both banks was. I could see that the path beside it was long and looping. Beyond the beautiful neo-classical colonnades and the domes of the Royal Naval College it soon began to wind around building sites and unexpected little coves. One was sandy, a miniature beach fringed with willows and an exotic tree I didn't recognise. But I could see that far in the distance the path would go around the Greenwich Peninsula and what used to be known as the Millennium Dome, now the O2. However, should weariness cause me to stumble, there were reassuring signs at regular intervals: 'In Emergency Ring 999. Ask for Coastguard'. Perhaps the Thames had become the sea.

It was certainly growing broader and probably deep enough for ships on that morning of high tide. Its scale seemed to dominate the eastern city. On an information board near the Maritime Museum I'd seen archive photographs showing sailing ships, tugs, barges and all sorts of industrial activity on the riverbanks. But now the Thames was empty. The only craft I saw that morning was an Uber Boat taking visitors up and down the river. London had ceased to be a commercial port with the advent of container ships in the 1960s and 1970s. All of the particular, traditional skills of dockers with their billhooks, ropes and swinging quayside cranes were no longer seen on the banks of the Thames. Wharves and quays are only names now, often attached to new high-rise flats built where cargoes used to be unloaded. Huge ships, their open decks stacked with multicoloured containers, now dock at Harwich or Felixstowe, massive international ports on opposite banks of the River Stour, further north on the Essex coast. Ferries to and from Europe also operate from there, and Harwich is a base for the companies building wind farms in the North Sea. And now the Thames flows quiet and empty.

In contrast to the wide and vacant river, its southern bank buzzed with activity. There were groups of cranes in many places, and the bustle of building work was intense. To cross the road leading to the Blackwall Tunnel I had to follow a long diversion up and down stairs and ramps. An advertising hoarding for high-rise flats in the Greenwich Peninsula had prices ranging from £330,000 to £1 million. The Greenwich Millennium Village was 'close to the world famous O2, and Ecology Park and a Yacht Club, and just one stop from Canary Wharf'. And one more stop from anonymity. 'Come friendly bombs . . .'

Having navigated my way through building sites and temporary paths, I had managed to avoid walking around the loop of the Greenwich Peninsula. But when I emerged on the bank of the river once more the Thames Barrier still seemed a long way away, its distant towers glinting in the morning sun. As I got closer it struck me that their design looked odd, like giant rowing boats stood up on their sterns, and, more than that, they had the air of a series of ritual objects, like a steel version of Stonehenge, shining altars to river gods. And indeed, something magical seemed to be happening. On an otherwise bright and calm morning I could see that the barrier was at least partly closed and what is called an underspill, a flow of turbulent water, was running below its sections.

On that same morning, 8 April 2024, across Mexico, the USA and Canada tens of millions of people were craning their necks, tilting their heads to the sky and watching in wonder as day turned to night. For many it was a unique experience, even spiritual, cosmic, to watch the moon moving precisely between the earth and the sun, extinguishing its light in a total solar eclipse. On the other side of the world I was watching its effect on the North Sea. Solar eclipses cause unusually high tides. The double blob effect of the moon's gravity is made much more pronounced when the sun's is in the same alignment, and so when the eclipse began over the Pacific Ocean it created higher than usual tides in the North Sea, and the Thames Barrier rumbled into action.

As a response to the catastrophic floods of 1953 the barrier was a long time coming. It was completed in 1982 and opened by the late Queen in 1984. The design had endearingly domestic origins. Reginald Charles Draper built a working model in his parents' house in Wood Green, a northern suburb of London. The barrier he envisaged works by rotating huge, hollow cylinders from a prone position level with the riverbed through ninety degrees to an upright position. Reginald based his design on the taps on his gas cooker. And it worked. On 9 November 2007 a storm surge thought to be comparable to the floods of 1953 blew up the Thames Estuary. The barrier closed and prevented widespread damage and possible loss of life. If it had not been there, and raised quickly, more than 116 square kilometres of Greater London would have been inundated, the Tube system rendered useless and dangerous, virtually the whole network filling with seawater; there would have been unprecedented damage and inevitably very significant loss of life. In all there have been only 209 closures since 1982, and Reginald Draper's ingenious design is predicted to repel future surges, even allowing for the rise in sea levels as a consequence of climate change.

Sadly, it isn't possible to go out onto the Thames Barrier, and so I turned back west towards the National Maritime Museum at Greenwich. Walking back along the Thames Path was never an option, and, without checking if such a thing was possible, I'd decided to use public transport to return to where I'd started early that morning. It could not have been simpler. In comparison to Scotland's, London's transport infrastructure works, and works well. Once I had registered my debit card online with Transport for London, it was all I needed. There were no tickets and no difference between using it on the Tube, the over-ground trains and, as it turned out, the famous red buses. It is so rare in Britain now to experience efficient and inexpensive public services that I added an exclamation mark in my notebook to 'London works!' The rolling stock and the buses also seemed new or newish, well maintained and for passengers like myself who are unfamiliar with the routes, information is constantly available, both graphic and on audio. I feared that my excellent experience in navigating my way through the river of people would be unique as I continued my journey up the North Sea coast to Shetland.

The National Maritime Museum struck me as odd. While there was a good deal about Britain's seafaring and naval past (the section on Horatio Nelson and Trafalgar was very good, clear and atmospheric), it also included a lot of information and material about the places Britain's ships reached and helped to colonise. No matter. What had brought me to Greenwich were not the Pacific island outrigger boats, the Māori costumes or the kit used on polar expeditions. I'd come to look at a straight line and a clock.

When Julius Caesar crossed the Channel and Cicero worried about the tides, the Roman sea captains knew a good deal about navigation. Each time Pytheas of Massalia came ashore both at North Foreland and as far north as the Isle of Lewis in the Hebrides and several places between, he calculated his position by measuring latitude. Using a stick called a gnomon, he took readings as he travelled further and further up the length of Britain. They were very accurate, and Pytheas' methods were simple. Like a set square but with one side much longer than the other, a gnomon works somewhat in the same way as a sundial. By setting it up under the midday sun on a flat surface Pytheas could calculate the length of the shadow cast by the long side of the stick. Having taken a measurement of the shadow cast by the midday sun on the longest day of the year before he left Marseilles as a base point, he was able to measure latitude at each place in Britain where he came ashore, and by recording the variations in the length of the shadows cast he could work out how far north he had travelled. Pytheas' calculations of northern latitudes were reliable, and they were used by geographers who came after him. Longitude was quite another matter.

Marinus of Tyre was another pioneer. In AD 114 he published his *Geography*, in which he set out north-to-south lines of longitude. To do this Marinus had to start somewhere, and this involved choosing where his prime meridian should be, what was to be known as zero longitude. He set it on the Isles of the Blessed, out in the Atlantic Ocean, far beyond the Pillars of Hercules, the Strait of Gibraltar. Even though he had never visited the archipelago or spoken to anyone who had, it didn't matter because Marinus knew exactly where he would place zero latitude. The island of Rhodes would do, for it was familiar to many and close to where he lived, Tyre on the Syrian coast. A gifted theoretical mathematician, Marinus knew that if zero latitude was fixed, the location of zero longitude could be arbitrary. A semi-mythical set of islands that might or might not lie off the coast of Africa was fine because as lines of longitude approached what is now Portugal, Spain and the coast of North Africa, they would make sense when plotted with line of latitude. Marinus came up with the idea of equirectangular projection. When both sets of lines, latitude on an east-to-west axis and longitude north-to-south, inter-sected at consistent spacing, this allowed a flat map of the globe to be drawn without too much distortion. In turn, this also meant that the locations of distant places could be accurately plotted and found by travellers or sailors using a straightforward series of coordinates of latitude and longitude measured in degrees. A very similar set of calculations is still in use today.

Marinus' use of longitude worked because the Med-iterranean is an epeiric sea, one that is almost completely surrounded by land and with plenty of reference points in the shape of landmarks and islands. The North Sea is bounded on three sides by land, but Greek and Roman geographers had never had the opportunity or inclination to calculate degrees of longitude across it. Those who did cross between Europe and Britain used other naviga-tional aids. But, as we will see, the problem of longitude was to have a profound influence on the history of the North Sea.

Along with groups of other so-called barbarians, the Angles, Saxons and Jutes had close contact with the garrison of the Roman province of Britannia. First as mercenaries, or *foederati*, federates, they fought on behalf of the empire against Pictish raiders from the north and Irish warbands from the west. Long before Bede wrote of the first landings at Pegwell Bay in 449, people from the European shores of the North Sea already knew a good deal about Britain and also about how to get there. Archaeology for the period is sparse but eloquent. Two ships dating from the early seventh century have been discovered on both shores of the sea, one famously at

Sutton Hoo near the coast in Suffolk and another at Gredstedbro on the west coast of Jutland in Denmark. Both were about the same size, between twenty-five and twenty-seven metres long. But neither was a sailing ship – no mast block on the keel was found by the archaeologists – and it seems certain that these substantial, sea-going boats were powered by about thirty oarsmen.

Bede's traditional location of the homelands of the Jutes, Angles and Saxons has been broadly supported by recent ancestral DNA research. The characteristic genetic markers of their descendants can still be found along the North Sea coast of Britain and further inland – even as far as Kelso, for when I had my own DNA tested in 2012 it turned out that my marker originated in what is now Denmark. Since that surprising, defining moment, I've had to put up with a good deal of teasing.

It seems that the Jutes did indeed originate in Jutland. The Saxons came from Old Saxony in what is now north-western Germany, where the estuaries of the Elbe and the Weser drain into the North Sea. Their name derives from a favoured weapon, a long knife known as the *seax*. The arms of the old county of Middlesex (the Middle Saxons of early England) remember that ancient link with its three *seax* knives under a Saxon crown. The arms of the East Saxons of Essex also carry three *seax* knives. In addition to these heraldic devices, the origins of these North Sea migrants are recalled in one very familiar place name. The Angles came from the part of the Danish peninsula that lies between Jutland and Old Saxony. It was known as Angeln, and because of the shape of its eastern coastline the name probably translates as Hook-Land, the name surviving in angling, the old formal term for fishing with rods and hooks. It is also the derivation of England, Hook-Land.

The shorelines of these three homelands are frayed, deeply indented and sometimes radically altered by the tides and storms of the North Sea. From the Dutch Frisian Islands (where the local dialect remained very close to English for many centuries) and northwards up the Danish coasts, there are many scatters of islands, and the low-lying coast is pierced by fjords. In Jutland Lim Fjord reaches far inland to Aalborg and almost to the Baltic. This was and remains the watery landscape of seafarers. The large rowing boats like those found at Sutton Hoo and Gredstedbro were highly manoeuvrable, and their oarsmen and helmsmen could avoid rocky reefs and sand-banks more adroitly than a craft driven by sails and the chancy power of the wind. The frayed and fractured shores of the homelands of the English more than imply a tradition of capable seamanship and confident naviga-tion, they insist on it.

However, there are no helpful islands in the middle of the North Sea, and after the boats of migrating warriors and families were rowed past Heligoland, they were on the open sea and reliant on one obvious and comforting fact of geography: Britain is a long target, more than 1,300 kilometres from Kent to Shetland, one that mariners who could keep a westerly course were very unlikely to miss. Much more than sailing ships, rowing boats were influenced by the tides and currents, and it may well be that when those crossing the North Sea from Jutland, Angeln or Old Saxony came within sight of land, the great tidal wave that washed south down the British coast carried boats with it as their helmsmen searched the shore for safe harbour or a flat beach like Pegwell Bay where they could make landfall. Where the tides collide off the Thames Estuary and the Kentish coast may have been a destination chosen by the power of the North Sea more than any other factor. An eloquent record of early migrant settlement was compiled by the eminent archaeologist Sonia Chadwick Hawkes. Her map of Anglo-Saxon cemeteries and single burials in England by the end of the seventh century shows a dense concentration on the Isle of Thanet, Kent and the southern shore of the Thames Estuary. It seems that many more from Jutland and elsewhere followed the muddy footprints of Hengist and Horsa.

As well as a vehicle for migration, the North Sea may well have been a cause. There exists evidence of widespread flooding in the sixth and seventh centuries along the coasts of Jutland, Angeln and Old Saxony in particular, and communities may have been forced to abandon their inundated farms, the now useless earth saturated with sea salt, and seek new lives in England. In 1953 the great storm surge did far greater damage along the Dutch and German coasts, where the lie of the land is much lower, and 2,551 people were drowned. When migrating communities took to their rowing boats they will have brought everything they could carry: food, seed corn, even domesticated animals, hobbled and made to lie prone between the oarsmen. Even if they decided to travel down the eastern coasts, staying within sight of land, beaching their boats to seek water and whatever shelter families could find, it could be a long and arduous journey. And if the weather turned, and the boats shipped water from high waves, it could take even longer.

Many migrants will have been drowned, but many more also succeeded in making the crossing. When they were forced to leave the coast behind, experienced Anglo-Saxon oarsmen and helmsmen had no charts or compasses to guide them, but they would have known from others who had crossed the North Sea, depending on the season (and almost all voyages will have happened in the summer when the days are longest), how long a voyage should take. Early mariners also relied heavily on observation, sea lore and common sense. Distances travelled were estimated on the basis of shifts at the oars, although these calculations will have varied depending on the mood of the sea and of the sky. It is not clear when another traditional method of estimating speed came into use, but it is so simple, the likelihood is that the Anglo-Saxons used it. A floating log was put over the side and attached to a line that had knots in it at consistent intervals and how quickly these passed from bow to stern was an indicator of how quickly the boat was moving. This method eventually supplied the names of two characteristic items of maritime language: the ship's log and its speed reckoned in knots.

When the night sky was clear over the North Sea, experienced helmsmen knew enough astronomy to use the stars as direction finders and as an aid to plotting their approximate position. On cloudy days some may have used a sunstone, a piece of feldspar whose minerals polarise sunlight and change colour as the stone is turned towards where the sun might be. The presence of seabirds and also seals was usually encouraging, because sightings meant that land might lie just over the horizon. Mariners also looked at the sea itself, its swells and patterns, the run of the tides and currents, how they played on the surface. These Anglo-Saxon sailors managed with their skill and experience, but the lack of a consistent way to measure longitude was to become a greater challenge as voyages became longer.

The magnetic compass originated in China and began to appear in Europe in the fourteenth century. It was certainly a vital aid to navigation for those crossing the North Sea in both directions, as well as those venturing much further. Accurate lines of latitude also helped Christopher Columbus to sail over the Atlantic Ocean to the West Indies in 1492. His ships' logs show that he also used the dead reckoning method of navigation. The distance from the port of departure was estimated by reckoning the speed of the ship in knots, and after a day's sailing that distance travelled was plotted on a chart, and that point would be the starting place for the next day. So long as Columbus could 'follow the parallel', as he called the line of latitude, without deviation, and could keep his course consistent, he would continue to sail westwards. Using a version of a sextant, formerly known as an astrolabe – a device with a lens that can measure the angular distance between two visible objects – he avoided sailing too far south or too far north. In the open ocean Columbus measured the angle between a star or the moon (which is visible in the sky for about twenty-five days of every month) and the horizon, and his ships' logs recorded many readings.

Many sailors followed in the wakes of the *Santa Maria*, the *Pinto* and the *Nina* across the Atlantic. By the end of the seventeenth century more than 300 ships a year were crossing from Britain to the West Indies and the Americas. The risks were very great, but the riches and rewards were irresistible. As the Portuguese and the Spaniards plundered and exploited, ships laden with treasure and spices sailed eastwards and some were attacked and captured by English privateers – a slightly more polite term for pirates, but essentially the same thing. But many ships were lost in the open ocean, particularly when there was fog or bad weather. The most intractable problem was the inability to reckon longitude accurately when out of sight of land, and as a result there were no accurate charts.

Matters came to a head on the night of 22 October 1707. The splendidly named Sir Cloudesley Shovell was commander-in-chief of the Royal Navy. After leading a successful attack on the French fleet at Toulon (in what was known as the War of the Spanish Succession, in reality a struggle with France for control of the Spanish Empire, and especially its lucrative possessions in the Americas), he and the captains of his small flotilla were sailing northeastwards towards the English Channel and their home port of Plymouth. Or so they thought. It was 'dirty weather', complained the admiral, a foggy night with poor visibility. None of his captains were certain of their position, for there was no way even to guess at a reading of longitude. Not until Shovell's flagship, HMS *Association*, smashed into the rocky coastline of the Scilly Isles, a long way west of where his flotilla should have been or thought it was. The flagship went down like a stone, sinking in only three or four minutes. Three other ships, HMS *Eagle*, HMS *Romney* and HMS *Firebrand*, all foundered on the jagged shore and went down in minutes. Two thousand sailors were drowned, including Admiral Shovell, and the disaster was mourned as one of the worst in British naval history.

Shock was followed by petitions. They led to action and the passing of the Longitude Act in 1714. It established the Board of Longitude which offered very substantial rewards to anyone who could solve this ancient problem. The transatlantic trade had become lucrative, and Britain had begun to acquire an overseas empire, so the cost of such losses at sea could no longer be borne.

★   ★   ★

After the excellent red bus from Woolwich and the Thames Barrier had dropped me outside the Maritime Museum at Greenwich, where the original text of the Longitude Act is on display, I walked up the hill behind the Georgian splendour of the old Royal Naval College to have a look at what the legislation achieved: a line and a clock. They were the solutions to the great problem. Set into the cobbles outside the observatory is a long brass line, the meridian, zero longitude, what marked Greenwich Mean Time. And inside the museum is the clock that put it there. Marinus of Tyre would have smiled to see both of them, despite his fondness for the Isles of the Blessed.

In order to establish lines of longitude in the open sea

it is vital to know exactly what the time is, and to know exactly what the time was when the ship began its voyage, when it sailed out of its port of departure. There were, of course, clocks in use all over eighteenth-century Europe, but their mechanisms were problematic. As ships pitch and roll at sea, pendulum clocks do not work reliably, and even if the weather is calm, temperature changes can thin or thicken lubricating oils, causing them to malfunction or simply stop, as well as expand or contract their metal components. Variations in barometric pressure also affected pendulum clocks.

Accurate time measurement mattered because if the time was taken from port to, say, a ship's position at noon on the following day, then its position could be established in conjunction with calculations of its speed, the wind, currents and other factors. The time gap can then be easily converted into geographical distance and the position plotted on a chart. And if Sir Cloudesley Shovell had been able to record accurately what time he had sailed out of Gibraltar and compare it to the time he found his ships were close to the Scilly Isles, he would have realised he was off course and changed it.

The genius of John Harrison would solve the problem of longitude, but not until after a long and titanic struggle and his single-minded dedication had overcome entrenched attitudes and what sounds like straightforward snobbery. Born in 1693 in the village of Foulby near Wakefield in the West Riding of Yorkshire, Harrison was the child of a carpenter, and he himself became preternaturally skilled in working with wood. By the age of twenty he had built his first long-case clock, made entirely out of wood, mainly oak and lignum vitae, a very dense and hard wood that resisted wear.

Aware, as most clockmakers were, of the Board of Longitude's great prize, Harrison designed and built a sea clock in 1730. Also made out of wood, which was not affected by temperature change as much as metal, it worked very well on board a ship because of two radical inventions: the grasshopper escapement and 'dumb-bell' balances. Harrison created the grasshopper escapement, an almost frictionless means of keeping the pendulum swinging regularly. Crucially, it needed no lubricating oil that might be affected by heat or cold. This first sea clock, labelled H1, was also well adapted to cope with the movement of ships. Instead of a conventional pendulum of the sort that swung in the long case below the clock face, H1 had two balances that resembled a pair of dumb-bells linked together. The Board of Longitude was sufficiently impressed to recommend a sea trial, and in 1730 Harrison sailed on a return voyage to Lisbon on board HMS *Centurion*. Despite suffering from acute seasickness, he was able to maintain and wind the clock. Even though it lost time on the outward voyage, it was more accurate on the return trip and more reliable than any other clock had been up until that time.

Despite this, the Board of Longitude did not award John Harrison the prize of £20,000, although they did agree to advance £500 for more research. But war then intervened. The Board was nervous of H1 falling into enemy hands, and in any case the designs for two more versions of the clock, H2 and H3, were not satisfactory.

Some time in the later 1740s Harrison realised that a watch might keep time just as accurately as any of his larger sea clocks. Developments and refinements in steel production may have had a determinant influence. By 1759 Harrison had perfected the design of H4, his sea watch. Resembling an old fashioned pocket watch but slightly larger at fourteen centimetres in diameter, it sits alongside H1, H2 and H3 in the Royal Observatory in Greenwich. All of them are still quietly working, ticking in their glass cases in a darkened gallery. Harrison was exultant:

> I think I may make bold to say, that there is neither any other Mechanical or Mathematical thing in the World that is more beautiful or more curious in texture than this my watch or Timekeeper for the Longitude . . . and I heartily thank Almighty God that I have lived so long, as in some measure to complete it.

He was sixty-six by the time the watch was completed, but his view of it was not shared. Despite the elegance of the design, its accuracy and the fact that the small size of the watch made its likely use more practical and widespread, the Board of Longitude thought its successful sea trials across the Atlantic were more a matter of luck than a result of any improvement in operation. Frustrated, and perhaps sensing more than a degree of condescension to a common carpenter, Harrison appealed to George III. After his majesty had used the watch himself for a few weeks and was much impressed by its accuracy, he intervened. Even then, the Board did not award Harrison the full sum of the prize, only giving him a little more than £8,000.

On his epic voyages around the world and especially across the vastness of the Pacific Ocean, Captain James Cook, another Yorkshireman, used a copy of H4 known as K1 and was delighted with its reliability. By the beginning of the nineteenth century chronometers of this sort were common, and many maritime disasters were avoided by good charts and accurate navigation. By that time Britain had built an empire that was held together by the Royal Navy and exploited by fleets of merchant ships. The safety of almost all these vessels and their crews had been made possible by the genius and persistence of John Harrison.

Outside the Royal Observatory two young boys were walking in as straight a line as they could along the prime meridian. Perhaps they thought of it as neither east nor west. As Marinus of Tyre knew, its location was arbitrary. So long as it was fixed somewhere, zero longitude could have been anywhere. At first, most Western countries nominated their capital cities as its location and consequently created charts with different lines of longitude. But in 1884, in Washington, DC, a conference agreed that Greenwich should be where the prime meridian was marked. It allowed maritime navigation to speak a common language. Only the French disagreed, continuing to site zero longitude in Paris. But by 1911 even the French accepted Greenwich. As much as H4 and the other clocks, the brass line that so delighted the little boys was confirmation that John Harrison had created a small object that had solved a huge problem.

II

Humber

Waterworld

Invisible until they moved, damselflies flitted from lily pads up to the tall stems of sedge, their diaphanous wings and blue bodies showing only for a moment against the pools of black water. With taproots drinking long and deep, stunted, wind-bent willows and aspens made occasional canopies, their leaves dense, lustrous and lush at their fullest, greenest burst. In the shadows, chiffchaffs darted from branch to branch before swooping, scooping up the tiny insects hovering over the dark pools below the trees. Beside the path, in clumps of marsh thistles, bees harvested pollen, and beyond them stretched the fen, its hundred shades of green glowing under a wide sky.

Windless and very warm, with temperatures in the high twenties Celsius, it was a perfect day to slip through a crack in time, to go back to a world that had all but disappeared. The warm air was thick with memory. From the shaded, secret pools and the tangle of ancient trees, ghosts murmured and the sedge whispered as men and women hunted and children searched for the nests and eggs of waterbirds. As I walked slowly and quietly amongst the stunted trees and bushes, I sensed this was an ancient place, somewhere the old gods were close. Perhaps they watched mortal men and women, not looking down from the blue vaults of Heaven but up from the bottomless depths of the still, black pools, their surface a shimmering mirror of the temporal world. Beneath it, dark spirits swam in the deeps of the world.

In the drowsy sunshine there was no engine noise to be heard, no sign of buildings or any other vestige of the twenty-first century, only the constant chorus of birdsong and the distant echoes of a long past stretching back into the mists of prehistory. I had come north to Wicken Fen, a nature reserve not far from Ely, a surviving remnant of a lost landscape, the vast tracts of eastern England where the tides of the North Sea had once washed far inland, where wide rivers had meandered, often flooding over their banks, where the land was uncultivated, where people lived off the bounty of the natural world, hunting and gathering for millennia, long after their prehistoric ancestors had become farmers and herdsmen in the valleys and uplands across the rest of England.

Owned and maintained by the National Trust, Wicken Fen's 237 hectares is fringed by boardwalks and dotted with hides where visitors can watch the waterbirds without disturbing them. Walking in the shimmering heat, the reserve seemed to me much larger, its flat vistas stretching beyond the horizon, reaching back to a world shaped by the sea and land, and yet unlike either, somewhere unique and truly liminal. Shading my eyes, I watched a heron slowly flying high and grey against the blue sky, its angled wingspread tilting and swaying in the updrafts.

These wetlands, the Fens of England, once covered a huge area. Best known are the wide flatlands around the Wash, reaching almost to Lincoln in the north, as far west as Peterborough, south to Cambridge and east to King's Lynn, an area of more than 3,100 square kilometres. Settlements were built on naturally occurring clay mounds at Boston, Spalding, Holbeach, March and famously at the Isle of Ely, which, until recent times really was an island rising up out of an inland sea. But often forgotten are the northern Fens that covered large areas on both sides of the Humber, and across the Thorne and Hatfield moors west of the River Trent and around the confluence of the Ouse and the Derwent in South Yorkshire. To the north and south of York there were large areas of wetland, and well south of the Humber, in the ancient Kingdom of Lindsey, there were wide fens on either side of the Lincolnshire Wolds. Oliver Rackham, the author of the canonical *History of the Countryside*, reckoned that a quarter of the landmass of England had once been fenland.

Organised, well-funded and sustained schemes for drainage began in the early seventeenth century. Encouraged by the Stuart kings, companies of 'adventurers', led initially by the Earl of Bedford, financed the back-breaking shovel-and-basket or barrow work of digging ditches and raising embankments in return for grants of what they hoped would be fertile land. These cartels of incomers met with fierce and sustained opposition from native communities. For millennia these people had fished, caught wildfowl, cut peat, harvested the tall sedge for roofing and fired the clay for bricks and tiles.

Drainage would destroy an immensely productive and endlessly renewing fertile environment that had defined a way of life for countless generations. Fenlanders may have been materially poor, living in 'soggy hovels', but they were rarely hungry. The work of the adventurers was repeatedly disrupted by local gangs known as Fen Tigers, and at Wicken the villagers drove off the king's men in 1637 and their fen was ultimately, and accidentally, preserved. But by 1853 the widest stretch of open water, Whittlesea Mere, had been drained, and with its disappearance it was believed that the Fens had been almost completely reclaimed from the North Sea, and the meandering rivers, now canalised into straight courses, fed directly into the Wash.

And yet, as I made my way around the boardwalk in the baking sun, I had the sense not of a lost world, a living exhibit in an outdoor museum; instead, it felt like a window had opened on a past and a place that had been important in the story of the North Sea and its shores for many millennia, stretching far back into the mists and uncertainties of prehistory. But, as I discovered, the fen and its history also had much to say about the story of Englishness itself.

In the shade of a stand of willows and aspen, I sat down on a welcome bench to look out over Sedge Fen, an apparently vast area of biscuit-coloured tall grasses. A breeze soughed through the sedge, riffling and bending the fluffy heads of its long stems, keeping the flies at bay and loosening the oppressive warmth of the air. Looking at the ground below the boardwalk, I realised that on this day of high summer it was dry, the black earth of the damp marshland caked and cracked. When I jumped down into the sedge, into the heart of the fen, the grasses turned out to be considerably taller than I am, more than two metres high. A few paces away from the boardwalk immediately told me how easy it would be to get lost and quickly disoriented. There were no reference points to be seen, no landmarks on higher ground, nothing but the fen and the dense, tall grass crowding around me, brushing my shoulders. I was standing in a wilderness, somewhere men could hide, somewhere strangers should fear to tread. Before it was drained the huge area of the English fenlands was a trackless wilderness, deep and dangerous to outsiders and a natural rampart for natives from a time out of mind. This lost world reminded me powerfully of my impression of another lost world, one that had fascinated me for many years.

★   ★   ★

As darkness fell and the evening tide turned, Captain Pilgrim Lockwood piloted his trawler, the SS *Colinda*, out of Lowestoft harbour and into the waters of the North Sea. It was late September 1931, and the skipper set a course for the Leman and Ower Banks, a reliable fishing ground about forty kilometres off the East Anglian coast. Once the wide net had been shot, weighted to sink thirty-five metres through the shallows to settle on the seabed, Lockwood set his engines to a steady trawling speed. When at last he judged the net to be heavy with a decent catch, the captain stopped so that it could be hauled up. Having heaved their catch on board, the crew set about the awkward business of making sure the fish were pulled free of any seabed debris. Having scraped along the bottom, trawl nets often picked up shells, bones, bits of wood and other sunken flotsam and jetsam. As the net spilled its contents on that autumn night, the boat's arc lamps showed up a large black lump, what the fishermen called 'moorlog'. It was a saturated peat-like chunk too heavy to lift, and so Captain Lockwood picked up a shovel to break it up. And at that moment he discovered something extraordinary, a remnant of a vast, lost world.

'It was like I'd hit a piece of metal,' the skipper later recalled, 'something really hard.' Hidden in the middle of the lump of moorlog was a bone harpoon. More than twenty centimetres long, it was a piece of deer antler that had been carefully carved so that one edge was barbed. Lockwood had the presence of mind not only to keep the little harpoon but to pass it on to a Cambridge University scientist. What was extraordinary was not the harpoon itself – others very like it had been occasionally found around the coasts of Britain – but where it had been found. Typological comparisons dated the object very broadly (archaeological techniques were much less sophisticated in the 1930s) to some time between 4000 BC and 10,000 BC. But the real question was what was it doing under the North Sea, forty kilometres from the coast of East Anglia? It was discovered too far out to have been dropped from a boat by a prehistoric hunter intent on killing seals or large fish, and in any case it had been found encased in moorlog, a peaty sediment. What was the harpoon doing there, not lying on the seabed but buried some way below it?

Twenty years before, an archaeologist called Clement Reid thought he knew the answer. From the shallows of the Dogger Bank oyster dredgers had pulled up other prehistoric tools and also the bones of reindeer and walrus, all of them found 110 kilometres out to sea. In 1913 Reid published *Submerged Forests*, and the book put forward a theory that a large landmass off the eastern coast of Britain had been reclaimed by the North Sea, a place where prehistoric hunters hunted reindeer and killed walrus. It might even have been a land bridge connecting Britain with Europe. Reid's theories were patronised, laughed at and dismissed.

In the 1970s a Dutch archaeologist, Dr Louwe Kooijmans, began to record a series of finds made by fishermen trawling over the Brown Banks, immediately to the south of the Leman and Ower Banks where Pilgrim Lockwood had found the bone harpoon. Not only did Kooijmans' work support the discredited speculations of Clement Reid, comparisons with similar prehistoric artefacts found around the shores of the North Sea convinced him that the ancient population of this drowned landscape had been culturally slightly distinct, something that implied both scale and a long continuity.

Public awareness of these remarkable finds had to wait for a name. After more work on collating what had been discovered and new findings of her own, Professor Bryony Coles of the University of Exeter called the submerged sub-continent Doggerland after its most famous feature, the Dogger Bank. And she drew a dramatic map that showed a vast landmass lying between the coasts of East Anglia, Essex and Kent and those of northern France,

Belgium, Holland and northern Germany. To the north rose the Dogger Hills and near the centre was an inland sea called the Outer Silver Pit. In 2001 the University of Birmingham began to access much of the surveying of the bed of the North Sea that had been carried out by companies prospecting for oil and gas and later for the construction of offshore wind farms. A detailed map of Doggerland began to emerge from under the waves as its hills and rivers flickered on screens showing seismic reflection data.

Researchers could see that a major river once ran through the subcontinent for at least forty kilometres, and it was named after Fred Shotton, the eminent geologist who had taught at Birmingham University. There was evidence that herds of mammoths had splashed across the vast wetlands and grasslands of Doggerland. Hunters had gone out after the giant wild cattle known as the aurochs as well as the reindeer mentioned by Clement Reid. Traces were also found of an ancient species of lions that stalked the landscape. Most poignant was the discovery of the jawbone and teeth of a Doggerlander who hunted and gathered the bounty of the lost landscape 8,300 years ago.

All historical memory of Doggerland was lost. The surviving mythical tales of Atlantis, Lyonesse, Hy-Brasil and Tìr nan Òg (the Land of the Ever-Young) were all located somewhere to the west of Britain and were, in any case, clearly little more than romantic fables. Doggerland was real, vast and home to many of our prehistoric ancestors for many millennia – and yet its cultural legacy has completely disappeared.

Some time around 5800 BC those who lived on the eastern shores of what is now Scotland and those on the northern shores of Doggerland were transfixed by what must have seemed like an apocalypse. As seabirds shrieked and took to the air, the North Sea disappeared in moments, rapidly receding with a deafening roaring, sucking noise. The seabed was suddenly revealed. Fish, dolphins, seals, even whales were stranded, asphyxiating, flapping and writhing as the water rushed past them. In the deeps of the Storegga Trench that curved around the coast of Norway, a vast submarine landslip had convulsed the bed of the North Sea. A huge area, perhaps as big as the landmass of Scotland, disappeared in moments under a tectonic plate, and to fill the immediate vacuum the sea was dragged behind it. Only a few minutes later those onshore, already no doubt in a state of shock, heard a thunderous rumble that quickly grew louder. A giant tsunami was racing across the exposed bed of the sea towards them at 480 kilometres an hour. When the twenty-five-metre high leading wave smashed into Shetland, at that time connected to the British mainland, it destroyed communities in seconds and surged far inland. Down the eastern coasts and onto the northern shore of Doggerland, the leading wave was still nine metres high as it roared up and over beaches, snapping trees like matchsticks, thundering up river estuaries, covering the land with white pelagic sand, drowning thousands of fleeing people and animals.

It was the Storrega tsunami that almost certainly saw the submergence of most of Doggerland. By 5000 BC at the latest, only Dogger Island may have survived, its sole memory the fact that the Dogger Bank is occasionally revealed at low tide as a wide sandy area. Some fishermen claim to have played cricket on it for a daredevil hour or so. Perhaps it was at that moment of inundation that the North Sea broke through to link with the mighty Atlantic to create the English Channel and isolate Britain, creating an archipelago as the Northern and Western Isles broke away. It may be that the suddenness of this catastrophic disappearance washed away all memory of Doggerland. Except perhaps in one place. As I walked through Wicken Fen, it struck me that this singular landscape may well be a remnant of somewhere much larger, somewhere that closely resembled the wide world where a hunter lost a bone harpoon more than 6,000 years ago only for Captain Pilgrim Lockwood to find it.

Doggerland did leave one undisputed and enduring legacy. When the earth's climate began to change some time around 24,000 BC, and ice covered much of the northern hemisphere, its great accumulated weight pressed down hard on the crust of the planet. Often around existing land mountains, huge ice domes began to form, perfectly spherical and with constant winds whistling around their gleaming flanks, some of them more than 300 metres high. To the south of the domes that had formed over Scandinavia, an effect known as a forebulge was created. The land that was either ice free or frozen tundra began to rise. It was like leaning on one end of a pillow and seeing the other side bulge upwards. When temperatures at last began to climb and meltwater filled the seas and oceans, the North Sea was created only slowly and was at first much smaller. On the higher land to the south of the Dogger Hills that was created by the forebulge, the ancient subcontinent was, like the fen, a good place for hunter-gatherers to live, somewhere teeming with fish and wildfowl as well as larger prey. But since the devastation of the Storegga tsunami, an effect known as isostatic rebound (the rise of land masses after the huge weight of ice sheets has been removed) has had profound, if less dramatic, effects.

Since the disappearance of Doggerland, both the seabed and the lands around the southern shores of the North Sea have begun to sink at the rate of about a millimetre a year, while Scotland has been rising. This is the aftermath, the continuing and lasting effects of the weight of the ice domes on the earth's crust. The impact of the rebound has affected for many centuries the coast of East Anglia in particular. After tremendous storm surges in both 1286 and 1287, the town of Dunwich began to disappear under the waves. It had been the capital place of the early kings of East Anglia in the seventh and eighth centuries and the seat of a bishopric. Seven of its eight churches have all been claimed by the sea, and now Dunwich is little more than a village. At places such as Happisburgh, Norfolk, the erosion of the coast continues to see homes slide into the North Sea, and in Norfolk and Suffolk around 2,500 houses are thought to be in imminent danger. The gradual effects of isostatic rebound have been compounded by climate change causing sea levels to rise and bringing more frequent storms.

Before I came to Wicken Fen I had managed to find a second-hand copy of *The History of the Fens* by James Wentworth-Day. It was first published in 1954 and is, sadly, no longer in print. The author had bought part of what is now Wicken Fen so that he could recreate what the landscape was like before drainage. By having the drains dammed to hold back the retreat of the winter floods, the ancient meres reappeared, and the wild fowl quickly returned at the same time as the vegetation regenerated. Wentworth-Day wrote that he did this to

preserve it, to save for all time the essential Englishness of it, to love and enjoy the sight of birds and clouds, the wind in the reeds, herons fishing in summer shallows, gulls wheeling against May skies, the sting of winter sleet.

There are many beautifully written, evocative passages in *The History of the Fens* that seemed to me to summon up atmospheres, that most elusive of all impressions. His words capture moments when the water, the land and the sky conjure something unique to the Fens, something elusive, things outsiders might miss or mistake. All of Wentworth-Day's senses were employed in the writing of this extraordinary book, a labour of an intense love:

in the witch hours before dawn, the smell of the fen. A strange indefinable smell, scent of reeds and peaty waters, of sallows, and meadowsweet and rotten lily pads – and of fish. The smell of freshwater fish which is penetrating, ineluctable, indefinable. And old, strange, blended smell, a smell as old as Time, compounded of scents that belonged to an untamed, undrained England, the England of the Saxons.

Why it was that this notion of an essential Englishness should settle on the Fens rather than, say, Kent – where, according to the stone erected in Pegwell Bay, the history of the English had begun – or even London and its national institutions, intrigued me. It cannot be an unconscious memory of the broken link with Europe that was Doggerland that prompted it. The Storegga tsunami almost certainly washed away any vestige of that long-lost world. But nevertheless Wentworth-Day was by no means alone in seeing the Fens as something ethnically unspoiled. Perhaps it was the simple fact that many of the Angles and Saxons and others who migrated from the fragmented, watery shorelands of Frisia, Holland, northern Germany and Denmark recognised and felt more immediately at home in a very similar landscape. Having crossed the North Sea, they knew how to survive in the fen.

As a cavalry commander, Pliny the Elder travelled widely around the Roman Empire. For several years he was stationed in Emsland, between the rivers Weser and Ems (in modern-day Germany), and in his *Natural History* he left a vivid description of how these shore communities lived, one that might have applied to England's Fens:

We have discussed that at least in the east there are several peoples along the coast of the ocean [the name the Romans gave to the North Sea] who have to live without trees and shrubs . . . Twice a day over an immeasurable distance the ocean comes up with enormous amounts of water, and covers an area eternally disputed by nature, and of which it is unclear whether it belongs to the mainland or is part of the sea.

There, this poor people occupy high dwelling mounds or dams that they have single-handedly raised to the highest water level they experienced. With their huts they have built on it, they look like sailors when water has covered the surrounding land. But they look like [they have been] shipwrecked when the water has withdrawn, and they hunt around their huts for fish that flee with the sea . . .

From reed and bulrush, they weave rope to tie fishing nets. They collect mire [animal dung] that they let dry through the wind, more than through the sun. With this peat, they heat their food and their bodies churned by the northern wind. They drink only rainwater, which they keep in pits at the entrance to their houses.

One of the earliest descriptions of the English wetlands was written by a monk, Felix of Burgundy. He was ordained bishop of Dunwich in 630, and, to his evident chagrin, his see may have included the Fens:

There is in the midland district of Britain a most dismal fen of immense size which begins at the banks of the River Granta not far from the camp which is called [modern] Cambridge, and stretches from the south as far north as the sea. It is a very long tract, consisting now of marshes, now of bogs, sometimes of black waters overhung by fog, sometimes studded with wooded islands and traversed by the windings of tortuous streams.

Since his was a mission of conversion, it may be that Felix thought that too many pagans lurked in the shadows of such a dismal, inaccessible place. And in any case, as James Wentworth-Day might have remarked, he was a Burgundian, not an Englishman. How could he understand the nature of the fen and its people? Who they were in the seventh century is certainly elusive, but there exist some clues and names in a fascinating scrap of documentary evidence that sheds a dim and partial light on the secret world of the marshes and a gossamer-thin sense of how their people saw themselves.

The Tribal Hidage was compiled some time between the seventh and the ninth centuries, and it lists thirty-five tribes, or kindreds, in England. Their relative size and importance are measured in hides, a term that probably meant a farmstead. Wessex is by far the largest at 100,000 hides, and some of the smallest, such as the East Wixna, had 300, but all are round numbers, probably no more than rough estimates. The Tribal Hidage was probably a tribute list, an assessment of what client kindreds should pay to their superior, and since no kingdoms or kindreds north of the Humber appear on it, it may have been written by Northumbrian scribes in the later seventh century when their kings were known as Bretwaldas, Britain-Rulers, powerful men who claimed dominion over all the kindreds to the south. Some of the tribal names they recorded are more or less clear. In addition to Wessex, there were the East Saxons of Essex, the Cantwarena of Kent, the South Saxons of Sussex, the East Anglians and the Mercians of the Midlands. These names have all survived into modern times in various forms.

By far the greatest concentration of named kindreds lies in and around the southern fenland, implying a patchwork of different identities and perhaps a surprising density of settlement. Some are pinned to the map by modern place names, and it seems certain that the territory of the Spaldingas survives in the town of Spalding. More tenuously, the East and West Wixna may have survived in the first element of Wisbech. The Sweordora have not only left their name on Sword Point near the site of what was Whittlesea Mere, it might also be a hint of the origins of the endonym, for what that kindred called themselves is cognate to Sweden and Swedish. Best documented of the Fens tribes are the South and North Gyrwa who lived to the east of what is now Peterborough.

Æthelthryth was an East Anglian princess who died in 679 after a very eventful and surprising life. Deeply religious, she took a vow of perpetual virginity, but this did not prevent her from being married in 652 to Tondbehrt, a prince of the South Gyrwa. Surprisingly, Æthelthryth succeeded in persuading her husband to respect her virginity. Perhaps to the relief of both of them, Tondberht died three years later, but not before the princess had extracted a promise of a dower, a gift of land that would sustain an aristocratic wife should she become widowed. That gift was the Isle of Ely, and Æthelthryth , also known as Etheldreda, later went on to found a double monastery there, one that housed both nuns and monks, presumably in separate dormitories.

Life for the abbess became complicated when she was persuaded to contract a dynastic marriage to Ecgfrith of

Northumbria in 660. He was only a young teenager, and it seemed that Etheldreda's perpetual virginity was safe, at least for the time being. But in 670 the boy became *Bretwalda*, king of Northumbria, and as a dynast anxious to secure an heir, he demanded his conjugal rights. There followed a dramatic pursuit down the length of England. The fen saved Etheldreda from capture as she and two companion nuns found sanctuary on the Isle of Ely, and the high tides that lapped around the clay island successfully defended her virtue.

After all of this effort, Etheldreda was later sanctified and became more popularly known as St Audrey. Hers turned out to be a curious legacy, a mixture of tastes in fashion and religion. At Ely St Audrey's Fair became established, and it eventually supplied the English language with an adjective: lace goods were sold there, but by the seventeenth century Puritans had come to disapprove of showy or frivolous clothing, preferring to wear plain black, and they described the decorative lace work sold at St Audrey's Fair as 'tawdry'.

Some of the names listed in the Tribal Hidage are descriptive, like Gyrwa. It simply means the marsh dwellers. But others are obscure, impossible to parse but somehow romantically mysterious. 'These are the lands of the Herefinna' or 'I am of the Noxgaga' must have been sentences uttered in Anglo-Saxon England in the seventh century, and they were meaningful, describing clear identities that have long since withered and vanished into the darkness of the past. Nevertheless, the concentration of kindred names in and around the southern Fens is very striking, and it may be an important piece of a faded map, a concentration of Englishness that has somehow endured. For endure it undoubtedly has.

The 300 hides of the Sweordora or the 600 of the South Gyrwa are unlikely to have been farmsteads in any conventional sense, since almost all of the fenland was uncultivable. They were more likely to have been areas where the customary rights of families were accepted, places where they could hunt, trap and fish, or areas where peat could be cut or sedge harvested by them and by no one else. And also places where the old identities clung on for longer than across the rest of England. When the adventurers came to drain and tame the Fens in the seventeenth century, their goal was to create fields and farms out of the wild marshland and thereby destroy a way of life that had endured since herds of mammoths, aurochs and reindeer had roamed the watery plains of Doggerland 8,000 years before. There is in all these struggles and passages of history a powerful sense of Fenlanders as somehow elemental, the sons and daughters of the earth, the sea and the sky.

It was late afternoon when I left Wicken Fen, bound for Ely, a hotel, a cooling shower and another world. I left behind a wilderness of sorts, one that was preserved by human intervention, and I entered what looked to me like a manmade landscape. Beside many of the roads rose high dykes on one side, below them were ditches known as lodes, and beyond lay a billiard-table-flat vista of fields. Chocolate-box villages and hamlets with gardens full of red, yellow and white roses were shaded by many stands of mature, broadleaf trees, and it was as though the detail and variety of the architecture, the lanes that linked houses, their gardens and outbuildings and their setting were like oases in a green desert, turning their backs, keeping at bay the vastness of the drained fen. But even though I was travelling on unfamiliar roads, my destination was never in doubt. Ely Cathedral, the Ship of the Fens, was visible on the horizon long before I reached it.

I'd come north to the Fens in the week before the general election of 2024 and was struck by how little evidence of it there was in the communities I passed through. Even though Ely and East Cambridgeshire was a solidly Conservative seat with the sitting MP a cabinet minister, I came across no posters or placards urging the electorate to support her. There were a few yellow 'Winning Here' posters for the Liberal Democrats and one very prominent garden display on behalf of the Reform Party. It was a strangely muted atmosphere, perhaps a portent of the result, for early in the morning of 5 July 2024 the tide of Conservatism had dramatically receded around Ely, and a Liberal Democrat candidate won the seat. But the far-right Reform Party won a historic victory in Boston and Skegness on the north-eastern shores of the Wash. Perhaps it was not unexpected. In 2016 Boston saw the most enthusiastic Brexit vote in Britain, when almost 75 per cent of the electorate in and around the town voted to leave the European Union. An analysis of the referendum reckoned that eight out of ten of the highest Leave voting areas of England lay along the North Sea shore. Douglas Carswell, the former Conservative MP for Clacton who defected to the UK Independence Party, the predecessor of the Reform Party, later claimed that the momentum leading to Brexit began to rumble along the Essex and East Anglian coasts. Why it should be that the communities who live closest to Europe voted to sever links with the continent is difficult to understand. The reasons may simply be economic. As the popularity of foreign package holidays helped bring about the decline of most of these North Sea resorts, they felt left behind, their sad promenades and empty fun fairs relics of an England that was disappearing. When little was done by politicians to change the situation, the residents of Canvey Island, Clacton, Skegness and the others simply expressed their frustration and voted Leave in an effort to bring about change, any sort of change. And perhaps there was also a sense of returning to a good old England of the recent past, a time when crowds from the cities flocked to the seaside to spend their money on the simple, traditional pleasures of ice cream, fish and chips, candy floss and the fairground.

★   ★   ★

Ely stands on a clay island which, at all of twenty-six metres above sea level, is the highest point in the southern Fens, and until the seventeenth century it was an island reachable only by boat or at low tide on reliable paths. As I drove into the town, I had the unusual sensation of moving uphill. I'd come to stay there so that I could understand better an earlier episode in Ely's history, one that had lodged itself in my memory a long time ago.

Like many teenagers, my introduction to English literature, especially books published in the nineteenth century, like the works of Dickens and Austen, was not through reading but through television, the BBC's Sunday serial, usually broadcast in the late afternoon. On 12 September 1965 I sat down to watch *Hereward the Wake*. It starred Alfred Lynch. who, despite a costume of furs loosely stitched together, a Celtic torc around his neck and a chunky sword at his waist, looked as though he might have been more at home with a microphone in his hand as the lead singer of a group from Liverpool. The series was riveting and the plot straightforward: goodies against baddies. The son of Earl Leofric and Lady Godiva (I was disappointed that there was never any sign of her taking off her clothes and getting on a horse), Hereward led a rebellion against William the Conqueror some time after 1066. He was the 'Last of the English' (resistance) to the Norman (foreign, French-speaking) yoke. The rebel army bravely held out on the Isle of Ely and were so difficult to dislodge that the Normans employed the services of a witch to curse Hereward. I clearly remember a shaky, rickety wooden platform and a wild-haired woman clutching a railing while hurling curses across the Fens. Hereward was ultimately betrayed, but before he could be captured he disappeared into the Fens, like Robin Hood into Sherwood Forest, and then into legend. The sixteen-part series is completely lost, the BBC having erased all the tapes for reuse. Tragic.

The show was closely based on a novel published in 1865 by the Reverend Charles Kingsley. It became phenomenally popular, going through many editions, and it made Hereward the Wake into a national hero. Rumbling under all the action, wobbly film sets and swordplay was the central idea that an incoming Norman aristocracy had somehow suppressed not only traditional English liberties but also a fundamental set of identities, an Anglo-Saxon England, the real England, oppressed by the mailed fist of foreign tyranny. (For the moment I'll resist an analogy with the Brexit vote of 2016.) Before I came to the Fens I had bought a copy of Kingsley's novel in an attempt to understand why it had struck such a profound chord. It is all but unreadable now, the prose sometimes difficult to penetrate, the narrative wandering, subplots simply fizzling out. Not only are there convoluted sentences that can extend to a long paragraph, the sentiments behind it are also not attractive.

Even though Charles Kingsley was a priest of the Church of England, a Christian socialist who promoted the provision of education for working people and the formation of workers' cooperatives, he held deeply repugnant and racist views. In the middle of the nineteenth century several academics and some politicians developed a belief system known as Anglo-Saxonism. They held that the English (and some Lowland Scots) were a fundamentally Germanic people whose language and institutions had first developed 'in the free forests of Germany' before they sailed across the North Sea to give England its name and language. The Reverend Charles Kingsley was of the view that the Church of England was 'wonderfully and mysteriously fitted for the souls of a free Norse-Saxon race'. Mysterious it was because, remarkably for a priest, he also believed that Queen Victoria was directly descended from the pagan god, Odin.

Much of this stuff might have been excused as fairly harmless fantasy were it not for the inevitable corollary that always accompanies extreme nationalism: the necessity to create a clear sense of 'the other', those who are not us, in this case not of the Anglo-Saxon race. In 1860 Kingsley was in southern Ireland, only fifteen years after the potato famine had seen the death of almost a million people from starvation, and he wrote to his wife to complain:

> I am haunted by the human chimpanzees I saw along that hundred miles of horrible country . . . to see white chimpanzees is dreadful; if they were black, one would not see it so much, but their skins, except where tanned by exposure, are as white as ours.

Some Anglo-Saxonists were a little more inclusive. Thomas Arnold was headmaster of Rugby School where he introduced reforms that would 'turn boys into Englishmen'. His new curriculum was based on history, mathematics and, above all, on the study of Latin and Greek. He wrote that

> Boys at a public school never will learn to speak or pronounce French well, under any circumstances . . . [they should] learn it grammatically as a dead language.

Arnold was an enthusiastic promoter of Anglo-Saxonism, although his definition was more elastic than Kingsley's:

Our English race is the German race; for though our Norman fathers had learned to speak a stranger's language [French], yet in blood, as we know, they were the Saxons' brethren [not in the plot of *Hereward the Wake*, they weren't] both alike [and] belonging to the Teutonic or German stock.

From the writings and speech-making of other academics, intellectuals and politicians, there was a great deal more in this vein. Leaving aside the vile and un-Christian views of Charles Kingsley and others, Anglo-Saxonism developed as both an explanation and a justification of history. By the middle of the nineteenth century the Crown had taken over the rule of India from the East India Company and the British Empire was at its zenith, the greatest, largest and most lucrative empire in history. The unique nature of the English as a Germanic-Norse master race neatly explained how such an amazing geopolitical feat was possible and also in some ways inevitable. The sun would never set on English exceptionalism. The Indians and all of the other non-Anglo-Saxon races (including the chimpanzees in Ireland) who were governed by the English were in fact fortunate to have become subjugated colonials, the beneficiaries of the bringing of civilisation to their benighted lands.

As the British Empire began to wane after the slaughter of the First World War, Anglo-Saxonism's even more warped descendent, the Nazi ideologies promoted in Adolf Hitler's Germany, had catastrophic consequences in the manifold horrors of the Holocaust and the blood-soaked attempt to convert Europe into a network of states subject to the *Herrenvolk,* the Germanic master race. After the Second World War the inevitable independence of India and Pakistan and the very rapid evaporation of the empire across the rest of the world, the notion of English exceptionalism did not fade away and become redundant, a historical quirk best forgotten, it changed and found a new focus as immigration to Britain from former colonies began to accelerate in the 1950s.

Associated Rediffusion was the first ITV company to broadcast to London and the Home Counties, beginning transmission in 1955. *People in Trouble* was one of several current affairs series presented by the journalist Dan Farson. Broadcast live, as most television was until the later 1960s, it sought 'unconventional opinions'. A regular contributor was James Wentworth-Day, the author of *The History of the Fens.* In a discussion about mixed-race marriage between Black and white people, the historian referred to any children they might have as 'coffee-coloured imps', and he went on to assert that Black people were inferior because 'in many cases their grandfathers were eating each other'. Smirking as he uttered these views, speaking in impeccable received pronunciation, Wentworth-Day reminded Farson that he had been a Conservative parliamentary candidate and that 'no first-class nation [like England] can afford to produce a race of mongrels', and added that 'France is a third-class nation – too much mixed blood.' Most alarming for Dan Farson, who always ended these exchanges with 'I couldn't dis-agree with you more', was that during a programme about transvestism, Wentworth-Day said that he thought all homosexuals in England should be hanged. At that time sexual relationships between men were illegal (although not a capital crime) and Farson became very alarmed. He himself was gay and feared that his interviewee's views might prompt some investigation. But the programme was dropped, and so was Wentworth-Day.

The contrast between these appalling prejudices and the beautifully written, lyrical and intensely emotional passages in *The History of the Fens* seems at first to be stark, but they are not irreconcilable. Wentworth-Day was a twentieth-century Anglo-Saxonist, the heir of views held by Charles Kingsley and many others, and like Kingsley a believer that the essence of Englishness was bound up with the ancient nature of the fenlands where Hereward the Wake had defied the Norman incomers, Normandy no doubt being part of a third-class nation even then.

More recent political shifts have revealed that versions of Wentworth-Day's views still rumble under the surface of British political discourse. In the general election campaign of 2024 the prime minister, Rishi Sunak, made a bad blunder when he left early from the eightieth-anniversary celebrations of D-Day in Normandy. In a last photocall Foreign Secretary David Cameron stood in for him alongside the presidents of France and the USA and the German chancellor. The first British-Asian to become prime minister, Sunak was immediately attacked by Nigel Farage, the leader of the far-right Reform Party, as someone 'who doesn't understand our culture' and 'whose instincts are not in line with those of the British people' – implying that, as a Hindu, Sunak could not possibly be seen as an Englishman. The dog whistle was clearly audible to all, and it was meant to be. When the results of the election were declared, the Reform Party polled more than four million votes, more than the Liberal Democrats. They did particularly well in the constituencies in and around the Fens, winning a seat at Boston and Skegness.

When I reached Ely and my hotel I was pleased to find it was only 200 metres from the cathedral, the Ship of the Fens. The heat had at last come off the day, and I walked around this very beautiful, striking great church as the evening sun glinted off its spires, taking many photographs. The successor to Etheldreda's abbey, it was first dedicated to her and to St Peter, and the present building was begun in 1079, when William the Conqueror was still on the throne. The interior is awe-inspiring, wonderfully well proportioned. I had noticed that it was almost time for evensong, and I went into the cool of the nave to sit for a few minutes and listen to the choir singing the old metrical psalms. I had read that the first would be Psalm 80, 'Give ear, O Shepherd of Israel, thou that leadest Joseph like a flock'. Its gentle cadences seemed to soar like a flock of birds rising into the wide skies above the fen. The high notes echoed and died around the nave, and a peace seemed to settle as I listened to another, kinder sort of Englishness.

Billy Butlin

His name seemed synonymous with fun: jaunty and alliterative like the contemporary comedians Arthur Askey and Tommy Trinder. Catchphrases like 'Good morning, campers!' echoed Askey's 'Hello, playmates!' and Trinder's 'You lucky people'. And like them Billy Butlin was a showman who understood how to give people a good time. His seaside empire of holiday camps have entertained millions of people since the first was opened near Skegness in 1936. In the same year Parliament passed an act that entitled workers to a week's paid holiday each summer, and Butlin's slogan 'A week's holiday for a week's wage' neatly capitalised on that. The camps were an immediate success.

Christened William Heygate Edmund Colborne Butlin in 1899, Billy was born in South Africa but spent much of his early life in Canada. Estranged from his father, the young boy followed his mother's example. Bertha Butlin was part of a family of travelling showmen, and when Billy came to Britain after the end of the First World War he hired a hoopla stall in his uncle's fair. Very quickly he realised that if he set the stall closer to where people stood and thereby made it easier to throw the hoops over the prizes, more customers would pay to try to win a teddy bear, a goldfish in a jar or a bag of boiled sweets. As he became increasingly successful, Billy began to buy other fairground attractions, and by 1927 he had established a permanent site at Skegness. Business continued to be good, but Butlin began to believe that if he could supply inexpensive accommodation for his customers it would become even better, and the idea of a holiday camp was born.

Other companies and organisations had built camps with basic accommodation, but none had developed a wide variety of attractions on the scale of Butlin's. In addition to the traditional stalls of the funfair, Billy bought the European rights to run dodgem cars and added scenic railways, helter-skelters and even zoos. Construction began at Ingoldmells on the coast of the Wash just to the northeast of Skegness, and plans included rows of chalets that could accommodate up to 500 people. Dining and recreation halls, a theatre, a gymnasium, a swimming pool (instead of the cold North Sea), a boating lake, tennis courts, bowling greens and cricket pitches were all created, and the whole site landscaped. On 11 April 1936, Easter Saturday, the holiday camp was opened by Amy Johnson, the first woman to fly solo from Britain to Australia. It was an early example of celebrity endorsement. To add to the publicity, Butlin spent a very large sum, £500, on advertising in the *Daily Express*. It offered a week's holiday at £3 for accommodation, three meals a day and free entertainment. The camp was immediately overwhelmed with bookings as the railways brought campers from the Midlands cities and London, and accommodation had to be increased from 500 to 2,000.

As a showman, Billy Butlin was very aware of how much people were enjoying themselves. Fun was his business. And it seemed that although the camp at Skegness was very busy, campers were not taking part in the activities that were offered. Families and friends were tending not to mix with others. Some people seemed bored. Billy expressed his concerns to Norman Bradshaw, the senior engineer on the site and a naturally cheerful, outgoing and friendly man. That evening Norman got up on stage in the main recreational hall and told a few jokes, but more than that he explained how the attractions worked and what were the best times to get the most out of them. Apparently the atmosphere changed immediately. 'The place was suddenly buzzing,' one colleague recalled. Campers started to mix beyond their families and groups of friends. Billy recruited more cheery individuals to act as smiling facilitators but realised that if campers wanted to approach them they needed to look distinctive. Norman Bradshaw was sent to Skegness and returned with a choice of three blazers: blue, yellow or white. Not convinced, Butlin remembered his upbringing in Canada and settled on a red jacket, the same bright colour worn by the Mounties, the Royal Canadian Mounted Police. And the Redcoats were born. Billy Butlin had understood that the British needed encouragement to enjoy themselves, and the ever-smiling, ever-helpful Redcoats supplied it.

In 1937 work began on building a second camp at Dovercourt near Harwich on the Essex coast, but it was not used as a holiday camp. As war in Europe became increasingly likely, the government requisitioned Dovercourt to house refugee children, most of them Jewish, who arrived on the *Kindertransport* trains from Germany. Another camp opened at Clacton in 1938, but once again it was soon requisitioned, this time as a training camp.

The holiday-camp business was put on hold after the declaration of war in 1939, but Billy Butlin was sufficiently astute and far-sighted to see that the needs of the wartime economy and what might happen when and if peace came might be compatible. More training camps were needed, and Butlin agreed to oversee construction, but on condition that he could buy the sites after the war ended and convert them into holiday camps. These were built at Filey on the Yorkshire coast, Pwllheli on the Lleyn Peninsula in North Wales and at Ayr in the west of Scotland. All of them eventually opened as holiday camps in 1947. By the early 1960s the Butlin's empire was complete (despite a failed attempt to set up an outpost in the Bahamas) with further camps at Bognor Regis on the Channel coast, Minehead in Somerset and Barry Island in South Wales.

Before foreign package holidays and their guaranteed sunshine began to drive deep inroads into the British holiday market in the later 1960s, Butlin's holiday camps were extremely popular and affordable for ordinary people. Encouraged by the Redcoats, campers' children enjoyed the fairground attractions, played tennis and crazy golf and much else. Butlin's offered a nursery service for the under-fives, something that was important in the post-war baby-boom years, and there was an evening chalet patrol to check on older children while their parents went for a drink or to the dance hall. And, of course, the camps ran Bonny Baby and Mother and Child competitions where everyone was given a prize.

Before the age of mass TV viewing, there were cinemas at Butlin's, concerts and, naturally, dancing every night. Many of the black-and-white archive photographs of the camps in the 1950s feature bathing beauty competitions and line-ups of often awkward-looking young women by the side of swimming pools and diving boards. At Skegness there were also Miss Personality competitions and Glamorous Grandmother contests. With many single men and women also on holiday, and with access to one another's chalets and some privacy, all sorts of other entertainments were also available. Interviewed long after their retirement, several former Redcoats smiled when they recollected summer in the camps. 'We didn't do it for the money,' said one.

Through the later decades of the twentieth century, and especially after Billy Butlin's retirement in 1968, the empire began to shrink. There are only three camps (now called resorts rather than camps) still open: Bognor Regis, Minehead and Skegness. The latter was difficult to find. As I drove through the town, which had a sad and faded, run-down look characteristic of many resorts on the North Sea coast, there were no signs I could see. But by the time I left Skegness I could make out the white outline of the huge Skyline Pavilion in the distance. To counter the vagaries of British summer weather, Butlin's had erected these enormous marquee-like structures at their resorts so that no one's holiday could be dampened. Once I had explained to the security guard that all I wanted was to look around, I parked and began to follow the signs to the attractions under and around the Pavilion.

Most of the campers I saw did not look happy. It was a sunny morning without a cloud in the sky, and yet the resort was most crowded under the Skyline Pavilion. When I looked up at the white roof, I watched the shadows of seabirds as they flew over it. Before I reached one of the entrances, I passed rows of chalets in Breakwater Grove in Pacific Wharf, the first sign of a strange, awkward cultural mash-up. Later I came across Lagoon Bay and Studio 54, ten-pin bowling and a sandwich board advertising happy hour (between 2 and 4 p.m.). Alongside these geographically illogical American imports there were attractions that Billy Butlin would have recognised. In a wooded copse, or perhaps a grove, was Adventure Golf, what looked like a version of crazy golf, played with a putter off a hundred promenades in the 1950s and 1960s. It was deserted. There was a miniature merry-go-round with small rocking horses that might have bobbed up and down to carousel music and a game I played as a boy with pennies in amusement arcades. Sealed under glass, it was a slow-moving shelf of two-pence pieces, and the idea was to roll one of yours onto it so that it dislodged others and they came tumbling out. No one was playing it, and I had no change in my pocket.

Under the vast pavilion there was a wide auditorium with a curtained stage at one end. It was being used as a very large dining room, seating perhaps 150 people. In the middle of the morning it was full. There seemed to be food outlets everywhere, from the Rock & Sole fish and chip shop to the Pasty Shack, Papa John's Pizzas, the Firehouse Grill, the Beachcomber Bar and many more. In the shops more food and drink were for sale, including tubs of candy floss, Parma Violet sweets and Refreshers, all of them billed as 'retro'.

Most of the families and groups I passed that morning were either eating or drinking or both. Several groups were studying menus on boards outside the restaurants or cafés, making decisions about an early lunch. It was striking how many obese adults and children there were, some of them using mobility scooters to get around, many in skimpy holiday clothing that exposed more flesh than seemed possible. And it appeared that every second person wore tattoos. Often their clothes, or lack of them, were designed to show off the elaborate designs.

I realise this is beginning to sound more than a little precious, even sniffy, and no doubt what I saw at Butlin's Skegness is only a reflection of a national picture as an obesity epidemic takes hold and grows into a huge problem for the NHS. But it was the atmosphere that seemed strange to me. These people were on holiday, and while I know I was there for only one morning, I saw no one smile, heard no laughter or felt little sense of ease. It seemed to me that the main attraction was not the fairground rides or even the American imports like the flumes and the ten-pin bowling, but rather the food and the drink.

3

Over the Night Sea

On a late September evening in 1943 the BBC radio journalist Wynford Vaughan-Thomas and his sound recordist
Reg Pidsley boarded a Lancaster bomber. Its squadron was
to take part in a massive 700-bomber raid on Berlin, and
Vaughan-Thomas planned to record what happened on
what was an extremely risky assignment. On the flight he
supplied commentary, but in that recording, made on a
disc so that it would endure as a piece of history – if the
plane returned from its mission – the voices of the crew
can also be clearly heard above the thunder of the engines.
It is a unique and very vivid record of how the war was
taken to Germany in the years before the D-Day landings
of 1944. Night raids across the North Sea were launched
from the airfields of Lincolnshire and the flat fenland
around the Wash and in East Anglia. Much later, in 1972,
Vaughan-Thomas was interviewed by Thames Television
and the sound recording has survived.

Thirty-three years old when he crammed himself in
the cockpit of F-Freddie, the reporter remembered that
the crew was, on average, ten years younger than him
but that they 'nursed me through it'. When his Lancaster

reached the North Sea coast, guided by a single search-light, a rendezvous point for the massive raid, Vaughan-Thomas looked behind and saw the squadrons of bombers come together 'like fireflies' before his captain, the skipper, confirmed they had left the coast behind. Even after all the navigation lights had been switched off, the following flights of Lancasters could be seen against the fading light of the westering sky, 'their wings rising and falling'. Even though the skipper told the reporter that the sea crossing would take an hour and ten minutes, the crew could quickly see 'a film of light' in the distance, the searchlights of the air defences on the Dutch coast. As they approached, the Lancasters began to be picked up by the long beams raking the sky 'trying to claw you down'.

I thought 'this is it'. The searchlights lit up the inside of the aeroplane. But suddenly they seemed to go past us, and they caught the Lanc following us like a moth. Two, three, four more were on it and up the line of the searchlights came flak, streams of it. And to my horror I suddenly saw the wings of the plane starting to slowly come apart and flame going right through and it turned and [went] down and down and down. My insides went down with it. And at that very moment, we were through the search-light screen . . .

'Berlin,' said the flight engineer. He'd a lovely Scottish accent [he was Jock Scotty Stewart]. 'You're going to enjoy this, Mr Thomas. You're really going to enjoy this'. Behind us the whole sky was clearing [of cloud] and a mass of black specks [Lancasters] following and ahead of you a bullring of light. You could see the whole of Berlin. It was a nightmare. Tracer bullets going past, there was flak coming up. And we looked down. We were dropping the big Cookie [an 1,800kg bomb also known as a Blockbuster, the origin of the term] and the ritual took over and you could hear the captain saying 'steady, steady', and the bomb aimer saying 'left, left, steady'. Then 'bomb away'. Down goes the big Cookie, and you follow it down, and it was as though jewellery was being thrown on black velvet. It sparkled, it shone. The whole of Berlin looked like the most beautiful, dazzling sight you ever saw, until you realised that that this was civilisation burning below you.

At that moment – I will never forget it – a slow East Anglian voice came into my left ear on the intercom, 'Night fighter attacking, sir.' Suddenly the whole aircraft seemed to be filled with fumes. The captain said, 'Steady, steady. Where is he?' He calmed the whole thing down. Never will I forget – talk about heroism or coolness, but that East Anglian rear gunner, he had it absolutely taped and the captain held the whole crew together. And I think I suddenly saw the tracer bullets drop right below the nose, and suddenly another burst of gunfire and then the cool East Anglian voice saying, 'Night fighter shot down, sir.' He went down like a burning piece of oily waste rag. Suddenly we were out [of the searchlights around Berlin] and the cloud came round again . . . We made a huge circle [over Sweden] and came down over the North Sea and there came the blissful moment when we knew we had made it. And then the crew sang a song.

> 'There's many a Lancaster back from Berlin
>   bound for Old Blighty's shore,
> Carrying its cargo of terrified men, shit-scared
>   and thrown on the floor.
> There's many a Heinkel that's shooting the shit
>   and many a Messerschmitt too.
> They've ruined our hydraulics and shot off our
>   bollocks.
> What are we going to do?
> Fuck 'em all, fuck 'em all,
> The fast and the slow and the small.
> Fuck all the Heinkels and FW1s
> And fuck all the pilots and fuck all their guns
> For we're showing our arse to them all,
> As back to our billets we crawl.
> For Christ's sake give Margate as our next
>   target,
> As for Berlin, fuck 'em all.'

For some reason Reg Pidsley failed to record the song, but Wynford Vaughan-Thomas remembered that the chorus was exultant, belted out by each crew member, showing immense relief mixed with an unequivocal sense of a dangerous job well done.

Known as Bomber County because its flat fenlands were home to forty-nine airfields during the Second World War, Lincolnshire was also bordered by the North

Sea, a welcome stretch of calm before the storm that waited on the opposite shore. As Wynford Vaughan-Thomas discovered, the coast could be reached in ten minutes and the Nazi-occupied European mainland in little more than an hour. But in order to carry the war to the Germans and to achieve the powerful propaganda coup of regularly bombing Germany itself, hitting back after the Blitz and the destructive raids on Britain's cities, the right aeroplane was needed. And none were available. Before the end of 1941 the RAF's heavy bombers – the Wellingtons, Blenheims and other types – had proved ineffective. New designs with greater range and more capability were urgently needed. As often, wartime necessity gave birth to brilliant invention, for in the formidable shape of the Lancaster, Roy Chadwick created a deadly weapon. It was a killing machine, an aircraft that could carry more bombs than any other – one American pilot described the Lancaster as a plane attached to a bomb bay – and its superb aerodynamics meant it handled well and could evade attacks from fighters. More than that, the Lancaster inspired great affection. Harry Yates, a pilot with 75 Squadron, wrote in 1944:

> Some products of the hand of man have that uncanny capacity to pull at the heart-strings and the Lancaster was one such. Everything about it was just right. Its muscular, swept lines were beautiful to look at. It flew with effortless grace and had a precise weighted feel. It made the pilot's job easy. You could throw it all over the skies if you had the inclination and the physical strength.

When the first Lancaster bombers became available in later 1941 and Sir Arthur Harris took over Bomber Command after February 1942 a new strategy gradually emerged. Not in favour of precisely targeted raids – which in any case had to take place in daylight and were much more dangerous – he believed that a policy of area bombing would achieve much better results. This involved large-scale raids like the one Wynford Vaughan-Thomas took part in, and they saturated a chosen area, usually large towns and cities in the heart of Germany. This meant the wholesale destruction of civilian as well as military targets and all the concomitant casualties. Having fought in the First World War, Harris never forgot the slaughter of the trench warfare in Flanders, and his strategy was designed to weaken Germany so profoundly that when the time for invasion came casualties on that scale could be avoided. It was more than ironic that the scale of the sacrifice of the aircrews of Bomber Command far exceeded what happened in the First World War. More than 125,000 men flew Lancasters and other aircraft, and a staggering 55,755 were killed. This was a casualty rate of 44 per cent of all British personnel compared with an overall rate of 9 per cent between 1914 and 1918. And most of those who died were very young men, often between nineteen and twenty-three years old, barely out of their boyhoods. Because of the very high casualty rate, after aircrews had survived thirty missions they were not asked to do more – although some did volunteer to continue. That immense sacrifice was unparalleled across all of Britain's armed forces, and its grim scale should not be forgotten.

At each airfield the prelude to a mission was nerve-racking. In the morning, battle orders were pinned on a central notice board listing the names of the crews who would fly that night. But for security reasons, there was at that point no mention of targets. Bob Woolf, a gunner with 9 Squadron, remembered:

All those listed for the trip felt the tension, and this would continue right up through [to] the briefing, the preparation for the flight and the pre-flight meal. Sometimes the reaction would be instant. Sometimes some fellows would need to go to the toilet in great haste. Others would try a forced kind of levity, cracking jokes and laughing too easily. Others would become quiet and withdrawn. Nobody wanted to reveal the fear they felt inside but it was deep in our souls.

When at last the briefing began, men crammed into a Nissen hut, and RAF Special Police manned the doors. On a dais at one end there was a large map of Western Europe covered with a curtain. When the senior officers arrived, one of them pulled off the curtain to reveal 'the target for tonight'. If it was Berlin, there was always a murmur of disquiet, whereas if it was France, there was relief. All Lancaster raids took place at night, and the shorter the journey the better. Bill Jones was the intelligence officer at the Lincolnshire airfield of Elsham Woods:

Although I had my briefing notes in my hand, I always made sure I could do the briefing without having to read from them. If you had to read your notes, you couldn't look at the crews and, in any case, it gave the impression that you were simply reading from a prepared speech. As I take the platform with my three foot long black pointer in my hand, I give a quick look round. It happens at every briefing – how many of them will return to be interrogated in the early hours of the morning, I wonder?

Before the crews boarded the Lancasters, each man had to hand over the keys to his locker to avoid it having to be forced open if he did not return. Benzedrine pills were offered. Known as 'wakey-wakey' pills, they helped keep tired men alert on the night missions. And when each crew reached their Lancaster a strange ritual took place. To relieve themselves before a long flight and to wish themselves luck, each man urinated on the tail wheel. Bomber Command issued orders forbidding this practice, but they were ignored. Luck mattered almost more than anything. Once all were aboard and each man in his station, the four Merlin engines were fired up, and as dozens of planes queued for take-off, the noise was thunderous. It was the din of battle, one that would only be stilled by disaster or safe return.

The need for the continual production of Lancasters dominated the war economy after 1941, and their success, their ability to hit back, undoubtedly boosted home morale. Between November 1943 and March 1944 Bomber Command sent sixteen raids of hundreds of Lancasters to attack Berlin with devastating effect. On the night of 22–23 November the western suburbs suffered devastating damage, with firestorms consuming entire neighbourhoods because of the dry weather conditions. But the sixteen raids in the winter of 1943–4 saw terrible losses, with more than 500 aircraft shot down and their crews killed or captured. Many Bomber Command prisoners were brutally treated by their German captors. And many lockers in the airfields of Lincolnshire were opened and their contents sent to relatives or disposed of.

Even though the aircrews were only 10 per cent of the personnel on RAF stations, their losses were felt very keenly but dealt with almost brutally, as all traces of the dead airmen were quickly removed. Each base was like a temporary rural town with more than 2,500 living in Nissen huts and other buildings. There were usually two squadrons of bombers led by wing commanders, and in each, two to three flights of eight to ten aeroplanes under squadron leaders. To reduce the risk of bomb damage, most buildings were well spread out on either side of runways, and a bicycle was considered an asset. Bases had shops, the NAAFI, hospitals and even dance halls where aircrews could partner the many WAAFs, the Women's Auxiliary Air Force recruits, who did much of the administration and communication. Returning pilots sometimes remarked that the WAAF who was in radio contact when the Lancasters approached their home base had a particularly lovely voice. Most people slept in the Nissen huts, and diaries remembered icy winds blasting across the Fens. And with the exception of the traditional breakfast of bacon and eggs after returning from a raid, the food was meagre and of poor quality. Nevertheless, crews knew how to party, and alcohol seemed a regular and necessary means of letting off steam.

Almost all of the forty-nine airfields in Lincolnshire have reverted to farmland or found other uses. But one of them has been converted into a shrine. At East Kirkby, not far inland from Skegness, is the Lincolnshire Aviation Heritage Centre. It is home to one of only two remaining Lancaster bombers left in Britain, and that was something I wanted very much to see.

Harry Yates was right. It was strangely beautiful, monstrous and monumental, like a massive sculpture laid on its side. The sheer size of the Lancaster surprised me, perhaps because I'd only seen photographs of it flying, with no reference to judge its scale. It was brutally elegant, its nose and its gun turret in the air, the lines of its wingspread clean and perfectly proportionate. And the tail wheel seemed dry. Below the framed Perspex and glass of the cockpit were the Lancaster's battle honours, its successful missions counted in rows of little painted bombs, and, such was their disdain, two ice cream cones for raids over Italy. The aeroplane had been meticulously and lovingly rebuilt by a band of devoted enthusiasts, and although one day it might fly, on that warm summer afternoon it would taxi out from in front of its hangar and run up and down on what remained of the grass runway of the old RAF base. More than a thousand people had come to this green and leafy corner of Lincolnshire to watch a deadly killing machine show itself off.

The tarmacked area outside of the hangar was roped off, but I managed to get close to the huge aeroplane, standing opposite the cockpit. The pilot and the flight engineer seemed to be checking their instruments while the ground crew removed the chocks from the wheels under each wing. On the far side, where the pilot could clearly see him, a man wearing headphones appeared to be orchestrating the starting procedure. Once thumbs went up in the cockpit and all seemed to be in order, he made a circling movement with his hand, and the first of the four Merlin engines spluttered into life, and the propellors became a blur. When the engine nearest me started, fire flickered out of its vents. It seemed that a dragon was waking, coming to life. The roar was deafening. And then something magical, menacing happened. As the pilot eased off the brakes, the Lancaster moved slowly forward towards the grass runway, and the shadow of its mighty wing passed over me, and on that hot afternoon, I shivered. The dragon was awake, a creature that could spit fire and death from the skies.

With the watching crowd, I walked quickly over to the long, open field to watch the great aircraft taxi. Many long lenses were adjusted and shutters clicked, but the spectators were oddly silent with none of the excited chatter of groups of people on a day out. All that could be heard was the rolling thunder of the four Merlin engines as the Lancaster went up and then back down the runway. The undulations of the ground put me in mind of Wynford Vaughan-Thomas looking behind at the vast fleet of Lancasters flying out of the westering sky towards the darkness of Europe and seeing their wings dipping up and down. Even on the ground, the lines and movement of the aircraft seemed almost graceful. But as it turned and moved towards the crowd, grace became menace as its propellers sliced through the summer air.

Then something unforgettable happened. The bomber came to a halt, and with the brakes fully engaged, the pilot revved all four engines to what might have been full throttle. The noise shattered the afternoon as the dragon roared. Its visible power became all too audible. Some people put their hands over their ears. But one woman stood very still by the barrier, staring steadily at the great aeroplane. I noticed that tears were running down her cheeks.

Near the group of outbuildings opposite the hangar, I'd passed a grove of young trees, and some had white metal plaques by their trunks. Each was dedicated to men who had flown in the Lancasters: 'In loving memory of John Chatterton DFC MSc . . . Returned home again'. He had served with three squadrons, survived the war and died at the age of eighty-four in 2004, only twenty-three when he flew with Bomber Command. And here he was, returned to East Kirkby airfield, the place where life had been most precious, perhaps most vivid. Maybe the woman had wept for someone like him, someone she had known.

After the Lancaster's engines were shut down, I joined the long queue in the NAAFI, noting that its name stood for Navy, Army and Air Force Institutes, something I hadn't realised. I wondered if they had the sort of soggy, stodgy slices of cake my dad remembered from his wartime days in the Royal Engineers. It was known as 'wad', and was tasteless but filling. Balancing a plate with a safe-looking sandwich and a teacup and a saucer, I saw that all the tables were taken. On the line of benches outside I saw the woman who had wept sitting on a bench. When I asked if she minded if I joined her, she smiled and wondered where in Scotland I came from.

'I've been coming down here for a long time,' she said in response to my question. Pointing at the Lancaster, she added, 'That's a piece of our history we shouldn't forget. But we nearly did.'

Wearing white, very pretty and carrying only a handbag, not a camera with a long lens, she seemed an unlikely enthusiast. But she turned out to be very knowledgeable indeed. I asked if she minded if I took notes and again she smiled.

'It was a friend of my father's. He flew Lancasters, and unlike many other men who came back after the war, he did want to talk about what it was like. I think he did that, talked to us, because he couldn't or didn't, talk to other people.'

As I sipped my tea and scribbled, she explained at the end of the war Winston Churchill had made an important speech when victory in Europe was certain. He thanked and praised all the branches of the armed services except Bomber Command.

'It must have been calculated,' she said, 'not a mistake or an oversight. Churchill took a lot of care over his speeches.'

Public opinion had turned against Bomber Command, especially after the area bombing of Hamburg and Dresden towards the end of the war, when terrible fire-storms had raged and incinerated thousands.

'It became so bad that my dad's friend was abused,

called a murderer. And so, when people enquired about what he did in the war, he just said he had been a pilot in the RAF.'

Sitting forward on the bench and turning slightly towards me, she said, 'It was worse than wrong. All of those young men, boys really, they weren't criminals. They were heroes. They knew what the chances of their survival were. But they flew anyway.' She pointed again at the Lancaster on the tarmac in front of the hangar. 'And that beautiful aeroplane, it won the war.' And then she shook her head. 'They had to wait almost seventy years for a proper memorial.'

I'd stopped taking notes. It seemed somehow disrespectful, and I was sure I'd remember what was said.

'And even then, the money to build it had to come from private donations, not the government. My dad's friend couldn't go. He was too old and unwell, and so I went in his place.' She stopped, and then seemed to gather herself. 'A Lancaster flew over London at the end of the ceremony and dropped thousands of poppies.' Turning to face me, she took off her sunglasses. 'And I cried then, too.'

Since the arrival of Caesar and his legions, the war bands of the Angles, Saxon and Jutes and the Vikings in their longships, the North Sea had brought war west to Britain. The pilots of Bomber Command reversed history as they flew up and over Britain's great moat when they carried destruction in the opposite direction. And the sea also became a friend to aircrews, a prelude before they met the raking searchlights over the coasts of the Low Countries and a welcome sight after they had dropped their bombs, survived the flack and flew home to its welcoming English coast. But for some, forced to ditch in the North Sea, it became their grave, and their memorial of sorts, perishing as they did in Britain's greatest natural defence as they sought in their way to defend our islands.

III

Tyne

The Holy Coast

On a windless May morning the land lay still under an open sky, the sun brilliant and warming. I was driving down country roads made into glorious avenues of white blossom on hawthorn hedges, the colour of strawberries and cream from the occasional crab apple, egg-yolk yellow gorse, and everywhere the lustrous green of new leaves on birches and beeches. Where a night wind had blown, there were occasional drifts of blossom snow as the road swung around a corner.

I'd left very early to drive to the coast along a quiet B road that would take me up to the breast of a ridge, a vantage point where I had often stopped. To the east are revealed long views of the North Sea shore, where the patchwork of farmland – technicolour rapeseed and fields of pale-green barley – meets the blue vastness where the land undulates gently to its edges.

But a kilometre or so before I planned to stop and get out of the car to look at the sea and the coast, a haar loomed up. I disappeared into its grey shroud, visibility quickly shrinking to less than a hundred metres, the air suddenly cold. Known in Scotland by the Dutch word, haar, and called a sea-fret in England, it is a weather phenomenon characteristic of the North Sea. Haar occurs most frequently on its northern coasts in spring and early summer. When warm and moist air passes over the cold sea, it causes condensation to form, and easterlies blow the damp mist towards the land. It rarely penetrates far in daytime. In spring the land warms more quickly than the sea, and higher temperatures keep the haar at bay by dissolving it as the sun climbs, but at night, when the air is colder, the mist can move far inland.

Haar can be dangerous as well as inconvenient. When inshore fishermen find themselves suddenly enveloped, they can quickly lose their bearings, all reference points on land having disappeared. It is not so much the sea that fishermen fear as what lies beneath it. When line of sight courses can be set from daymarks on land such as headlands, bays, buildings and even church steeples, rocks and reefs can be safely avoided. When nothing can be seen, those fishing from small, open boats without any sophisticated navigational aids can often become disoriented and find themselves at the mercy of tides and currents that might drive them towards invisible danger.

Even those on a beach can get into difficulty, especially if a haar is blown quickly onshore. Tynemouth has become an unlikely centre for surfing (only unlikely when compared to the images of Californian beaches conjured up by the music of the Beach Boys). Big waves can crash onto Longsands Beach, and there is a shop and a surf school for those hardy souls who can afford a wetsuit. Paddle boarding is also popular. But some years ago, a haar came in very quickly, and a group of children who had been splashing around in shallow water were suddenly engulfed by a big wave they couldn't see coming. The ebb, the riptide, was powerful, and it dragged them out to sea. But fortunately local paddle boarders found the children quickly and brought all safely to shore.

As I drove into the heart of Gateshead the haar billowed above the tall buildings, sometimes hiding them, sometimes suddenly revealing them. But I could read the road signs for Jarrow and others told me that I was close to my destination: Bede Industrial Estate, Bede Metro station and the Bede Motor Company. They were surprising examples of the enduring memory of a very great man who lived on the shores of the North Sea and made an indelible mark on history and identity. I wanted to visit St Paul's Church and the site of the early medieval monastery where Bede lived almost his whole life. There he wrote about sixty works of scholarship, much of it biblical commentary, some of it poetry, history and science. But immensely learned and prolific though he was, Bede rarely left Jarrow, except perhaps to go south to York and north to the Holy Island of Lindisfarne. His was the life of the mind and his world the library he constantly consulted. Bede's achievements were towering, and his work dominated the intellectual life of Europe for four centuries. And he was fascinated by the nature of the North Sea.

Despite their immediate surroundings and wider context, certain locations can doggedly retain a powerful sense of place, a unique *genius loci*, places of spirits long fled. Almost perfectly preserved, the chancel of St Paul's is the same little church where Bede prayed and sang every day. It was where, as a thirteen-year-old boy, he and his mentor Abbot Ceolfrith went together and kneeled to praise God, all of the other brothers having died in a devastating visitation of the plague by the end of 686. It was where divine office was observed every three hours and where at least one mass a day was said and sung.

The western end of St Paul's is much younger, erected in 1866 on the site of the seventh-century basilica and its successor churches. The Victorian building is bright, welcoming, with a gift shop in one corner and Fenwick Lawson's stunning 1983 wooden sculpture, the *Risen Ascended Christ*, suspended from the roof of the nave. Perhaps not surprisingly, visitors seemed to prefer to spend their time there and not in the plain seventh-century chancel. I sat for a long time in the old church – not in prayer, for I am no Christian – but much moved that I could be exactly where Bede once was, look at the solid stone walls he saw every day of his life at the monastery. Such moments aren't mysterious or even spiritual, at least not for me. They are miraculous.

Outside St Paul's the twenty-first century is utterly dominant. Immensely tall pylons that carry power lines from across the River Tyne tower over the church. Traffic thrums along a very busy road only a few metres from its walls. Containers are piled up alongside rows of cars for export at the Port of Tyne only 200 metres away and factories and warehouses crowd around. In the midst of all this, the little church has miraculously survived for more than thirteen centuries. Perhaps there are spirits swirling around it. Perhaps the brilliance of Bede, the sanctity of Ceolfrith, Cuthbert and others have cast an invisible protective shield over St Paul's, an island of peace and contemplation in the racket and hubbub of modern life.

Outside Bede's church the haar had at last burned off. To the south of St Paul's stand the substantial ruins of the later medieval monastery founded from Durham Cathedral in the eleventh century. Under its walls and archways lies the complex of buildings the great scholar knew so well. When Abbot Ceolfrith came to Jarrow with ten monks and twelve novices to found the monastery in 681, when Bede was only eight years old, they chose the site carefully, setting the church and the monastic buildings on the banks of the River Don, a tributary of the nearby Tyne. The landscape Ceolfrith and his followers saw in the late seventh century was very different. Now covered by the quays and warehouses of the Port of Tyne, Jarrow Slake was a wide, tidal expanse of mudflats close to the monastery, and the Don meandered along its southern fringes. The Anglian name for Jarrow was Gyrwe (pronounced 'Jeer-way') and it meant the 'Place of the Marsh-Dwellers'. It is clearly cognate to the Fenland kindreds of the North and South Gyrwa. When the port was built up after the Second World War the little river was canalised and the mudflats drained.

In 674 Ecgfrith, king of Northumbria and frustrated husband of Etheldreda, had gifted land near the mouth of the River Wear for the building of the monastery of St Peter. Its abbot was Benedict Biscop, a determined, energetic, innovative and apparently wealthy churchman. Born into a noble Northumbrian family, he decided that

St Peter's would be different from the humble timber-and-thatch buildings of other contemporary monasteries (which Bede later described as built *in more Scottorum*, in the manner of the Irish). Biscop's church would be built *in more Romanum*, in the Roman fashion, meaning that it would be a stone structure. The abbot crossed to Europe to recruit masons who had the necessary skills, and also glaziers to make stained-glass windows, something not previously seen in Britain.

This was not only a well-organised extravagance, it was also a political statement. From his trips to Rome and from his Bible study, Biscop was making a series of conscious links. His king, Ecgfrith, claimed *imperium*, according to Bede's later assessment – that is, authority over all the Anglo-Saxon kingdoms of England as their *Bretwalda*, their Britain-Ruler. And so his new church would make those links with the glories of the Roman Empire manifest and much stronger, Ecgfrith's legitimacy was further under-pinned by a biblical comparison. The Angles, Saxons, Jutes and others had been Christian converts for a short time, fifty years or so, and it was only in the seventh century that their kings had finally overcome the native British, confining their power to the west, to Devon, Cornwall and Wales. By building the new church with the help of foreign masons and glaziers, Biscop was inviting compari-sons with Solomon. For the construction of the temple in Jerusalem the great king had imported the skills needed from beyond his realm, from gentiles. And more than that, the claims of the incoming Israelites to Judaea and the surrounding territories were justified because they were God's chosen people – and to give praise and thanks to their God Solomon had built a temple. And so did Benedict Biscop with the help of King Ecgfrith. The Angles and Saxons had come to dominate England, incomers like the Israelites to the promised land, and they needed to give thanks to God for making them his chosen people.

Building in the Roman manner at Jarrow was also made much easier by the efforts of the Roman army. Nearby, in what is now South Shields, stood the large depot fort of Arbeia, and across the Tyne was the greatest Roman monument of all, Hadrian's Wall, and its terminal fort at Segedunum in the middle of Wallsend. Already cut-and-dressed stone was almost certainly robbed out of these huge complexes to make the job of Biscop's foreign masons much easier.

There is, of course, no direct written evidence to support this thesis of a link between the children of Israel and the Anglo-Saxon kings of the seventh and eighth centuries. Except for one defining document. When Bede sat down to write his great masterpiece, *The Ecclesiastical History of the English People*, he intended to produce an account of how the chosen people came to rule over England, and how their churchmen honoured God in several ways. The idea of the twin monasteries of St Peter and St Paul probably grew in Benedict Biscop's mind. He had visited Rome six times and prayed at the tombs of the apostles Peter and Paul, the founders of the Christian Church. The twin monasteries, dedicated to the great saints, were perhaps an attempt to extend the frontiers of the Kingdom of God from Rome to faraway Northumbria.

Biscop's energy and determination are striking. A

journey from the shores of the North Sea to the Continent and then overland to Rome was long, arduous and potentially dangerous, especially when the abbot brought back objects like sacred paintings and jewelled reliquaries. But perhaps his most valuable baggage on the return journey would not have interested brigands or thieves. Benedict brought back many books. And when Abbot Ceolfrith later visited Rome, he did the same. The library of the twin monasteries grew vast for the times, with around 300 books on its shelves. It was without doubt the communities' most enduringly valuable possession, and it was also a matter of great good fortune, or perhaps an act of divine providence, that a great scholar emerged who could use the library to create an extraordinary cultural legacy.

The authors of ancient Rome did not write books, they wrote volumes. Cognate to the English word 'revolve', the Latin *volumen* meant a roll of script, or a scroll. When Pliny the Elder compiled his encyclopaedia *Natural History* in the years leading up to his death in the eruption of Mount Vesuvius in 79 AD, he wrote on scrolls, rolls of papyrus of roughly thirty pages each. But when Benedict Biscop brought back a copy of his great work, as well as those of several other great classical authors, a volume had become a codex. From *caudex*, it carries the sense of being made of wood. But in fact this was a reference to covers made from boards of either oak or elm.

By the sixth century the book looked completely different. Instead of writing on papyrus, scribes had begun to use vellum, calfskin or parchment, the hides of goats or sheep. They did this in part as a response to the demand for Bibles and gospels. Vellum and parchment were much more durable, and wooden boards protected pages from damage. This mattered very much because of the nature of Christianity. Above all it was, like Islam, a religion of the book, the Holy Bible, and the Word of God was sacred and should be venerated, even worshipped. Bibles were often laid upon altars with the pages open for that reason. After the skin from legs had been trimmed off animal hides, the shape was broadly rectangular, and this determined not only the form and size of codices but also of modern books. A piece of vellum or parchment could make at least four pages if it was folded in the middle. This in turn dictated how books were bound and the way pages were laid out in fascicles of four or its multiples.

Scholars believe that Bede consulted at least 200 of the 300 or so books in the libraries of the twin monasteries (St Paul's was only eleven kilometres from St Peter's) in his research for all that he wrote, and he knew intimately what knowledge each of them contained. Compared to scrolls, codices were easy to rest on a table, either laid flat or at angle on a reading stand, and that made note taking (with a metal stylus and wax tablets) much more convenient. In St Paul's Church I bought a postcard with an enlightening quote on it from the great scholar: 'I am my own secretary; I dictate, I compose, I copy all myself.' This is, I believe, revealing. We are nowadays surrounded by vast reservoirs of knowledge held in media of all sorts, whereas Bede had a library of only 300 books. The quote suggests that he owned what he read, knew his sources intimately, probably held a great deal of information in his head. Copying was the sole means of publication and it is also a reliable means of internalising information, and from that store a great stimulus to making connections and seeing relationships between different writers and their ideas.

Benedict Biscop's ambition to build a Kingdom of God in Northumbria extended beyond the stone churches and walls of monasteries. The Word of God would be remade on the shores of the North Sea. Under Abbot Ceolfrith, three complete single-volume (or single-codex) Bibles were copied, the earliest surviving versions in Latin. It was an immense and enormously expensive labour. Each Bible needed 1,550 calfskins, a huge investment from an agrarian economy that measured its wealth in livestock, and especially cattle. Many skins must have been donated. Known as the *Codex Amiatinus*, only one of these Bibles has survived. It was taken to Italy in 716 as a gift to Pope Gregory II, and it eventually found its way to the Abbazia di San Salvatore at the foot of Monte Amiata in Tuscany. It can now be seen in all its vibrant glory in the Medici Library in Florence. There can be little doubt that, as the twin monasteries' greatest scholar, Bede was heavily involved in the planning and perhaps part of the execution of this great project, perhaps the most impressive product made in the new northern Kingdom of God.

Beyond the library, Bede appears to have spent some of his time observing the natural world. From classical authors like Pliny and Isidore of Seville, he knew that the world was a globe in a cosmos of stars and planets (although he did also think that the solar system revolved around the earth). When he looked at the variations in the length of the shadow cast by a sundial and understood that the length of daylight varied according to latitude, that was further confirmation that the earth was round.

Other conclusions drawn by Bede imply that he reached beyond the walls of the library and beyond the immediate environs of the monastery at Jarrow. He wrote to the communities at Lastingham in North Yorkshire, in East Anglia, Wessex, London, Barking and Canterbury asking for information. From replies Bede learned a great deal, received information he could not have found in the library. That constellations looked slightly different in Canterbury compared to Jarrow was further confirmation that the world was a globe. But his most profitable set of responses concerned the investigation of a phenomenon that was very close to home.

By the time I'd left St Paul's the spring sunshine had returned, and I walked along a path that threaded through trees down to the banks of the canalised River Don. It was low tide, and on the steep-sided banks I could clearly see the high-water mark. The fall was substantial, perhaps five metres. When I later looked at the Port of Tyne Tide Tables for 2024 I saw that my guess was about right.

Thirteen centuries before Maritime House at Tyne Dock issued its annual tables, Bede completed the first set ever to be calculated. In his *On the Reckoning of Time*, written some time in the early eighth century, he used a nineteen-year lunar cycle as the basis of his workings. He then used information supplied by other monastic houses around the coast, as well as what he observed at Jarrow Slake and on the banks of the Tyne, to corroborate his findings. Bede clearly understood the effect of the moon's gravity on the tidal cycle, and he also studied solar eclipses. He wrote of 'this union of the ocean with the orbit of the Moon', and also that it was as if the tides were unwittingly drawn up by some 'breathings of the Moon' and 'when the Moon's force had ceased' it was as though the sea 'was poured back into its proper basin'. But more than these evocative metaphors, Bede must have realised from his own regular observations on the banks of the Don and the Tyne and how the sea covered and uncovered the mudflats of Jarrow Slake, that the time of high tide changes each day. He linked that with the slightly different time at which the moon rises through each lunar month.

The responses to Bede's enquiries from other coastal monasteries, some as distant as Iona on the Atlantic shore of Scotland, and also what visitors to St Paul's and St Peter's reported, helped him understand something fundamental, something that would be of great benefit to sailors and fishermen. Bede was the first to realise that around the coast of Britain it could be high tide in one place at exactly the same time as it was low tide in another. More than that, he understood that north of Jarrow high tide occurred before it took place along the coast to the south of the monastery. Although he could have had no knowledge of how the incoming Atlantic tide divided at Land's End, he did understand the direction it took and how its northern wave moved around the coast of Britain.

As it was in his church, I found it moving – and revealing – to stand on the banks of the Tyne and Don, where this truly great man stood, and to see exactly what he saw.

What lay behind much of Bede's mathematical and

chronological research was a great controversy that had convulsed the Christian communities of Britain fifty years before he wrote *On the Reckoning of Time*. Easter was the most important and sacred date in the calendar, the time of the Passion, when Christ died on the cross and when he was resurrected. But its calculation had become complicated and entangled with the Jewish Feast of the Passover. In Britain the Celtic Church of Ireland, Scotland and parts of England, including Lindisfarne (founded by monks from Iona), reckoned that the movable feast fell on one day while the so-called Roman church believed it fell on another.

These dates had to be reconciled for a simple, arithmetical reason. In the seventh century and long afterwards, the physical, actual presence of evil, of Satan and his devils, was an absolute belief. And the best defence against the hellish hordes lurking in the shadows was prayer. The different dates for Easter had a simple effect: at a crucial moment in the calendar, when the threat of evil was greatest, they divided the army of God. For prayer to be most effective, numbers mattered, and all Christians had to pray at the same time so they could banish Satan and his devils with unanimous praise for God.

Of course, politics was also in play. The kings of Northumbria, Britain-Rulers, sought approval not from an emperor in Rome but the next best thing, the bishop of Rome, the Pope. And so, at a specially convened church council at Whitby in 664, King Oswy (Ecgfrith's predecessor) ruled in favour of the Roman formula for calculating the date of Easter. For some considerable time before that pivotal moment great efforts had been made in support of both interpretations. Dates and the calculations of the correct one for Easter had almost become a separate discipline, what was known as *computus*, but it was Bede who finally persuaded a widespread adoption of how time ought to be measured.

The BC and AD dating system now universally adopted (and recently and irritatingly modified as BCE, Before the Common Era, and CE, the Common Era – a clumsy attempt to remove Christianity from the making of history) was not invented by Bede. About 150 years before he wrote *The Ecclesiastical History of the English People*, Dionysius Exiguus (his name translates as Little Denis), a monk who lived on the western shores of the Black Sea, had worked out that Christ was born in 1 AD. From that, he devised a computus that determined all subsequent dates for Easter. Dionysius' Easter Tables, projecting the correct dates well beyond 1000 AD, were accepted by the Synod of Whitby as standard, and it was Bede in his great history who popularised the use of the tables. The acceptance of AD gradually cleared up a great deal of confusion. Alternatives had been to use the AUC formula, a calculation of the year number *ante urbe condita*, since the foundation of the City of Rome in the 8th century BC. Regnal years were also used and in Spain and Portugal the system of counting dates from the Roman invasions of 39 BC persisted until the fourteenth century. The habit of using BC for the millennia before Christ's birth in 1 AD first came into use in France in the early seventeenth century.

Bede's was a modern intellect, his thinking based on evidence, sources he could verify and also observation.

Few dragons flew across his pages. He has often been hailed as the 'Father of British History', and the way in which he tidied up dating and got most things in the correct sequence is testament to that claim. But most striking is the fact that his achievements changed the world not by force but by the power of words, research and clear argument. Bede was the first in Britain to show that his quill pen was not only mightier than the sword but also that he could take a central role in the development of European culture from a monastery built on the windy shores of the North Sea, a long way from Rome, Greece or Constantinople and the great intellectual glories of early Islam. And more, he did this as his own secretary and copyist, often working alone. That was what drew me to Jarrow, to Bede's story, an immense admiration for a mighty intellect, a dogged enquirer and a great writer. It was a privilege to sit in the place where he prayed and said mass and to be able to hear his voice echo across thirteen centuries in all that he wrote.

2

Fish and Chips

The view was perfect. From my table I could look out all the way along the shore road in South Shields. Not strictly a promenade, for it did not have a beach on the other side – that lay beyond a fun fair, arcades, car parks, burger bars and other, more exotic food outlets – nevertheless it offered a long and satisfying perspective of many traditional, essential aspects of the British seaside.

The weather was perfect: grey, the sky heavily overcast, the temperature bracing, the wind freshening. Rain had been threatening all day. The beach, the white-crested waves and the blurred meeting of the sky and the sea were also characteristic. On the beach no one was lingering, and all the dog walkers kept up a brisk pace, their pets trotting behind them, getting it over with. On the shore road itself I had been one of only a handful of well wrapped-up walkers, and most of the burger shops and amusement arcades I passed were shuttered.

My plate of fish and chips was perfect. Like sad people on holiday, I took a photograph of it. In contrast to the muted, neutral colours of the view from my table, the chips were golden and satisfyingly chunky, the batter that crinkled around the fish was a light but rich brown and the mushy peas gloriously green. In the middle of the table was all I needed to complete the picture: salt and vinegar. The walk along the shore road had been much longer than I'd been led to believe, and this wonderful feast seemed like a just reward.

I wasn't sure of the protocol. As a phrase, salt always comes before vinegar. But boyhood memories of chip shops in Kelso suggested it was the vinegar first and then the salt. The former made the latter stick. And in any case, if the vinegar is sprinkled on second, it would wash off the salt. The first and best chip was crisp on the outside and soft and fleshy on the inside. Channelling my twelve-year-old self clutching a poke of chips on the pavement outside Halliday's in Kelso, I started to eat with my fingers (except for the mushy peas) and broke off bits of battered haddock. The underside of the fish was just as crunchy, and the white flesh had real texture and taste. Perfect.

I was lunching at Colman's Seafood Temple, a modern structure wrapped around the pillars of an old bandstand, its main dining area projecting over the beach like the superstructure of an ocean liner. It had been recommended by the owner, Richard Colman, after a warming cup of tea and a fascinating conversation at his original fish and chip restaurant in Ocean Road.

The story of Richard's family and their business seemed to run in parallel with the development of days at the seaside, and to be an integral part of that experience. Many Italian immigrants, including Richard's ancestors, arrived in Britain at the end of the nineteenth century, fleeing from poverty, sometimes walking across Europe to the English Channel or the North Sea coasts and a passage on a ship or a ferry. Richard explained that his grandmother had married William Colman but that his original family name had been Turrichi. They came from Barga in northern Tuscany. Several other families made the same journey from the village, an example of chain migration. Those who arrived in Britain first often wrote to relatives at home encouraging them to follow, sometimes sending the cost of the fares. Almost all immigrants will have had no English or a place to stay after disembarkation, and the pathfinders, the original arrivals, could make the transition to a new life much easier. Some went back to Barga after having put away some money, and now about 40 per cent of the villagers there have relatives in either Scotland or the northeast of England. There is even an annual fish and chip festival.

The Italian immigrants pioneered street food in Britain, especially at the seaside. Those who had the skill to make ice cream sold it at first from barrows with either wafers (known as sliders) or cones (known as pokey hats) that could be eaten after all the ice cream had been licked off. Sophisticated consumers pushed the ice cream down into the cones with their tongues to make the crunchy cone more tasty. Fish and chips needed no plates or cutlery and was instead served in old newspapers to be eaten with greasy fingers which could be wiped on the paper before it was thrown away. Most of the working people who came down to the seaside on day-trip trains had neither the cash to patronise restaurants nor any experience of them, but the sea air created an appetite that needed to be fed.

Richard Colman showed me a photograph of his great-grandfather, Federico Turrichi, and his son Joseph, or Giuseppe, standing beside a hut on South Shields beach. It was set up not far from where Ocean Seafood Temple now stands. The contrast between the two is striking, emblematic and, for me, moving. Impressively moustached and waistcoated with a flat cap pulled down tight so that his eyes are barely visible, Federico looks confidently at the camera, his hands in his pockets as he stands ramrod-straight at the counter of the wooden hut. He seems like a proud man. Behind the counter is Joseph, much younger and fresh faced, and he stands in front of shelves of what look like bottles of lemonade or cordial. By deed poll, Federico changed his name to Frankie because, as Richard remarked, it was not always easy being an immigrant and his great-grandfather wanted to integrate. There is another photograph of a much larger and more permanent looking hut with 'Frankie's Ices and Fish and Chips' on its fascia. In the interwar period, the Turrichi family opened a 350-seat restaurant on the beach as well as two more chip shops in the town of South Shields.

'It was the railways that made it all work,' said Richard. 'They could get fresh fish all over the country quickly, and in the 1930s there might have been 30,000 or 40,000 chip shops all over Britain. Now, there might only be 7,000 or 8,000. Between the wars, and in the early 1950s, that was the boom time.'

Steam trawling in the North Sea in the second half of

the nineteenth century had also made fish a cheap staple that working people could afford. As the large nets were slowly dragged along the bed of the shallow sea, they increased the volume of catches dramatically. Across the Tyne at North Shields, the Fish Quay was developed between 1870 and 1890, and it became much easier to unload catches quickly. An ice factory known as Tyne Brand was built and since the railway line from North Shields to Newcastle had been integrated into the North Eastern Railway network since 1854, chip shops from York to Northumberland were kept supplied by catches from the North Sea.

The origins of fish and chips are not clear. Italians did not invent the classic combination. Jewish communities were in the habit of frying fish in batter before the weekly Sabbath and its restrictions began so that it could be eaten cold on the Saturday when cooking was forbidden. No one is sure where fried chipped potatoes came from, although Charles Dickens mentioned them in 1859 in *A Tale of Two Cities*. By the later nineteenth century fish and chips were being sold as a takeaway in the East End of London and in Mossley near Manchester. Whatever the genesis of the dish, what Winston Churchill called 'the good companions', Italian families were certainly closely involved in making it popular and widely available, particularly at the seaside. During both the First and Second World Wars, governments made great efforts to ensure that neither fish nor potatoes nor the fat needed to fry them were rationed.

In 1926 the Colmans bought 176 Ocean Road and had it fitted out. The fish and chip shop is unmissable, a busy place in an otherwise quiet street, and very efficient. When I arrived a young woman offered me a menu, a table and a cup of tea. Before Richard joined me I noticed that a nearby table of four older ladies had been served with four identical meals, what I'd enjoyed at the Ocean Seafood Temple. When the waiter laid down the plates, a hush descended, and no one spoke as vinegar and salt were reverently passed from hand to hand and carefully shaken. In the right order.

'The business has changed,' said Richard. 'We used to be open from 11 a.m. until midnight, and that didn't count the prep time in the morning and cleaning up at the end of the day. That didn't make it attractive to young people. A lot of shops closed. But now it's different. Since the 1980s pubs have changed. They're now quiet after 9 p.m., except maybe at the weekends. Now we close at 6 p.m. And maybe 60 per cent of our customers sit in, and the takeaway trade has declined. It used to be the other way round.'

Virtually all of Colman's fish is caught in the North Sea and potatoes come from local farms in Northumberland and Durham. Richard explained that the sustained success of Colman's was not because of secret recipes for batter or anything like that. 'We just love what we do,' he said, 'and I suppose that after a hundred years we've got quite good at it.'

As we walked to the door, Richard smiled as we shook hands. 'Not many people don't like fish and chips.'

And it is true. What I'd been served at the Ocean Seafood Temple was superb, memorable, far superior to anything shop bought and heated in the oven, or indeed served up by any other fish and chip shop I'd ever been in. But the meal was properly rounded off about a hundred metres along the shore road. I stopped at Minchella's ice cream parlour and ordered a vanilla cone. Not one drop was allowed to melt.

3

The Edge of Beyond

The heavy rain tripped whatever sensor my car has to convert the steady, hypnotic rhythm of the windscreen wipers to frantic. Which doesn't really help. The crazy flicking back and forth reduces rather than improves visibility, and I ploughed through too many sudden roadside puddles. I was driving up the North Sea coast from South Shields to the little harbour town of Amble, built around the estuary of the River Coquet. Rising at the watershed of the Cheviot Hills, it flows east through some of England's most beautiful but least-known landscapes. Not that any view could have been much enjoyed, or even seen, on that sodden morning.

Formerly a harbour for fishing boats and coal ships, Amble has adapted itself for visitors. On the seafront there are several 'attractions' – places to eat, drink and buy stuff – but, rather than park my car and retreat into a comfortable and dry café for a warming cup of coffee, I had hoped to sail out of Amble harbour into the North Sea. One of the town's main attractions lies a couple of kilometres or so offshore. Coquet Island is home to around 40,000 nesting seabirds, most of them puffins, and regular cruises take visitors to look at them and also a colony of seals. But even though one of the vessels that makes the hour-long round trip is a restored lifeboat, the bad weather meant that there would be no sailings that morning. In any case, visitors are not permitted to land on the island and disturb the bird population, which is especially fragile now after outbreaks of bird flu. Only six hectares, Coquet Island is very small, and the nesting birds need every bit of space.

My own interest was not in puffins, terns or seals but in the human beings who had first endured a strange and harsh existence not only on Coquet Island but also on the Farne Islands and Lindisfarne, a little further up the coast. The most famous of these was St Cuthbert, a man who fascinated Bede of Jarrow and is perhaps England's most revered native saint, even though he was born in the Tweed Valley in what is now part of Scotland. Such was Cuthbert's prestige that the magnificence of Durham Cathedral was raised on his bones, and the great patrimony of its prince-bishops grew out of reverence for him as both poor and wealthy pilgrims left great and small gifts.

Bede wrote two lives of the saint, and in the second, the great scholar recounted an incident that took place on Coquet Island in 685. For some time, Cuthbert had been withdrawing from the monastic community on Lindisfarne, where he was prior, wishing to spend more and more time alone with his prayers and meditations. Having persuaded Eata, his abbot, to allow him to lay down his office and go to Inner Farne, about a kilometre and a half offshore and eleven kilometres south of

Lindisfarne, the saint built an oratory where he could worship and a cell for shelter from the bitter winds. As his reputation for piety grew, Cuthbert was drawn into the dynastic politics of Northumbria, ruled at that time by Ecgfrith, the Bretwalda. The king's sister, Ælfflæd, sent a message to the saint asking him to meet her on Coquet Island. Wishing to associate Cuthbert's great prestige with her dynasty, she made him an offer. Here follows Bede's account:

Now she knew that Ecgfrith proposed to appoint Cuthbert bishop, and wishing to learn whether this proposal would be carried into effect, she began to ask him in this way, 'How the hearts of mortal men differ in their several purposes! Some rejoice in the riches they have gained, others who love riches always lack them. You despise the glory of the world, although it is offered, and although you may attain to a bishopric, than which nothing is higher amongst mortal men, will you prefer the fastnesses of your desert place [meaning Inner Farne] to that rank?'

But he said, 'I know that I am not worthy of such a rank, nevertheless I cannot escape anywhere from the decree of the Ruler of Heaven; yet if He had determined to subject me to so great a burden, I believe that after a short time He will set me free, and perhaps after not more than two years, He will send me back to my accustomed rest and solitude. But I bid you in the name of our Lord and Saviour not to tell anyone before my death what you have heard from me!'

Cuthbert accepted the king's offer, and for two years was bishop of Lindisfarne, the most exalted and powerful of all the churchmen in Northumbria's Kingdom of God. In 687 this clearly charismatic and vulnerable man resigned his office and once more returned to Inner Farne, where he died a short time later.

These small islands off the Northumbrian coast, now the resort of wildlife and, in the case of Lindisfarne, a magnet for hundreds of thousands of visitors, were once central to the religious, cultural and political life of seventh- and eighth-century England. It occurred to me that the morning's heavy rain was appropriate in any effort to understand something of the power and practice of early Christianity. As I peered through the grey mirk towards the outline of Coquet Island, perhaps I was looking at a place where men believed they were on the edge of eternity, where, through privation, prayer and suffering, they might move closer to God and to Heaven.

In its early centuries Christianity was frequently outlawed, and believers were persecuted by the imperial authorities, especially in the provinces of the eastern Mediterranean. When devout Christians were arrested and refused to recant their faith, many were tortured before being put to death, often publicly. This was known as red martyrdom, and those who gave their lives – executed or attacked by ravenous wild animals in the amphitheatres of the cities – were certain that they would find a place in the Kingdom of Heaven and enjoy everlasting life. Others fled the horrors of persecution in the cities to remote places, especially the deserts of Egypt and Syria, where they became hermits. In caves and other shelters, these men, and sometimes women, suffered what was known as white martyrdom. They fasted and mortified their flesh in other ways, all the while praying, chanting, meditating and worshipping God. Many believed in the power of repetition, reciting the Jesus Prayer over and over again. As they whispered 'Lord Jesus Christ, Son of God, have mercy on me, a sinner', they counted the repetitions on a knotted prayer rope (originally there were thirty-three knots, one for each year of Jesus' life), running it through their fingers – an early version of what became the rosary and its beads.

These monks, the term coming from the Greek *monachos*, meaning a solitary, began to cluster in loose groups in the desert. They spent most of their time alone at their devotions but came together to eat in silence. At least twice a week, they fasted for a day, taking only water. Early Christianity was transactional. If red and white martyrs gave their lives to God alone, however uncomfortable that may have been, then the glorious reward of everlasting life in Heaven would be theirs.

Cuthbert had been prior of the community of monks at Old Melrose in the Tweed Valley and had abandoned his role (something Bede did not mention since it might have blemished an exemplary life) to wander as a white martyr in the wild moors of Northumberland. When he eventually returned to the communal life on Lindisfarne, he found that his yearning for solitude had not lessened, and he returned to the hermetic life on Inner Farne.

There are very few islands off the North Sea coast of Britain, few places where men might live a life apart from the world. I wondered how they saw these bleak wave-battered and windswept places. The deserts of Egypt and Syria that had kept the first white martyrs out of the sinful, temporal world were substituted around the coasts of Britain by the wastes of the sea. And the memory of that replacement has survived in the Gaelic language, in which the word for a hermitage or an early monastery is *diseart*. In his account of the meeting of Ælfflæd and Cuthbert on Coquet Island, Bede clearly understood the link, for he put the phrase 'desert place' into the mouth of the king's sister.

There is also a sense of Lindisfarne, Inner Farne and Coquet Island as liminal places, islands on the edge of beyond, between a mortal life and eternity. The grey eastern horizon of the North Sea and the huge skies encouraged a distinctive atmosphere in these barren tree-less places open to the elements, with little detail and shelter. They were also open to the sight of God.

The rain that fell all that morning on the Northumberland coast reminded me of how recently human beings have been able to protect themselves from the elements. Waterproofs are a modern invention. I never knew my great-grandmother, Annie Moffat, since she died rela-tively young, long before I was born. Died, my grannie said, because she was a 'done' woman, worn out, suffering what she called her 'pains', acute arthritis. Annie worked as a bondager, a female farm worker who was bonded by a six- or twelve-month contract made between her father, or her husband, or her brother and a farmer. In return for a fixed fee – paid not to her but to her male relative, with in-kind payments of oats, potatoes, coal and a tied cottage – Annie worked in the fields, weeding with a hoe and shawing turnips in all weathers, planting or bringing in the harvest. 'She always said to me that if it's going to rain, then let it rain in the afternoon,' my grannie told me more than once. 'For if it rains in the morning, that's you wet the whole day.' There was no question of downing tools and taking shelter. Bondagers and other farmworkers wore empty sacks tied across their shoulders to try to keep out the worst of the wet. Most simply endured the dampness and in later life suffered for it as their joints creaked and their bent fingers throbbed. Oilskins were not manufactured cheaply enough until the early twentieth century for farm workers to feel their benefit.

Now we would never tolerate the working conditions that gave Annie her 'pains'. In fact we no longer tolerate being cold as well as wet, and yet for almost all of human history people were often both for long periods, especially in the winter. Most owned few clothes, and so that made drying what they had been wearing on a wet day difficult. On winter mornings they sometimes put on damp clothes and hoped it did not rain and that the wind might dry them off. Monks living on the North Sea islands probably owned only one garment, something like the later ankle-length woollen habits seen in medieval illustrations, secured at the waist by a rope. If that became wet, as it must have often, then there was little to be done except get as close to the warmth of a fire as possible. The weather was seen as an expression of God's will, and to suffer because of it was part of the privations of white martyrdom. And on Coquet Island, the Farnes and Lindisfarne, there was plenty of weather.

On the much more fragmented Atlantic shore of Scotland there were many diseartan, many little islands where hermits prayed and strove to move closer to God. The place names of one of these remembered some of the metaphors of devotion. Eilean Mhàrtainn, or Isle Martin, is named after St Martin of Tours, a fourth-century monk who brought the ideas of the desert hermits to the West. The little island is uninhabited now, but it was once home to a community of solitaries. To the west of Eilean Mhàrtainn stretches the wide mouth of Loch Broom and beyond it the vastness of the Atlantic Ocean. West of a tiny lochan that sparkles like a natural font on the island's hill are steep sea cliffs known as Nuill Dhuirch. The name can mean something like the Edge of Beyond. Westernmost is Clach an Nuill Dhuirch, the Great Rock of Beyond. Perhaps Cuthbert and his monks on Lindisfarne had names such as these that are now lost. In the sea cliff below the Heugh – the long, steep-sided rock south of the ruins of the Benedictine priory where the earliest churches were built – there are openings and ledges known as prayer holes. When the winds drove the waves of the North Sea inshore and spray spattered the Heugh, monks used to crouch through the night in these narrow, hard places to pray, perhaps recite the Jesus Prayer and meditate on the elemental power of the Almighty.

The dogged piety of these leathery ascetics attracted great prestige and brought the sinful, temporal world closer to the shores of these holy islands. In addition to the *Codex Amiatinus* and the two other complete Latin Bibles made in the twin monasteries of St Peter and St

Paul, the great Lindisfarne Gospel was copied and painted under the direction of Abbot Eadfrith at the beginning of the eighth century. These magnificent objects, the most glittering adornments of the Kingdom of God in Northumbria, required a substantial investment of lay patronage. The tenth-century chronicler Æthelweard described the gospel book as 'adorned with gold and with gems and also with gilded-over silver'. Many treasures were given to Lindisfarne as the transactional nature of early Christianity was more and more understood by the laity. Wealthy noblemen and women gave land and gifts in return for prayers for their immortal souls and an easier passage to the glories of the everlasting.

Archaeologists have uncovered nineteen small headstones on Lindisfarne. Many carry names such as Ethelhard, Beannah or Osgyth, and some seem not to commemorate monks but lay people. Places such as Lindisfarne were different from the temporal world because the ground itself had been made sacred by the saints and pious men and women who had passed their lives there in the service of God. Their constant prayers meant that the Almighty looked down and saw them and saw the place where they lived. That made the soil itself powerful, almost magical. Lay people believed that if their bodies could be buried in holy places then the soil itself would cleanse them of mortal sin. As their flesh rotted under the ground walked on by saints, their bones attained purity and made the passage of their souls to Heaven much easier. And wealthy families were willing to make great gifts to religious communities if they could be assured of burial in holy ground. In the later Middle Ages, when noblemen believed that death was close, they sometimes entered monasteries as novices to ensure burial inside the sacred precinct. This was known as conversion ad succurrendum, in a hurry. Masses were also said for the sake of their souls and prayers offered up, all of which enriched religious communities. And few were more prestigious than Lindisfarne, or wealthier, for those who could afford to be buried on the island would be planted in the same soil as Cuthbert, Britain's greatest native saint. After his death on Inner Farne, his body was brought back and a shrine created on Lindisfarne.

★   ★   ★

In July 793 the world suddenly changed. Here is an entry from the *Anglo-Saxon Chronicle*:

This year came dreadful forewarnings over the land of the Northumbrians, terrifying the people most woefully: these were immense sheets of lightning rushing through the air, and whirlwinds, and fiery dragons flying across the firmament. These tremendous tokens were soon followed by a great famine: and not long after . . . the harrowing inroads of heathen men made lamentable havoc in the Church of God in Holy Island [Lindisfarne] by rapine and slaughter.

From out of nowhere, from beyond, it seemed, the Vikings sailed into history. As the startled and terrified monks fled in all directions, these sea raiders rasped the keels of their dragon-ships up the stony beach below the monastery and attacked it. Killing any who stood in their way, they stole whatever portable treasures they could find, threatening and torturing monks to tell them where valuables were kept. It mattered not at all that the island was holy, under the protection of God and St Cuthbert, for the Vikings were pagans, worshippers of Thor and Odin. A year later, and for many summers after that, they raided and pillaged coastal monasteries such as Iona and Applecross. Within a few years the Viking raiders began to take captives so that they could sell them for silver at the great slave market in Dublin. Because they were often literate and numerate, monks could fetch high prices, especially in the courts of Islamic caliphs in Spain and further east. Some suffered castration to make them even more saleable.

The shock of the first raid on Lindisfarne rippled across Western Europe. God's Kingdom of Northumbria had been breached and defiled, the sanctity of Cuthbert no defence against the heathen men whom the monastic chroniclers called the Sons of Death. Such had been the prestige and the glittering achievements of Northumbria in the eighth century that it sent missionaries and teachers to the courts of Western kings and magnates. Perhaps the most influential of these was Alcuin of York, a teacher and writer who had great influence at the court of Charlemagne and who tutored the royal children. He was appalled at the attack on the community and wrote to Higbald, bishop of Lindisfarne, his letters a rare contemporary record. How could a place more sacred than any in Britain . . . suffer in this way . . . The church of St Cuthbert is spattered with the blood of the priests of God, stripped of all its furnishings, exposed to the plundering of pagans.

Perhaps the Vikings had been sent as a punishment from God because the discipline and piety expected from the monks had slackened. Here is some finger-wagging from Alcuin:

Consider carefully, brothers, and examine diligently, lest perchance this unaccustomed and unheard-of evil was merited by some unheard-of evil practice . . . Consider the dress, the way of wearing the hair, the luxurious habits of the princes and people.

God's Kingdom of Northumbria had been desecrated, and Alcuin predicted that worse was to follow, there would be even 'greater suffering'. And follow it did. In the opening decades of the ninth century raiding intensified and some monasteries were abandoned. Some time around 845 what became known as the Congregation of St Cuthbert left Lindisfarne bearing the coffin of the saint, and they travelled inland, away from danger, to Norham on the River Tweed. 'They were like sheep fleeing before the face of wolves,' says the *Anglo-Saxon Chronicle*. By the late tenth century the wanderings of the Congregation had ceased, and a church was established at Durham where the great cathedral built on Cuthbert's bones would eventually rise.

Within decades of the first spasm of raiding, Scandinavians began to settle along the North Sea coast and up its navigable rivers. Roman Eboracum had become Eoforwic in the time of the Anglian kingdom and then Jorvik when the city fell to the Danes in the middle of the ninth century. In 886 King Alfred of Wessex concluded a treaty with Guthrum, king of East Anglia, that defined the Danelaw, the eastern part of England conquered and settled by Scandinavians. The frontier ran from the Mersey Estuary down the middle of England to the lower Thames Valley and London, Lundenwic. But by 954 the successors of Alfred of Wessex had reconquered the Danelaw and more or less unified England.

In the early eleventh century the twists and unexpected turns of dynastic politics almost stood recent history on its head. The early medieval chronicler, Henry of Huntingdon, reckoned that 'never before was there a king of England of such greatness . . . so glorious . . . the author of handsome and magnificent acts', and yet he does not rate much of an entry in the *Oxford Companion to British History* and rarely much more than a passing mention in the general histories of England. He was an aberration. Perhaps the problem with Cnut, Knutr, Knut or Canute is not that we cannot spell his name but rather that we do not think of him as one of us. Not a real king of England. And yet he was undoubtedly a very real – and very effective – king of all of England. Having married Emma, the widow of Æthelred the Unready (she was old enough to be his mother) and having been crowned king of England at an elaborate coronation in London, Knut gave the nation twenty years of peace, legislated wisely and firmly, was pious and without any doubt a highly successful monarch by any measure. His father, Sveyn I, was another king of England – an undoubted fact now almost entirely forgotten – and Knut's sons succeeded him, Harald I and then Harthacnut. And yet historiography still finds it hard to accept this dynasty as more than an episode, an interruption by a bunch of weirdly named Danish arrivistes. Knut is chiefly remembered as daft Canute who tried to rule the waves.

That odd story has an emblematic truth. The political reality is that Knut did rule over the sea. He was the first and almost the last Emperor of the North Sea, king of Denmark and Norway as well as England, and his longish reign was full of unrealised possibilities. If his sons had had sons of their own then the Danish kings would not have been dogged by dynastic failure, Edward the Confessor would have remained in exile, the Normans may not have dared to cross the Channel in 1066 and Britain might have looked east for its destiny. The North Sea, the Baltic, the new Viking kingdom of Kievan Rus', the river-route to Miklagard, or Constantinople, were all full of opportunity. The political focus might have been turned away from the southeast. London might have developed as a regional port depending on trade with France and the south while kings might have ruled England from York or Newcastle with an archbishop not at Canterbury but Durham, the shrine of the nation's greatest saint.

4

The Salt Sea

The map of the countries around the edges of the North Sea shown on page 11 of the *Philip's Modern School Atlas* of 1958 begs an interesting series of questions. From the great landmass of Europe, five major rivers flow into the sea from the east. Through the plains of Saxony run the Elbe, the Weser and the Ems, while the Rhine and the Maas meander almost in parallel across the Dutch landscape to reach the sea south of Rotterdam. Approximately 240 kilometres to the west the Thames Estuary opens. To the north are the outfalls of the Trent into the Humber, the mouths of the Tees, the Tyne, the Tweed and the Tay. River names are thought to be the oldest in the landscape, and it is striking that all of these begin with T.

At least two rivers may, according to the great toponymic scholar of Celtic Scotland, W.J. Watson, correspond with the name of a goddess. Tay and Thames may mean something like the Silent One, something that might suit their stately passage to the sea. Fragments of cartographic and documentary evidence support the notion of major rivers having characters or the characteristics of people or animals. The Tyne may mean the Rapid River, and Tweed could have come down to us from a Proto-Indo-European root word equating to the Surger, the Powerful River. The Rhine's derivation is more straightforward. It is from renos, a Gaulish word. It was a Celtic language related to Old Welsh that was spoken before and during the time of the Roman province and echoes of which might still be heard in modern Breton. Like Tyne, it meant something like the Fast-Flowing River. The Ems runs through Emsland. It was once a sparsely populated area of fenland flooded in winter, the place where Pliny the Elder was stationed on the northern frontier of the Roman Empire. The origins of the name of the Weser are cognate to those of the Wear in eastern England, a river Bede knew well. All three have the sense not of flowing but of oozing through marshland. The Elbe is from a High German word simply meaning 'the River'. Since it runs for 1,100 kilometres that was probably description enough.

Its major rivers form an important part of the nature and character of the North Sea. Their estuaries are gateways in both directions, and the origins of their names remember ancient links and similar landscapes on both its eastern and western shores. Before the inundation of Doggerland, the Elbe, the Weser and the Ems flowed north to the Storegga Trench, as did all of the British rivers apart from the Thames. Along with the Rhine it drained southwest, eventually reaching the Atlantic. After the tsunami had drowned Doggerland and the shores of the North Sea assumed their modern shape, the rivers became very influential in two ways.

The oceans and seas of the world are not naturally salty. They become so because of a simple cycle. Rain on landmasses, particularly over high ground, washes over mineral deposits, and gravity ensures that these reach streams which become rivers and deliver the minerals to the oceans and seas. In the case of the Elbe and the Rhine, their length and that of their many tributaries means that they collect and carry a wide spectrum of bits of Europe's geology. When the Atlantic flows into the North Sea between Shetland and Norway, it brings even more salinity.

Where the North Sea meets its great rivers, another set of natural interactions occur. On a late summer afternoon I drove to Berwick-upon-Tweed to watch these take place. There had been several days of intermittent but heavy rain and the great river was in flood. It had become the Surger.

Even though I know the town well, and despite its dramatic setting, Berwick-upon-Tweed has always seemed disconnected, somewhat forlorn, a place apart. Geography and ethnicity should mean that it is one of the related communities of the Tweed Basin, the river system that waters the Borders, and that it should be part of Scotland, the North Sea port from where all of the traditional products of the river valley – wool, grain, hides and much else – should have been exported to the wider world. But history decreed otherwise. After the Wars of Independence of the late thirteenth and early fourteenth centuries, and the intermittent flaring of conflict in the following 200 years that culminated with the slaughter at the Battle of Flodden in 1513, Berwick became part of England, an outpost in the far north, a place apart.

In January 1558, after two centuries under English rule, Calais was recaptured by the French. It was the last English possession, the last remnant of the wide territories gained in the course of the Hundred Years War. In the same month of the same year, Elizabeth I succeeded her half-sister, Mary I, and as a new queen anxious to establish her authority she was determined there would be no more losses. The Kingdom of Scotland was a traditional, if generally ill-advised, ally of France, and Berwick would at all costs be held as a bastion in the north. But it needed to be securely defended. Only days after the fall of Calais a plan was commissioned from an Italian designer, Giovanni Portinari, and Sir Richard Lee was put in charge of construction. Work began on the defences immediately, and the final cost was staggering at £128,648. Too much was at stake so early in Elizabeth's reign, and for the notoriously parsimonious queen, money was for once no object.

Up to very recent times Berwick remained a garrison town, until 1963 the depot of the King's Own Scottish Borderers. I parked on the old parade ground outside the barracks, now home to the excellent regimental museum. Berwick's Elizabethan walls loom up nearby, defending the eastern end of this open area where sergeant majors once roared their orders and nailed, spit and polish boots once clacked on the tarmac. I decided to walk almost the whole circuit to the place where I wanted to be.

The most obvious reason for the near-complete survival of Berwick's walls is their sheer mass. Designed by

Portinari to resist artillery fire, they consist of stout stone walls infilled with earth to make them very thick indeed, in some places more than nine metres across. A well-directed barrage would certainly damage such walls, but cannonballs could never hope to breach it. Even more substantial are the bastions at each corner. Shaped like compressed arrowheads projecting from the curtain wall, there are five facing the landward side of the town, the north, the direction from which trouble would most likely come. Cannons emplaced on the broad wallheads, the cavaliers of the bastions had an uninterrupted field of fire (where the houses of townspeople had been ruthlessly demolished) on attackers attempting to negotiate the ditches in front of the defences. Artillery could be ineffective in repulsing an enemy that had fought its way close to the walls of a fortress, and to deal with this difficulty an ingenious solution was devised for Berwick. Behind the bars of the compressed arrowhead of each bastion sit two pairs of cannon sited so that they can fire parallel with the curtain wall and be able to rake any soldiers who got close. These flankers ensured that no piece of ground below the walls was unprotected. By 1570, when the work was at last completed, her huge walls had made Berwick virtually impregnable and, after such an enormous outlay of cash to ensure that it would never fall into Scottish hands, they probably sealed the town for ever inside the English state.

The walls are at their most commanding on the southern, seaward side of the town, overlooking the Tweed estuary. Having consulted the tide tables, I'd come to watch the sea ebbing and the effect of the flooding of the great river. It was dramatic. The roiling brown water had spilled far out to sea in a wide curve, and from what I could make out there seemed to be a clear line with the blue saltwater to the east and the muddy flood-water pushing it back. And surprisingly the surface seemed calm, even placid. But in fact this was, as I knew, an optical illusion. Below the surface of major estuaries, there are powerful, elemental forces at work.

As admiral of the imperial Roman war fleet, Pliny the Elder was not only widely travelled but also an experienced sailor able to read the moods and the run of the sea. In the Bosphorus, the narrow straits that connect the Black Sea with the Mediterranean, he noticed that fishermen's nets were behaving oddly after they had been cast. The currents seemed to take them one way and then the other. From this, the great historian and naturalist deduced that the surface and bottom currents were flowing in different directions, pulling the fishing boats behind them. And though I could not see it from my vantage point on the ramparts of the Elizabethan walls at Berwick, the waters of the Tweed Estuary were behaving in a similar way.

Even though the floodwaters of the river were brown, thick with particles of mud, freshwater is significantly less dense than salt seawater. Although I couldn't see it as the tide turned, the outfall of the Tweed was rising above the incoming waters of the North Sea and spreading out into the wide arc that reached perhaps a kilometre or more offshore. But under that current the dense seawater was pushing its way upstream. It is this counterintuitive interaction that makes estuaries difficult and turbulent places to handle a boat and cast nets where they are intended to land. And the mixing of swirling water and suspended sediments has a profound effect on the story of the fascinating, noble creatures that had brought me to Berwick and the mouth of the Tweed. The confusion often disorients salmon, fish that have swum a couple of thousand kilometres through the North Atlantic Ocean to return to their home river, the end of a miraculous, profoundly mysterious and epic journey.

On Thursday 20 July 2023 it was overcast, but at least not raining, as an ancient ceremony was enacted. Preceded by a pipe band, pulled along a riverside road by a van from Greenwood's MOT and Service Centre, a coble, a boat of the sort traditionally used for salmon fishing, carried five young girls wearing long, formal and pretty dresses. Four attendants faced aft, looking at the Tweedmouth Salmon Queen sitting in the stern. She was on her way to be crowned in a ceremony that may have begun in the late thirteenth century and was revived after the Second World War. The Atlantic salmon return to their home river at all times of the year, but from July onwards numbers were thought to increase. It may be that the crowning of the Salmon Queen was at first both a blessing ritual and also a signal that fishing could begin in earnest. In Berwick and Tweedmouth, a village on the southern shore of the estuary, salmon fishing was once an industry that employed hundreds, not only in netting the fish but in preserving them in ice houses, in the key business of cooperage, or barrel-making, and in the vital process of pickling them in 'kits' or transporting fresh fish quickly to market.

What fascinates me is not so much the fishing as the mysterious journey, the life story of a beautiful, even majestic, fish that moves from an early life in freshwater to salt and how it returns to where it was born upriver. It is a story that brings together the North Sea and its deep hinterland of rivers that flow into it in Britain. How do Atlantic salmon find their home river after living far out in the ocean as they grow to maturity sometimes for four or five years? And then how do they find the place where they should spawn, where the hen fish lays her eggs and the cock fish finds them and fertilises them with his milt? After an immense and dangerous journey, how do they find their way back to the place where they themselves were born? In an atmospheric, deeply felt memoir, *A River Runs Through Me: A Life of Salmon Fishing in Scotland*, Andrew Douglas-Home wrote:

> I learned as a child what most salmon fishers never will, that the most important part of any river is its faraway upper reaches, not the Junction Pool [a famous fishing beat at Kelso] or whatever other grand beat they are fishing. The future is there, the calm, clear water of the Tweed's myriad spawning streams, at their most exquisite after a sharp frost . . .
>
> Running along the northeast boundary of our Easter Langlee farm [near Galashiels] was the Ellwyn Burn, not big enough to hold salmon for most of the year, but they would come in numbers to spawn. I cannot recall what year in the mid-1960s, but it was very cold and the Ellwyn was low and clear, and full of spawning fish.

I would walk up from our house to where the Ellwyn meets the Tweed at Upper Pavilion [a beat on the river], and then walk upstream from there, crucially coming up behind any salmon or sea trout before they could see me. For most of the way it was a steep-sided wooded glen but breaking into open countryside the higher it climbed . . . The pools were small but deep and in the shallower riffles there would be salmon spawning on the gravel.

The salmon born in the redds – the gravel nests of the Ellwyn Burn and many other spawning streams – begin life as a freshwater fish and they will stay in the Tweed for two or three years. Known as smolts, the young salmon then swim down to the estuary at Berwick and out into the saltwater of the open sea, where they appear immediately to adapt. The fish then turn to the north and swim an immense distance, 2,400 kilometres through the ocean to the continental shelf off the coast of Greenland. How they navigate the journey across all of that open, featureless vastness after a life enclosed by the banks of the Tweed is only the first of several mysteries. The northern feeding grounds are rich, and the salmon grow quickly into sleek and powerful fish as they consume smaller fish, crustaceans, herring and even large plankton.

At some point everything changes, and a trigger mechanism tells the Atlantic salmon that it is time to reproduce. For some, this happens after only one winter in the waters off Greenland, but for most it takes two or three more years. It is at that moment the fish turn south and seek their home river. How they find it is still a matter of speculation. Salmon swim near the surface, and it has been suggested that they can navigate by starlight. More detailed anatomical research has shown that fish are very sensitive to changes in the water around them. In what is known as their lateral line there are sensory organs that can detect movement around the fish, vibration and changes in the pressure of the water. These messages, conveyed from their sensors to the salmon's brain, allow it to navigate and hunt even when there is poor visibility and in darkness. Iron is present in the lateral line, and some scientists believe that the fish can detect changes in the earth's magnetic field as they swim long distances through the ocean. Strongest at the poles and weakest at the equator, the magnetic field weakens as the fish swim southwards, back to their natal river. It may be that the lateral line's sensors act like a living compass needle.

When returning salmon enter the North Sea it seems that many swim south down Britain's coastal waters as they search for where they were born. Researchers have discovered that each estuary, each river's water, has a particular odour that is different from all the others. After three or four years in the open ocean, how do the salmon recognise it? How do they remember it? But remember it they do, and if the great fish can evade those who would net or hook them, they move from saltwater to fresh and swim upriver to find their spawning stream, places like the steep-sided glen of the Ellwyn Burn. At that moment something strange and very moving takes place. After they enter their home river they cease to feed until they have laid and fertilised the eggs in the gravel redds. And then, when that is done, most of the salmon die, their bodies dissolving into the river that made them. Only a very few swim back downriver again and out into the ocean, perhaps only one in ten. Those that do sometimes grow to great lengths and gain a tremendous amount of weight. These salmon are often the monsters we see in glass cases in fishing hotels or displayed as trophies in the grand houses of wealthy fishermen.

Andrew Douglas-Home's book is elegiac when it speaks of another, lost era. When growing up on the banks of the Tweed he was fortunate to fish beats belonging to his extended family. Records kept in his fishing books record regular daily catches of a dozen fish or more. But since the late twentieth century salmon numbers have declined sharply in Scotland's rivers and now a catch-and-release policy is practised on the Tweed. Predation by seals and seabirds, overfishing with nets, changes in spawning patterns, inappropriate fish-farming practices and the effects of climate change may all be factors, and now conservation rather than the catching of the great fish is what matters. And the crowning of the Salmon Queen at Tweedmouth may be seen as a homage rather than any sort of symbolic assertion of dominion over the enigmatic, epic life of a creature that spends most of its life in the salt sea but is born and dies in the freshwater that flows into it from far inland.

IV

Forth

I

The Links

There was no clubhouse, no car park, no toilets, no scorecard and no clear idea of the layout of what is almost certainly the world's oldest golf course. Bruntsfield Links lies close to the centre of Edinburgh, about six hectares of gently sloping, undulating, treeless ground to the southeast of the Meadows, a billiard-table-flat area of wide grassland that was once a loch. The Bruntsfield Links is one of the places where the game of golf began in the fifteenth century and perhaps even earlier. It is the ancestor of almost 40,000 courses, from South Korea to South Africa to Argentina and across the USA. But what should be a shrine for the 450 million players all over the world looks at first glance anonymous, like a municipal park – and not a well-maintained one at that – and it's not even used exclusively for golf. Dog walkers and joggers cross its short fairways, children kick a football around and picnickers munch their sandwiches on its margins, and on the morning I went to play the links a large beer bottle sat in front of a green, empty crisp packets and squashed beer cans had been thrown into the long grass. Despite this despoliation and lack of care,

Bruntsfield Links is absolutely authentic, informal, a place where the early spirit of the great game still lives. And it is free to play. All anyone who has to do is turn up with a wedge, a putter and a ball and then just start.

And so we did, on a bright Thursday morning in July, my old friend and long-time, long-suffering golfing partner Tom Leckie and I. To our shame we had never played the course, only walked past it. Tom told me he used to live in a flat on the southern edge of the links but it had never occurred to him to play a round. Even though it was free and nobody had to join a club or pay a subscription.

The day before I'd found the website of the Bruntsfield Short Hole Golf Course and printed a map of its layout. There were not eighteen holes but thirty-six. All were short, between around forty and eighty metres, what is nowadays called a pitch-and-putt course. From the map it was clear that the first hole was close to an old building that resembled the police boxes that used to be found in Britain's cities, except it was green. But the location of the first tee and the first green was by no means obvious. So we started anyway.

Having played together hundreds of times over forty years, there is nothing that Tom and I could do with a golf club that could embarrass the other. Never mind keeping the ball on the fairway, for years I had trouble keeping it in Scotland. We have both posted double-figure scores for straightforward, even easy, holes, and in the course of only one round I once lost eleven balls. Despite these dark moments, there is always redemption. In each round there will be at least one hole well played, several shots worthy of a professional, even if most of them are short putts. Dreams of a perfect round, or at least a score under ninety, are not always completely crushed by the dismal reality of scuffed shots or wide, arcing slices into woods or the long grass. So it was cheering to see that this little golf course had no hazards, no sandy bunkers or ponds or streams and no long grass except at the edges. Only our incompetence stood in the way of a good round, the only consistent facet of our play over four decades.

Poor and often non-existent signage meant that we inadvertently missed out three holes at Bruntsfield (not all of the little metal flagsticks had the hole number on them) but by the time we had found the thirty-sixth tee we had played a game that had much closer connections to the origins of golf than the immensely long championship courses around the world with all their long avenues of magnificent trees, azaleas, sweeping fairways and perfect greens. Success on these manicured holes often depends on power, the ability to hit the ball off the tee for 275 metres and then get close to the hole with an immaculate approach shot before sinking a putt on greens cut to look not like normal grass, but a carpet. The Bruntsfield Short Hole Golf Course is not like that. All the greens are reachable in one shot, but most of the tees, when they could be found, are bare patches of earth (usually the sole clue to their location) and the greens were only patches of slightly shorter grass with a ruff around the hole which had not been trimmed, making it difficult to get the ball in the cup. The person cutting the grass had not bothered to take out the flagstick and just mown around it rather than across it. Both Tom and I agreed that this was a reasonable excuse for so many missed putts. More important was the realisation that early forms of golf were about precision rather than power. And that made it a game accessible to many in Scotland, women and children as well as men.

What does golf have to do with the North Sea? Well, the North Sea brought golf to Scotland, and the nature of its shoreline defined the game. It all began in an unlikely connection with the wool trade. Through ports like Berwick-upon-Tweed, Leith, St Andrews and others to the north, the Scottish wool trade boomed in the Middle Ages mainly with exports to Flanders, in what is now northern Belgium and southern Holland. Weaving had become well organised, with new and more product-ive vertical looms able to produce high-quality cloth for export all over Europe. When Flemish merchant ships tied up at Scottish quays to take on raw wool, they first unloaded not only finished cloth but also munitions, bells and tapestries. And golf. The widespread distribution of the surname of Fleming in Scotland shows that weavers settled permanently, having brought their skills as well as a game they called *het kolven*. Played in the streets of Flemish towns using what looked like a hockey stick, players hit a ball towards an upstanding target, something like a tree or a specially set-up stick. Whoever hit the target with the fewest shots was declared the winner. The nature of Scotland's North Sea shore took the game out of towns and villages, no doubt to the great relief of residents. The liminal stretches of sandy ground behind the dunes, often punctuated with clumps of gorse and stands of dense marram grass, were known as links.

The term derives from *hlinc*, an early English word for a ridge, perhaps a reference to the dunes and the undulation behind them. Too sandy to be ploughed, the links provided grazing for sheep (but not cattle, whose weight would damage the thin layer of turf and poach the ground in winter), and after the twelfth century it often came to be regarded as common ground. *Het kolven* became golf, or gowf, when Scots and immigrant Flemings began to play the game on the links.

Early golf balls were known as 'hairies' because they were small-stitched leather spheres stuffed with horsehair or wool. And not being perfectly round, they could not be hit very far, probably not more than 100 metres. Clubs changed. The Flemish hockey-style sticks were too clumsy and too thick to connect with a hairy and smaller ball, so wooden club faces were developed, often made by bowmakers. Carved from thorn wood, the faces of these early clubheads were lofted so that when a player hit a ball on the sandy turf of the links it would fly through the air and not bobble or bounce along the uneven ground. And instead of using only one club, several were carried around with different degrees of loft to deal with the different places where a ball might come to rest. The replacement of the target with a hole instead of a stick or tree is another consequence of playing on the links. There were very few, if any, trees, and so at some point players began to cut holes in the thin layer of turf with a knife, and a flat-faced club called a putter – the word is from the Scots language, and it means to push or shove, but gently – was made to putt the hairy ball in the hole.

By the fifteenth century golf or gowf had clearly become distressingly popular. In 1457 James II was worried that archery practice, essential for a medieval army in the age of the longbow, was being neglected, and his government issued an angry edict: 'It is ordained and decreed that football and golf be utterly condemned and not practised.' This cannot have had much effect, since the same edict was reissued in 1471 and 1491. But by the beginning of the sixteenth century the king had caught the golfing bug, and James IV not only lifted the ban but began to play the game. The Scottish exchequer records show that he not only had a set of golf clubs bought for his use he also appointed an official ball-maker and fixed the price. Handmade in a slow and necessarily patient process, balls were expensive.

During the sixteenth and seventeenth centuries golf was principally a winter game, because in an era long before the invention of mechanical mowers the grass grew too long in the summer to risk losing expensive hairy balls, and hitting them might also have been difficult. Hungry sheep and low temperatures kept the grass short, especially near the coast, in winter. The winds that blew off the North Sea also helped create an enduring feature of all the world's 40,000 golf courses. To find shelter on the treeless links ewes would scrape out depressions in the sandy soil that in Scots became known as *bunkarts*, or bunkers. There is also some evidence that the precious balls were painted red in winter to make them more visible, and if play was possible in summer they were white. Red balls were probably used in February 1567 when Mary Queen of Scots was recorded playing golf in Edinburgh, either at Bruntsfield or Leith Links near the sea; carrying her clubs were 'cadets', men who later became known as caddies.

By the early eighteenth century hairy balls had been replaced by 'featheries'. Surprisingly, stuffed with boiled feathers rather than wool or horsehair, the new ball was heavier, and when painted with several coats of lead paint, much harder. Featheries could also be hit further, approaching 200 metres. But the new ball was also more expensive, and that, of course, narrowed the appeal of the game. In 1738 the world's first golf club was formed by players who used Bruntsfield Links. Known as the Burgess Golfing Society of Edinburgh, and clearly a middle-class enterprise, it seems to have been played on a six-hole course that occupied approximately the present area of the links. Two holes look as though they were about 200 metres long, and four shorter ones on the higher part of the course were about half that distance. Since the expensive feathery ball flew further, 'fore-caddies' (their name giving rise to the shout of 'Fore!' if a ball looks like hitting a pedestrian, another player or an onlooker) were posted on the fairway to watch the flight and mark where a ball landed.

Golf was also played in the early eighteenth century nearer the Firth of Forth at Leith Links, and in 1744 players about to compete in a tournament found themselves subject to the earliest set of written rules. They make clear how close the game was to what my playing partner and I were attempting to do on Bruntsfield Links. The tees for the next hole were close to the previous green, and there are several references to non-players on the golf course, and to litter. 'If a ball is stopped by any person, horse, dog or anything else, the ball so stopped must be played where it lies.' And golfers were 'not to remove stones, bones or any break [broken] club for the sake of playing the ball'.

By 1800 there were only five golf clubs in Scotland, and it appears to have remained an elite game. However, in the second half of the nineteenth century balls, grass cutters and railways wrought radical change. In 1848 Robert Paterson, a divinity student at the University of St Andrews, received a parcel from Singapore containing an effigy of the Hindu deity, Vishnu. It had been packed in gutta-percha, dried gum resin derived from various species of trees in South-East Asia. It gave Paterson, presumably a golfer, an idea. He heated the resin and tried to make golf balls from it. And failed. But his younger brother persisted and eventually produced a workable prototype of a ball which he branded as Paterson Composite. These early gutta-percha balls had the great advantage of being made in moulds and were therefore perfectly spherical and smooth, and they could be hit further as a result. It was soon noticed that the ball performed better after it had acquired some wear, a few nicks and scratches. A saddler in St Andrews worked out a way of scoring regular grooves, and these improved the aerodynamics and enabled the ball to fly even further. And, most important, 'gutties' were much cheaper and quicker to manufacture. By 1860 they had replaced featheries, golf became accessible to many more in Scotland and the links grew busy – in the summer. Mechanical grass cutters created mown fairways and even more closely mown greens, and instead of remaining a winter game, golf could be played in warmer and sometimes better weather. As the rail network spread in the 1860s and 1870s the seaside links course became accessible to city dwellers, and the game grew very quickly and demand for new courses rocketed.

And new balls called for new clubs. Metal heads had often cut up the expensive featheries and were therefore not much used, but with gutties there were usually only nicks to contend with, and the modern range of metal-headed clubs began to emerge. Players would carry (often under their arms, since golf bags took a while to be invented) two or three woods, a driver to get away off the tee, a brassie – so called because its head was made from brass – for long fairway shots and a spoon for loft. A cleek was an iron club for use on the fairway at some distance from the hole, mashies had wider and more lofted club faces and niblicks were wedges used to get out of long grass or bunkers. These resonant old names are etched on my memory. When I started to play golf sixty years ago older men who had bought the new-fangled steel-shafted clubs gave me their wooden shafted cleeks, mashies and niblicks. They often carried makers' names, and I had two made by Ben Sayers of North Berwick and another from Auchterlonies of St Andrews. How I wish I'd kept them, not for their antique value but as a reminder that golf wasn't always played by numbers, with 2, 3, 4, 5, 6, 7, 8 and 9 irons.

By 1900 gowf had ceased to be a purely Scottish game. In a matter of less than twenty years more than 500 clubs had laid out courses in England, and hundreds of new ones opened in Scotland. It was almost as though a craze had gripped middle-class men. After a good deal of variety in their length, eighteen holes had become the norm, and the Royal and Ancient Golf Club in St Andrews had taken over the governance of the game's rules and the management of the Open Championship. In 1894 the first Open outside of Scotland was played at Royal St George's on the Kent coast at Sandwich, only a couple of kilometres or so south of Pegwell Bay. The club secretary kindly allowed me to walk around a few of the holes so long as I didn't interfere with play. It is a classic links course, very flat and with the fairways and greens like islands in a sea of marram grass and gorse bushes. It is also without doubt one of the most beautifully kept courses I've ever seen, and also a magical, atmospheric place.

In the twentieth century golf became global. American professionals began to dominate, many of them reared on inland courses – parkland as opposed to the windswept links. But some have come to love the sandy, apparently featureless stretches of liminal ground between land and sea, and they consider it a greater test to play well there, perhaps because it was where the game was born. Links golf cannot be played by numbers, clubs selected because precise distances need to be reached in a metronomic sequence from tee to green. Shots on the links have to be crafted, improvised. Wind and the squalls that blow in off the North Sea can transform in moments what seems like a benign landscape into the scene of nightmares. Balls hit high in the air to cut out the wandering and uncertain undulations of the sandy ground can be taken by a gust and dropped into a deep bunker. Jack

Nicklaus, one of the greatest ever to play the game, found himself bunkered on the Old Course at St Andrews; he took four shots to get out and saw his chances of winning the Open evaporate.

There are very many famous links courses in Scotland. In addition to the Old at St Andrews, Muirfield in East Lothian and Carnoustie on the Angus coast also host the Open Championship in rotation. But for me the greatest of them all is the West Links at North Berwick. Golf has been played there, on the southern shore of the Firth of Forth, since a time out of mind. The first documentary record is from 1611, but the links have seen golfers hit a ball there for much longer, and the club claims that after Bruntsfield Links it is the oldest course still being played. Like St Andrews, the layout evolved over time, and it too is owned not by the club but by the town of North Berwick. That means that visitors can get a tee time relatively easily and enjoy all that a traditional links course can offer. But unlike Royal St George's and Muirfield and several others, North Berwick is good to play on for the vast majority of golfers, those like me who have high handicaps. Many courses are heavily influenced by the professional game and are far too long and tough to play, with features like 140 metres of long grass in front of the tee that needs to be flown before the ball can safely reach the fairway, or a string of bunkers set at 180 metres, the average length of a decent opening drive. And there are other very punitive hazards. By contrast, the West Links is fun, perhaps because it evolved over centuries and was moulded by players who could never hope to hit the ball 275 metres or land it on a sixpence on the green.

These things matter because, unlike the vast majority of sports, golf can be played and enjoyed well into old age. My father-in-law played until he was eighty-eight, and even older people can still manage a round if they use a golf buggy. When Tom Leckie and I play, we are still competitive even though neither of us will see seventy again, but we are mostly competitive with ourselves. In addition to playing the game in beautiful places (mostly easier and shorter parkland courses now) in the open air and taking good if unhurried exercise, we also have an uninterrupted four-hour conversation. Apart from with spouses, few people do that, and in itself that's refreshing. What do Tom and I talk about? Golf, of course. Which club to use? What went wrong there? And occasionally we rejoice in not only our own, for once, sweetly hit approach shot to a difficult green but we also smile and applaud the other if something good happens. And just audible as we walk down the eighteenth fairway looking at the scorecard, always a record of mixed fortunes, are the echoes of men and women who have done the same thing in all the centuries that stretch out behind us. Golf is embedded in our history; it came to Scotland across the North Sea and is best seen in its purest form when played on the links by the seashore.

The Invention of Time

Time began on the shores of the North Sea. Bede of Jarrow established the AD system of dating in order to introduce uniformity and accuracy to the recording of historical events, but it was 100 kilometres to the north that the idea of deep time, the hundreds of millions of years BC, first came into currency.

Below Siccar Point, about fifteen kilometres southeast of North Berwick, three friends sailed their boat as close to the cliffs as they dared and managed to find a place to moor it safely. It was a fine day in the spring of 1788, and the sea was calm as they looked up at the red-and-grey rock formations that had been laid bare by the ceaseless washing of the waves and the tides. While James Hall made drawings, James Hutton explained what they were looking at, the processes that had led to what he called 'an unconformity', clear evidence of the immense age of the earth and the first stirrings of an understanding of deep time, the unimaginably vast aeons of geological time.

As late as the beginning of the eighteenth century calculations based on a biblical study of the moment and even the precise date of Creation had been widely accepted. The best known of these were made by James Ussher, the archbishop of Armagh, in 1654. Having studied scripture closely and made some assumptions, he believed that the earth came into being some time around 6 p.m. on 22 October 4004 BC. Other scholars made similar claims, and in an era when the hand of God in Creation was not often questioned, many accepted the literal truth of the narrative of the book of Genesis and found Ussher's assertions plausible and by no means as ridiculous as they seem now.

What James Hutton and his friends saw at Siccar Point and elsewhere in Scotland swept such antiquated thinking into the dustbin of history and replaced it with scientific observation. Here is what the third man in the boat, John Playfair, later wrote:

> On landing at this point, we found that we actually trod on the primeval rock, which forms alternately the base and the summit of the present land. It is here a micaceous [slate-like] schistus [rock that has changed through heat or pressure or both], in beds nearly vertical, highly indurated [hardened], and stretching from south-east to north-west. The surface of this rock runs with a moderate ascent from the level of low-water, at which we landed, nearly to that of high water, where the schistus has a covering of red horizontal sandstone . . . at the distance of a few yards farther back, rises into a very high perpendicular cliff. Here, therefore, the immediate contact of the two rocks is not only visible, but it is curiously dissected and laid open by the action of the waves.

On us who saw these phenomena for the first time the impression will not easily be forgotten . . . We felt necessarily carried back to a time when the schistus on which we stood was yet at the bottom of the sea, and when the sandstone before us was only beginning to be deposited, in the shape of sand or mud, from the waters of the supercontinent ocean . . . The mind seemed to grow giddy by looking so far back into the abyss of time; and whilst we listened with earnestness and admiration to the philosopher [Hutton] who was now unfolding to us the order and series of these wonderful events, we became sensible how much further reason may sometimes go than imagination may venture to follow.

What all of these and other geological observations meant was that the craton, the crust of the earth, had been dynamic over hundreds of millions of years as earthquakes shook and volcanoes roared, and that it continued to change, albeit imperceptibly. The vertical strata Hall described were laid down 450 million years ago and they were directly covered with horizontal layers of old red sandstone that were at least fifty million years younger. This unconformity had been created by ancient convulsions of the craton. Siccar Point is now seen as the most important geological site in the world, a point of comparison for many others, and James Hutton was hailed as the founder of modern geology. He later remarked that he could see 'no vestige of a beginning . . . no prospect of an end' to geological time.

Empirical observation constantly informed the development of Hutton's thinking and writing, and his *Theory of the Earth*, published in 1788 in Edinburgh, showed that the planet was the product not of divine initiative in 4004 BC but of natural forces over very long periods of time. His views were constantly informed by drawings and written records of geological phenomena from all over Scotland and one of the most spectacular examples lies in the mouth of the Firth of Forth, where it meets the North Sea, a couple of kilometres offshore from North Berwick.

James Hutton was the first to recognise the Bass Rock as an igneous intrusion, or volcanic plug. Many millions of years ago, magma (molten lava) had hardened as it reached the surface of an active volcano. As softer rocks around it were weathered or scraped away by the rumble of the glaciers at the end of the last ice age, the much harder solidified magma became an upstanding singular feature before much of it was submerged by the sea after the inundation of Doggerland. To the south of the town rises North Berwick Law, a volcanic plug that solidified in what may have been another vent of the same ancient volcano.

On a sunny July afternoon I had come to North Berwick to board a catamaran that takes sightseers out to and around the Bass Rock. Home to the world's largest colony of gannets, perhaps as many as 110,000 birds, the top and cliffs of the grey rock had been made white by their guano. Metaphor is another, less scientific but nevertheless informative form of observation, and to my eye the Bass Rock looked from a distance like an iceberg that had wandered south from the Arctic into the warmer waters of the North Sea. And, of course, most of it would be invisible under the waves, another means of imagining the millions of years of geological time that made it, that saw it thrust up through the crust of the earth as volcanoes roared and spat red molten lava into the darkened air.

The names of places also speak of the past, of more recent times when the landscape and its features needed to be labelled as geography followed on from geology. Old Welsh and Gaelic were spoken in Scotland long before Bede of Jarrow's ancestors brought their version of English to the north. While the detail of the agricultural hinterland, especially in fertile East Lothian, was named by them – Berwick is from bere-wic, barley farm – the names of more emphatic and dramatic features such as rivers and mountains are often older. The Old Welsh name for the Bass Rock has disappeared, but in Gaelic it survives as Creag nam Bathais, the last element rubbed smooth into Bass. It may mean the crown of the head, and looking out at the rock from the shore, that is what it looked like to me; the cranium of an underwater giant, the crown of the head of Neptune. Far from being idle, it seems to me that such musings make the landscape come alive.

Unusually for the rain-spattered summer of 2024, the sun beat down on North Berwick as I drove into the town and spent half an hour looking for a parking place. Its great charm is in its dual identity, simultaneously embracing and turning its back on the sea. Like many pretty Scottish coastal towns the streets in the old centre are narrow as the houses huddle together against the wind whipping off the winter waves. The harbour is a haven, its walls high, built with massive stones to shelter the moored boats. But when the railway brought day-trippers and golfers in the second half of the nineteenth century, terraces and splendid detached houses were strung out along the margins of the beaches on either side of the old harbour, and promenades built.

It was low tide when at last I arrived at the East Beach and found that the Scots were on holiday. Windbreaks had been planted in the sand; barefoot children ran around shrieking without hats or, it seemed, much protection against the glare, inappropriate, ill-fitting, rarely worn clothing was everywhere; people paddled aimlessly amongst the rock pools, their hands in their pockets; and a mother and son threw a tennis ball back and forth to each other without any evident enthusiasm or purpose. Perhaps the sudden appearance of the sun in Scotland engenders a spasm of bewilderment bordering on incomprehension. Continental Europeans seek the shade on a day like that, wear dark glasses and lightweight clothes, are comfortable and languorous. But what I saw on the East Beach was a wonderful, nostalgic tableau. I happily joined the long queue at the ice cream van, pleased that it was from S. Luca of Musselburgh. The initial stands for Scappaticcio, who with his wife Anastasia opened the Olympic Ice Cream Shop in 1908, not long after the Turrichis had set up in South Shields. In Scotland, Italian ice cream made by the company who sell it is unlike what is available in supermarkets for one simple reason: it tastes of cream and milk and nothing else.

Waiting to board the catamaran with what looked like

a full complement of passengers, I saw that part of the harbour wall on the seaward side had been fenced off for construction work. In October 2023 a huge storm surge had rolled along the shores of the Forth and smashed through the wall, dislodging huge blocks of sandstone and piling them like pebbles in the harbour. The North Berwick lifeboat's coxswain issued a sombre warning on a notice: 'Stay back from the water's edge. Don't risk it for a photo. Feel humbled by the power of the sea from a safe distance.'

A very poor and panicky swimmer, I am more than humbled by the power of the sea. I'm terrified by it, and for me that fear is not visceral but, for once, explicable, traceable. When I was four or five years old my dad decided it was time for me to learn to swim. His method was simple. One summer we were on Spittal Beach, on the opposite shore of the Tweed estuary from Berwick. Despite my mum's objections, he picked me up, carried me, wriggling and screaming, out into the North Sea, and when he reached waist height for him threw me in. I sank and had to be rescued, gulping in air, coughing and choking – and permanently scared of the depths and vastness of the sea. In safe and shallow swimming pools, many years later, I managed to learn a slow and ponderous breaststroke, with my chin held up so far out of the water that my neck quickly gets sore. If I were ever to fall into the sea I wouldn't be able to stay afloat for more than a few moments. And so, when the catamaran cast off and its engines gurgled, I immediately checked the pockets of my waterproof for my car keys, wallet, phone and notebook for the first but not the last time. 'Lost at sea' is a notion never far from the front of my mind when I find myself in a boat of any kind. And playing in an endless loop was the line from the famous nineteenth-century hymn 'Eternal Father, Strong to Save', which sent up prayers for 'those in peril on the sea'.

The harbour entrance seemed impossibly narrow as the skipper edged the catamaran out into the bay, and when he turned east into the open sea the Bass Rock rose up out of it. I had only ever seen it from the safety of the land. The Rock is 107 metres above the waves at its highest point, and I was told later by the skipper that apart from the reefs near the only possible landing place, the cliffs run down sheer under the water for a further forty metres. My reading over the previous few days had told me that the Bass Rock could be seen as a palimpsest for the story of the northern shores of the North Sea. It was a spectacular monument to James Hutton's intellectual brilliance and his establishment of geology as a means of understanding how the land and seascapes came to look the way they do. In more recent times the Rock had been occupied as a wave-washed diseart by a pious and brave hermit known as St Baldred. A castle and a prison were somehow built on the ledges of the Bass, and both were occupied until the early eighteenth century. In 1905 a lighthouse was constructed to a design by David Stevenson, the cousin of the great novelist Robert Louis Stevenson, who had been the Stevenson to carry on the family trade in lighthouse engineering. And now it is home to an impossibly huge colony of gannets, perhaps 55,000 breeding pairs of Britain's largest seabird and one that may be seen as emblematic of the

North Sea, as well as an abundance of puffins, kittiwakes and other seabirds.

Some time around 700, Baldred sailed north from Lindisfarne. Very little is known for certain about him except that he left his name in several places in East Lothian. Near Auldhame there is a cave and a well, and in 2005 archaeologists found the remains of a very early church, probably from the late seventh century, with 200 graves around it. It may well have been founded by Baldred. Near North Berwick is a coastal rock formation called St Baldred's Boat, while on the rocky headland directly above the harbour is the aisle of an early medieval church that may have been originally founded by him. On the Bass Rock St Baldred's Chapel may have stood about halfway up the sloping plateau, and it is often confidently marked on maps. As winter storms whistled around its walls and the old saint shivered, few could have doubted the strength of his faith and the mortification of the flesh he was willing to bear as he prayed and meditated amidst the roaring elements.

Baldred's fame has faded, but North Berwick's association with saints lasted throughout the medieval period and made the town one of the earliest centres of tourism. This was only lightly disguised as pilgrimage, as Geoffrey Chaucer wrote, and what attracted devout tourists to the southern shores of the Forth was a safer (than travelling overland) and shorter passage across the firth. On the northern shore lies Earlsferry, so called because the Earl of Fife established a ferry service to carry pilgrims the eleven kilometres across the water so that they could then walk northwards to the shrine of St Andrew and his great cathedral. He was a man who knew Christ, and his cult was tremendously attractive. Only at Compostela in northern Spain was there a shrine to another apostle in Western Europe. It was widely believed that physical closeness to the relics of St Andrew, especially when the reliquary was ceremonially processed around the streets of the town on feast days, would mean that God was more likely to hear prayers and entreaties. And the canons of the cathedral were always happy to accept gifts of money that were, by extension, more likely to enhance the donors' chances of being heard.

As the catamaran picked up speed, taking us out into the open sea, and I checked my pockets yet again, I could easily make out the houses of Earlsferry on the far shore. Overhead I began to notice more and more gannets wheeling, floating on the updraughts, the black tips of their two-metre wingspreads making them much easier to see against the brilliance of the blue sky. And then, as the boat slowed and turned, the vast mass of the Rock was revealed. I had been sitting in the stern, behind the wheelhouse, as the skipper made straight for it, and all that time it had been hidden from view. The sheer, looming monumentality of the Bass rising up out of the waves shocked me, and the chatter of my fellow passengers subsided as we all gawped. I realised that the white of the wandering iceberg I'd seen from the shore was not just the wide streaks of guano on the cliffs but the mass of living birds perched on the many ledges and up on the sloping summit plateau. The density of the nesting birds was staggering, impossible, gravity-defying, and the noise they made grating. There was also a powerful stink only mitigated a little by the breeze. I had read that 122 tonnes of ammonia are emitted every year from the streaked and mounded guano. The animated mass of these huge birds and their even larger fluffy chicks, 110,000 of them, made the great Rock come alive.

From the time of Baldred the gannet was identified closely with the North Sea. The famous poem, *Beowulf*, was composed some time after 700, and one of its lines describes the sea as 'the gannet-bath'. Perhaps even older than Beowulf is *The Seafarer*. Recited in Old English and written down much later, it is an account of a man sailing alone on the sea, almost certainly the North Sea. Here is part of it:

How I, wretched and sorrowful
On the ice-cold sea
Dwelt for a winter
In the paths of exile
Bereft of friendly kinsmen.

Hung about with icicles
Hail flew in showers
There I heard nothing
But the roaring sea
The ice-cold wave
At times the swan's song
I took to myself as pleasure
The gannet's noise
And the voice of the curlew
Instead of the laughter of men
The singing gull

Instead of the drinking of mead
Storms there beat the stony cliffs
Where the tern spoke
Ice-feathered
Always the eagle cried at it
Dewy feathered
No cheerful kinsman
Can comfort
The poor soul
Indeed he credits it little
The one who has the joys of life
Dwells in the city
Far from terrible journey
Proud and wanton with wine
How I, weary often,
Have had to endure
In the sea paths
The shadows of night darkened.

The ornithologist, writer and broadcaster James Fisher did a great deal to encourage responsible and informed birdwatching in Britain. Apparently fascinated by volcanic plugs and their bird life, Fisher was a member of an expedition that landed on Rockall in 1955, far out in the Atlantic, more than 320 kilometres from the Western Isles. With three Royal Marines and a commission from the queen, he hoisted the Union Jack and claimed the rock for Great Britain. Getting ashore was dangerous and difficult, and in 1971 the secretary of state for Scotland, of which Rockall had become part, remarked that more people had landed on the moon than on the tiny island. It also gave its name to a sector of the Shipping Forecast.

In 1966 Fisher published *The Shell Bird Book*, and in it he unexpectedly offered a fascinating gloss on *The Seafarer*. Where the poet sang of the calls of the swan (most likely a whooper swan), the gannet, the gull, the tern and the curlew, the ornithologist drew some conclusions. The only place around the coasts of Britain where the calls of all of these birds could be heard in the same place and at the same time is the Bass Rock. Further support for this hypothesis comes from the poem's use of the Old English phrase gannetes hlother. In the extract above it is translated as 'the gannet's noise', but it is rendered better and more vividly in Scots as 'gannet blether'. Fisher made the excellent and telling point that the birds do not call when in flight, searching the sea for fish. Only in their breeding colonies do the gannets blether, and the only breeding colony in the Anglo-Saxon world of the seventh and eighth centuries was the Bass Rock. And it is in April that the birds arrive to claim their nests. The poet's use of the phrase 'where on stone cliffs the seas came crashing' is also very suggestive.

Along the North Sea coastline settled by Angles and Saxons the bird was well known and, very unusually, it acquired regional names. Norfolk fishermen described it as the 'herring gant', in Lincolnshire it was a 'gaunt' and in Yorkshire the 'mackerel gant'. More formal taxonomic labels also tell a story. The gannet is known as *Morus bassanus*, the Foolish [Bird] of the Bass Rock. Foolish because the gannet is so big that it has no predator except for man and when hunters take the fat chicks off the nests (the adult birds' meat being too tough to consume), it offers little or no resistance. Now the only place where the *guga*, the young gannet chicks, can be legitimately taken is from the cliffs of the rocky islet of Sula Sgeir, to the north of the island of Lewis in the Hebrides. Each summer boats set out from the port of Ness and men take a set number of chicks to be killed, dried and eaten as a delicacy. Apparently salty *guga* is an acquired taste.

Northern gannets are migratory birds. In winter the Bass Rock is quiet, but when the adult birds return from four or five months in the Bay of Biscay or further south in the Gulf of Guinea off the coast of West Africa, the gannet blether begins again. With so many birds in a such a restricted place the pressure on nesting sites is acute, and when breeding pairs have mated and eggs laid, one of them is always on the nest while the other goes fishing. If it was left empty for any length of time another pair would quickly move in. Gannets mate for life, and most live for between sixteen and twenty years, completing the annual cycle of migrating and raising chicks again and again. Several generations of the same bloodline must coexist on the Rock. Like the Atlantic salmon seeking their home rivers, the great birds find their way back to the Bass and the location of their particular nest perched on a narrow ledge of the brooding cliffs. The gannets must have memory as well as instinct and navigational skills over long distances. Perhaps it is a collective memory, but then they are also aggressive towards each other, using their long, ten-centimetre beaks to keep their neighbours from encroaching on their tiny piece of territory, the nearest thing they have to a home.

Once their chicks have hatched the adult birds begin the feeding cycle, hunting the waters of the North Sea for mackerel, herring, sand eels and whatever else they can find. Some fly hundreds of kilometres in search of food for their young, and several tagged birds have been known to fly as far as the Norwegian coast. Gannets sometimes form flocks and follow trawlers returning to the Firth of Forth from the sea, because they know that before they reach port the fishermen will throw discarded parts of their catch overboard. Other flocks fly far out to sea. With their binocular vision the hunting birds can see schools or shoals of fish some way below the surface. At that moment they dive at an extraordinary 100 kilometres per hour, retracting their wings, leading with their long, sharp beaks, and they hit the surface of the sea like living missiles. Under their skin they have an elaborate system of small diverticula, tubes with pockets of air to cushion the impact – like air bags in modern cars. The birds' speed as they enter the water allows them to dive as deep as twenty-five metres to catch their quarry. Gannets swallow fish whole, fly back to the Bass Rock and regurgitate their catch for their ever-hungry chicks. Two hundred tonnes of fish a day are landed on the ledges and the sloping plateau.

At its peak in 2014, the population of the Rock was 150,000, that is 11.5 per cent of all the northern gannets in the world, a spectacular rate of growth in a century. In 1904 there were only 6,000 birds but when, a year later, shooting was banned and the gannets protected, numbers began to climb, but only slowly. At that time their nests were all on the cliff ledges, and the three hectares of the sloping summit were green and home to a population of rabbits. The lighthouse keepers shot them, and in the 1950s they died out during the myxomatosis epidemic. More gannets came, and by 1988, when the lighthouse became automatic and the keepers left, the population soared. By 1994 there were nearly 40,000 pairs of breeding birds.

In the winter of 2021–2 seabirds began dying in large numbers around the coasts of Scotland. The corpses of more than 13,000 barnacle geese who bred in the Solway were found on the shore and floating in the water. Originating in intensive poultry farms in Asia in 1996, a virulent strain of bird flu eventually spread to wild birds and reached Britain. Gannets on the Bass Rock were dying in very large numbers, and wardens counted more than 5,000 corpses in a single day. But the population did not collapse. It seems that many gannets caught the disease but survived, and these birds showed a slight but noticeable change in their appearance. Instead of a bright blue, their irises had turned black, and it seemed that they had developed an inherited immunity.

Having made a circuit of the Rock, the catamaran pulled away so that last photographs might be taken. And having survived peril on the sea and checked the pockets of my waterproof once more, I stepped ashore gratefully, much happier on dry land. But I was also grateful for the experience of seeing two elemental, deeply impressive phenomena up close. The majesty and the glowering menace of the Bass Rock cannot be understood from the land. Its sheer cliffs need to tower above a small boat bobbing on the sea, making the simple but often forgotten point that the planet and its geological history can and should put us in our place. The time it took for *Homo sapiens* to develop from our various ante-cedents is but a blink in the eye of geological time, and the thunderous, earth-shaking forces that made the drama of the Bass Rock could crush us in one apocalyptic moment. And then there were the remarkable birds, the descendants of the dinosaurs. Claiming their ancestral places on the cliffs, returning from epic journeys, exposed in all weathers, surviving storms and diseases originating in manmade environments and flying with an effortless grace over the North Sea, their sea, the gannet bath, they too put us firmly in our place.

3

Peril Under the Sea

In the summer of 1800 a man clambered out of a fishing boat and onto a slippery, shelving sandstone reef eighteen kilometres offshore from Arbroath. Well wrapped up against the weather, he had brought a theodolite, an optical level, a tripod for setting each of them up, a measuring tape and a notebook for his readings. Robert Stevenson had to work quickly. The sandstone reef known as the Bell Rock was only exposed at low tide and for only two hours. Local fishermen had brought him out from Arbroath harbour, and while he worked, steadying his tripod in the breeze, they scoured the crevices and small gullies in the rock for salvage. According to Stevenson, they found plenty:

> two hundredweight [more than 200 kilos] of old metal, consisting of such things as are used on shipboard . . . a ship's marking iron, a piece of a ship's caboose [deck kitchen], a soldier's bayonet, several pieces of money, a shoe buckle . . . a kedge anchor [a small anchor], cabin stove crowbars etc.

The fishermen had been gathering the detritus of disaster. Only months before they ferried Stevenson out to the 425-metre-long rock, a severe December gale had wrecked more than seventy ships off the Scottish coast, including the warship HMS *York*. It had run aground on the Bell Rock and gone down with all hands. Close to the mouth of the Firth of Tay, the reef had destroyed many hundreds of vessels, perhaps an average of six each winter as the volume of shipping increased in the later eighteenth century. Robert Stevenson's famous grandson and near-namesake, the novelist Robert Louis Stevenson, later wrote:

> Placed right in the fairway of two navigations, and one of these the entrance to the only harbour of refuge [he probably meant Dundee] between the Downs [off the Kent coast] and the Moray Firth, it breathed abroad along the whole coast an atmosphere of terror and perplexity; and no ship sailed that part of the North Sea at night, but what the ears of those on board would be strained to catch was the roaring of the seas on the Bell Rock.

Also known as the Inchcape Rock, this notorious hazard got its better-known name from early efforts to warn mariners that it might be dangerously close. The abbot of the monastery of Arbroath was said to have had a bell fixed to the rock so that, exposed at low tide, it would toll balefully across the waves, presumably audible to those who sailed too close. No records exist to tell how high the bell was set, but to be effective it will have needed to emerge from the water some time before the deadly rock did. And in windless fog, the bell would not have tolled at all.

★   ★   ★

At least the toilets were open. On a glittering, dazzling hot July morning I had come to Arbroath to sail out over the North Sea to the Bell Rock lighthouse. It was clear that a great deal of effort and money had been well spent on refurbishing, paving, erecting beautiful stainless-steel safety railings and building a splendidly designed, ship-shaped new visitor centre at the old harbour. But it was Tuesday. And it was closed, except for the toilets. Which were difficult to find because the lighting in the foyer had not been switched on. Closed on a Tuesday at the end of July, the height of the holiday season, the school holidays, the time when visitors come and most need a centre. And there were plenty; a large group of German cyclists who had, from the evidence of their carrier bags, had the transport and the gumption to go to a large supermarket on the outskirts of Arbroath and buy sand-wiches, sushi and bottles of water and squash, none of which was available around the spruced-up harbour. And I met a party of confused Americans who asked where they might find a cold beer and something to eat. I shrugged, and we smiled at each other. Tuesday didn't seem like an explanation. There was a nearby ice cream shop open with a long queue attached, but a vanilla cone, even one with a chocolate flake attached, was not what I needed to sustain me on a three-hour sea voyage in the afternoon. Eventually I found a fish and chip restaurant that was open hidden behind the darkened visitor centre and a barrier of roadworks. I wondered about the wisdom of fried food before going to sea, and remembered reading that the crews of Lancaster bombers had refused chips before an eight-hour flight. However, the battered haddock and well-cooked, dry chips (not cheap at £16.99, but then it was Tuesday, and I was grateful) were excellent, if not quite in the class of Colman's of South Shields. As I remembered vinegar first and then salt, I mused on the difference between North Berwick and Arbroath and their attitudes to visitors. The former welcomed them while the latter seemed uncertain, certainly disorganised.

The hot sun of high summer beat down from an azure sky as I made my way past the cluttered evidence of fishing on the quays; piles of lobster pots, coils of rope, orange fish boxes, drying nets. The iodine sea-tang mixed with diesel fumes seemed to fill the still air. I passed the premises of M&M Spink, producers of Arbroath smokies, a famous delicacy with a strong taste. De-headed and gutted but with the skin left on, two haddocks are tied together with hemp twine after having been salted overnight. Placed on a stick, with a fish on either side, the haddocks are suspended over a smouldering fire of hardwood chips in a specially adapted barrel. This is sealed with wet jute sacks (so that they don't catch fire) and cooked and smoked for about an hour. I've only ever eaten Arbroath smokies cold and once (all of) the bones have been safely extracted, they are tangy, meaty, delicious and distinctive. I had noticed that a shop selling smokies was open, despite it being Tuesday. There was even smoke spiralling from a chimney, and, although tempted, I did not divert on my way to the quayside.

Noticing a set of steps, I climbed up onto the outer sea wall of the harbour, shaded my eyes against the glare and looked out to sea. And I saw it. Faint on the furthest horizon stood the tiny white outline of the Bell Rock Lighthouse, the dark lantern at its top a dot against the pale meeting of the sea and the sky, perching on the very edge of the world. Every other thought fled as I stared, peered across the indigo sea, seeing its tiny pencil shape and then not seeing it as the light seemed to drift. It was a breath-catching moment as all of the quotidian irrelevance of the quirks and awkwardnesses of the town receded behind me, vanishing into insignificance. This was what I had come to see, a monument to determination, invention and necessity, the best of us, the very best human beings could do to defeat and confound the dangers that lay under the sea, to make distant echoes of the screams and shouts of dying, drowning sailors, to protect those in peril on the sea from the great power of the deeps and its jagged reefs.

The *Ultimate Predator*, skippered by Alex Smith, was due to cast off at 14.00 hours on the round trip to the great lighthouse. Others who had booked passages out to the Bell Rock sat on benches by the harbour wall, and we all agreed that the departure time was correct. But the *Ultimate Predator* was nowhere to be seen. Then a tall, fair-haired woman said she could hear engine noise, and moments later the boat nosed into the harbour entrance and chugged over to the quayside. Carrying buckets of mackerel, several fishermen disembarked while the skipper and his crew of two hosed down the decks and made all ready to sail. The rapid turnaround time would have shamed the tight schedules of budget airlines. Unlike the catamaran that took me out to the Bass Rock, there were no seats along the sides of the boat, only a few in the middle. I was soon to discover why.

Being of a certain age and vulnerable to overexposure in the beating July sun, I had gone into the RNLI shop at the harbour, delighted to find that it was open, and bought a hat. There was no canopy over the stern of the boat, where all the seats were. And as we turned out of the harbour into the open sea and the skipper made the engines roar, we ploughed through the blue water, sending spray from the bow wave up and over the sides. If anyone had sat there they would have been repeatedly spattered. As it was, I stayed mostly dry as we set what seemed to be an arrow-straight course towards the lighthouse. But as on the short voyage to the Bass Rock, the cabin and wheelhouse completely obscured any sight of our destination. And because of our speed the boat seemed to travel uphill as the bow rode up and over the water.

From the stern I watched Arbroath and the red sandstone cliffs of the Angus coast shrink and become no more than a line behind us as we made headway past buoys and groups of flagged lobster pots. Birds wheeled above, and I made out the black wingtips of gannets searching the sea for fish. A couple who both had binoculars spotted a large flock of birds at high altitude, and I wondered what they were. Standing, their legs splayed against the slight pitch and roll of the boat, these two frequently and thoughtlessly stood by the rail, directly in front of me and the other seated passengers.

Then at last they moved aside. The boat's engines slowed and went quiet as it turned. Like a giant appearing from behind a high building, the great lighthouse was suddenly revealed, towering over us. My first, instinctive reaction was that it should not have been there. Was this a mirage? How had this magnificent monument risen up out of the sea? Tremendous, primeval, volcanic forces had thrust the mass of the Bass Rock through the crust of the earth amidst the roaring thunder of the early aeons of creation. But here was a beautiful, slender white tower, stately and elegant, soaring above the indigo sea perfectly set against the pale blue of the sky. The first courses are sandy coloured as they rise up from the spread of a broad base to a platform in front of a door and metal ladder to reach it. Then, its outline becoming like the trunk of a tree, the lighthouse is a brilliant white, its smooth sides pierced by tiny windows and topped by its whole purpose, the lantern, protected by a rail around it and dark netting. The Bell Rock is a thing of breath-catching beauty, unforgettable, majestic in all senses, a sentinel set in the sea to protect sailors against devastation and death. Looking at the scores of photographs I clicked on my phone, these moments come racing back, vivid and indelible. As I write this on the day after I saw this wonder of the modern world, I feel tears prickle, and my heart swells with joy and pride for my fellow human beings, for their achievement, for the mastery of the thing.

After a time holding his position off the lethal rock, the skipper began to circle slowly around it and I heard him say that he had only five metres of draught. A friendly seal swam alongside and the other crew members threw him some mackerel left by the fishermen. I had looked at the tide table, and on that day low water was expected at 15.11, but very little of the rock around the lighthouse was revealed. There was only a waning crescent moon the night before, and so the tide range was narrow. The skipper told me that was as much as we would see of what Robert Stevenson surveyed more than 220 years before.

Once the circuit of the Bell Rock was complete, the engines grew louder, spray flew and we set off back to Arbroath. I realised that it was the furthest out to sea I had ever been in an open boat, and the round trip would equate to a crossing of the English Channel. The wake churned milky white, the bow wave spattering spray over me as I watched the great lighthouse grow ever smaller until it disappeared into the shimmer of the blue horizon. But its mark on my memory will be indelible. I had started this journey with a visit to another lighthouse, the North Foreland on the Kent coast, set in its manicured garden, surrounded by rhododendrons. Although its function was the same, it could not have been more different from the raw, enduring, towering power of the Bell Rock. The first sea-washed lighthouse ever built, it has stood for more than 200 years, the stonework needing no maintenance as the mighty waves of countless storms have battered its slender form.

When we tied up at Arbroath harbour and disembarked, I rocked slightly on the pontoon, taking hold of the handrail and not only because I was finding my land legs. And when I reached my car I had to find a cloth to clean the sea-salt off the lenses of my glasses. Dry land felt safe, and I felt as though I had visited a much more dangerous world.

★   ★   ★

Seven years after Robert Stevenson had surveyed the Bell Rock, the Commissioners of the Board of Northern Lights were at last persuaded that a lighthouse should be built on it. But not by Stevenson. John Rennie had designed and overseen the construction of canals and aqueducts as well as taking a leading role in drainage schemes in the Fens. At Kelso, my hometown, he was responsible for a beautiful bridge over the Tweed that has stood many tests of time. Rennie's insistence that its piers should be sunk more than two metres into the bedrock below the river, the diggers protected by coffer dams, made the structure immensely strong and durable. It was the model for London's Waterloo Bridge.

Economic arguments were also persuasive for the Commissioners. In the second half of the eighteenth century victorious campaigns against the French in Canada and India had given Britain a vast and potentially very lucrative empire. Merchant shipping was the only means of bringing raw materials to the mills and factories of an industrialising British economy, and far too many cargoes and men were being lost at sea. A light on the Bell Rock would also greatly enhance the developing economy of Dundee. Raw flax for the city's linen mills was being imported from Russia and the Baltic, while commercial whaling had begun in the 1750s.

These valuable cargoes needed safe access to the mouth of the Tay.

As preparations for building the new lighthouse were made before work on the rock was due to commence in 1807, Robert Stevenson began to assume a leading role, playing on the fact that John Rennie was very busy with other projects and unable to devote more than a fraction of his time to the Bell Rock. Meticulous preparation was absolutely vital since it would be possible to work on the reef for only two hours each day, and then only in the summer. At Arbroath a work yard was set up and a lighthouse ship commissioned, which would ferry men and materials the eighteen kilometres out to the Bell Rock. Directly overseeing operations, constantly cajoling and questioning, writing hundreds of detailed letters, Robert Stevenson hired more than a hundred men, and he took his time to get every detail correct and precisely to specification. For two years, masons, carpenters and blacksmiths worked on the materials that would be needed. Most important were the vast blocks of stone that were to be used to build the lighthouse. Masons had to carve and sand them exactly to Stevenson's design, each one of them slightly different in each course. Even the slightest inaccuracy would show when they were taken out to the rock.

On 16 August 1807, with a rousing send-off from Arbroath harbour, the first work party sailed out to the Bell Rock. Their immediate task was to clear it of seaweed and the melancholy litter left by shipwrecks. The plan was to build barracks so that workers did not have to be ferried back and forth from the shore or spend periods of high tide on board the lighthouse ship, and footings had to be prepared for the cast-iron skeleton of the structure. Most important was the digging of the wide foundation pit for the base of the lighthouse. Hacked out of the rock with picks, pinches and chisels (which needed constant maintenance from blacksmiths), the pit needed to be perfectly flat and perfectly circular. Sixty centimetres deep, it would hold the first two courses of granite in place, and eventually the whole lighthouse, planted like a post in a posthole.

It was wet, slippery and dangerous work – and at one point almost fatal. On one autumn day the lighthouse ship broke away from its moorings and left Stevenson and his work party of thirty-two men stranded on the rock. The tide was rising as they watched the ship drift further and further away, and disaster loomed. It was only a matter of time before the incoming tide engulfed them. There were two small boats used to transfer materials from the ship, but they could only take a few of the men. Stevenson later recalled:

> Not a word was uttered by any one, but all appeared to be silently calculating their numbers . . . The workmen looked steadfastly upon the writer [Stevenson] and turned occasionally towards the vessel, still far to leeward. All this passed in the most perfect silence, and the melancholy solemnity of the group made an impression never to be effaced from the mind.

But then good fortune suddenly intervened. One of the men thought he could make out a boat on the horizon, sailing out towards them from Arbroath. It was a supply vessel bringing letters – and salvation.

Landing granite blocks on the rock that weighed a ton, with nothing but simple, hand-winched cranes and muscle power, was proving very difficult, and as he did throughout the life of the project, Robert Stevenson had to be inventive, find a better way of doing things. To get the stones from the safe landing place to the foundation pit, he had a short railway built and a small bogey adapted which the workers could push. It was vital to move these blocks very carefully, without chipping them in any way. Their shape, carved by the masons in the Arbroath work yard, was crucial to the strength and the durability of the lighthouse. What, in essence, Stevenson had designed was a huge three-dimensional jigsaw, and it had to fit together perfectly to form strong foundations and the walls of the tower that would rise from them.

At the work yard in Arbroath wooden moulds were made and fitted together in what was both a trial run and a guide for the masons. Each stone was carved like a jigsaw piece that would fit only into the stones next to it. The blocks of granite forming each course would link together in a circular pattern with a curved outer face before tapering inwards in sinuous lines to where they were butted against the stones next to them so that they interlocked with them, and only them. When the first course had been laid and found to be perfectly level, the second was locked on to it using two techniques. Set at random intervals, joggles were small knobs, protuberances on the bottom of each stone that fitted snugly into exactly matching notches in the one below it. The second means of locking the courses together was to have two holes bored right through a stone and then part of the way through the stone below it. Oak rods known as trenails were then inserted and pushed down until their top ends were flush with the new stone's upper surface. The ends were then split and wedges driven in to make the trenails as tight as possible. Pozzolana, what the masons called Roman cement, was used to point the seams between the stones. It would set in the wet. All of this very precise and strenuous work was done at speed in the two hours of low tide and with little more than muscle power and determination to make the stones fit. And they did fit, perfectly, giving the tower the immense strength it would need when gales blew in and mighty waves battered its walls.

At the end of March 1808 Robert Stevenson sailed out to the Bell Rock to see what damage the winter's storms had done to the foundation courses. To his immense relief, not one stone had moved, the jigsaw had stayed in place, the design and all the care taken over the carving had proved itself. That summer the pace of construction quickened. Not only were the barracks completed, housing eleven men and Stevenson himself, but as one course was laid upon another, rising up out of the incoming tide, work could go on a little longer each day. By the end of August 1809 the lighthouse tower was nine metres high, its sheer weight also adding significantly to its strength. By June 1810 the first internal floor had been laid, where the entrance door now is. At the end of August all that remained was the difficult and delicate business of placing the lantern on top of the tower, the whole point and purpose of all that effort, skill and ingenuity.

In February 1811 the Bell Rock light flared for the first time, and since then it has only been extinguished in wartime. Waves thirty-five metres higher than the top of the lantern are whipped up by gales, but none of these mighty storms has made any impression. And nor could the Luftwaffe. Three times in 1940 and 1941 the lighthouse was strafed by machine-gun fire, and on 1 April 1941 a bomb was dropped. It exploded about ten metres from the base of the tower, but it didn't cause any damage. The Bell Rock light can be seen for thirty kilometres out to sea as its beam rakes over the waves. And almost as much of a comfort, it can also be seen fifty-six kilometres inland, a reassurance for those who waited at home for the safe return of fishermen and sailors.

When the *Ultimate Predator* circled slowly around the lighthouse, the engines quiet and the passengers all standing on one side, the effect was almost hypnotic. Like others, I stared at the white tower as the sun made it brilliant. Awesome is now a threadbare adjective, but that is how it seemed to me; awe is what I felt, a belly-hollowing sense of awe at this elegant, powerful testament not only to hard, dangerous work and ingenuity but also to selflessness. The Bell Rock was built to save lives, and Robert Stevenson patented none of his inventions nor guarded any of the secrets of his methods so that others could use them elsewhere. More lights needed to be built, more lives saved.

As we sailed away, back to safe harbour, from this structure that had no business being there, standing sentinel in the midst of the sea for more than 200 years, I knew that I had been privileged to see one of the wonders of the modern world.

★   ★   ★

On 24 May 1844 in the cellars of the Capitol in Washington, DC, directly below where the Supreme Court used to sit, a group of men watched history being made. Using a simple code he had invented, Samuel Morse transmitted a message along a cable erected next to the railway line that was instantly received in Baltimore seventy kilometres to the northeast. His dots and dashes spelled out 'What hath God wrought', a phrase from scripture that was far from portentous. The invention of electric telegraphy changed the world, and also saved many lives at sea.

Vice-Admiral Robert Fitzroy understood how the ability to communicate instantly over long distances would be of great value to mariners. In 1854 the Meteorological Office was established as part of the Board of Trade with Fitzroy as the grandly titled Meteorological Statist. He immediately grasped the importance of the accurate measurement of weather data – air pressure, rainfall, temperature, wind speed and so on – and also that the measurements needed to be uniform, recorded in the same way. Ships' captains were given instruments to record conditions and asked to supply the new Meteorological Office with regular and reliable information. Fitzroy also oversaw the design of a standard barometer that was sent to many ports around

Britain and set up in a public place near harbours so that fishermen and sailors could read it before going out to sea. At Stromness on Orkney, the Fitzroy barometer is still on display in its stone housing, and it is still working.

On 25 and 26 October 1859 a tremendously destructive storm raged in the Irish Sea. The worst to be recorded in the nineteenth century, with gale force winds blowing in excess of 160 kilometres per hour, mountainous waves were whipped up, and they drove a staggering 133 ships to the bottom of the sea. The *Royal Charter*, a steam clipper almost at the end of the long voyage from Melbourne to Liverpool, was carrying 112 crew and 371 passengers. Some were gold miners returning home, men who had struck it rich in the diggings at Ballarat. Many carried large sums as luggage, no doubt afraid to let it out of their sight, and there was also a consignment of gold in the cargo hold. As the gale roared, the skipper of the *Royal Charter* decided to ride it out and dropped both anchors off the northeast coast of Anglesey. But then, in the black darkness of early morning, the tremendous seas caught the clipper broadside and snapped both anchor chains. Helpless, driven by the gale, the *Royal Charter* was smashed to pieces on the rocks and cliffs north of Moelfre. Most of the miners were said to have drowned, weighed down by body belts containing gold, and many others were killed because they were dashed against the rocks by huge waves. Only thirty-nine passengers and crew managed to scramble ashore, and more than 450 died. This was by no means an isolated, freakish tragedy. Between 1855 and 1860 a total of 7,042 ships had been wrecked off the coasts of Britain, with 7,201 people losing their lives.

But it was the shock of the loss of the *Royal Charter* and 132 other ships in only two days in the great storm of 1859 that galvanised Robert Fitzroy. Fifteen 'land stations' were set up around the coasts to transmit by telegraph daily weather reports directly to the Meteorological Office in London at set time each day. This in turn allowed Fitzroy and his staff to create charts that would allow predictions to be made. Fitzroy coined the phrase 'weather forecast', and in 1861 these daily predictions were published in *The Times* newspaper. It was, in essence, the beginning of the *Shipping Forecast*. This real-time weather data began immediately to save lives and cargoes. If what quickly became known as the Met Office believed a storm was imminent, they would telegraph ports that would be affected, and storm cones, large drums, would be hoisted as a warning in the harbours. It was, wrote Fitzroy, 'a race to warn the outpost before the gale reaches them'.

These first weather forecasts were really a by-product of the storm warnings for shipping, and Fitzroy believed that there could be no harm in publishing them in *The Times*. Here is the very brief forecast for 1 August 1861:

The temperature in London – 62F, clear with a south-westerly wind.

The temperature in Liverpool – 61F, very cloudy with a light south-westerly wind.

Overcast in Nairn, Portsmouth and Dover.

Fitzroy himself was dismissive:

Prophecies and predictions they are not, the term forecast is strictly applicable to such an opinion as is the result of scientific combination and calculation.

In fact the early weather forecasts had an immediate and profound impact in Britain. With a changeable, unpredictable Atlantic climate, there was enormous interest in the apparent certainty of Fitzroy's forecasts. The first few turned out to be broadly correct, and they seemed positively miraculous to many. No one had been able to do more than guess at tomorrow's weather until the first publication of the 'weather forecast' in *The Times* (other newspapers all over the country also began to publish them), and each day's predictions were eagerly anticipated and pored over, and not just by sailors and fishermen. Organisers of outdoor events in the summer, the likes of country shows, local fetes, sporting occasions and important ceremonies began to plan with the Met Office's predictions in mind. The great crowds who were keen on horse racing were particularly obsessed. For them the most important date in the calendar was the Derby, run in early June at Epsom Downs in Surrey. One newspaper carried this somewhat sardonic piece:

With what eagerness in every quarter was the meteorological column consulted in the newspapers where Admiral Fitzroy records the forecast of the weather, and with what satisfaction did the experienced interpreters of the prediction see that he had set down for the south of England – 'Wind SSW to WNW moderate to fresh, some showers', which of

course indicated that it would be a remarkable fine
day, and that the umbrellas might be left behind.

Of course, the forecast was indeed sometimes wrong,
and in reply to criticism or scepticism, Fitzroy used the
letters pages of *The Times* in 1861, poking fun at 'those
whose hats had been spoilt from umbrellas being omitted'.

Long before these pioneering forecasts stimulated great
interest, the British had talked about the weather, mostly
because it was so changeable and difficult to predict. Each
day could be a surprise, something worthy of an opening
comment in a conversation. In Scandinavia and around
the shores of the Mediterranean long periods of consist-
ently cold or warm weather are the norm, and there is
therefore much less to say about it.

There are two prevailing reasons for our changeable
climate. The warm currents of the Gulf Stream mean
that, despite our northerly latitudes, Britain is much
warmer than similar latitudes on the other side of the
Atlantic such as Labrador, and as a result the weather
can often fluctuate, giving us warm days in winter and
much less frost. (This is the reason for the sad fact that
we rarely have white Christmases.) A second factor is our
geographical position offshore Western Europe. Britain
lies directly at the end of an Atlantic storm track, a narrow
zone sandwiched between warmer equatorial temperatures and the colder air of the north. Driven by the
prevailing westerly winds, cyclones blow across the ocean,
and although their force is often waning by the time they
reach Britain, they too create changeable and sometimes
dramatic weather. As the planet warms and the traditional

pattern of the seasons is upended, weather forecasting has become more important than ever – sometimes a matter of life and death – but understanding how these storm tracks influence our climate has long been seen as essential by meteorologists.

In the summer of 1881 Clement Wragge climbed Britain's highest mountain in 153 consecutive daily ascents. Ben Nevis stood directly in the path of storms blowing in off the Atlantic, and Wragge wanted to take precise measurements of air pressure, temperature, rainfall (and sometimes snowfall), cloud cover, fog and much else at the base, halfway up and at the summit. He hoped to create an unrivalled bank of data that would allow meteorologists to discern patterns and in the future be able to issue even more reliable forecasts that could be immediately telegraphed great distances to shipping and elsewhere. Clement Wragge's work, to say nothing of his flinty fitness and determination, created a unique resource, a model of recording that is still the most complete dataset of high-altitude mountain weather that exists in Britain. His work was greatly helped by the use of Stevenson screens, instrument shelters set up on the flanks and on the summit of the great mountain. These were invented by Thomas Stevenson, the youngest son of Robert, also a builder of lighthouses and the father of Robert Louis.

Like John Harrison and both Stevensons, Robert Fitzroy's work had an immensely beneficial effect on those in peril on the sea. With the introduction of weather forecasting, the incidence of shipwrecks around the coasts of Britain declined dramatically in the second half of the nineteenth century, even though the volume of shipping increased as imperial trade reached its zenith. After 1850 submarine telegraph cables greatly extended the reach of information, in both directions, and when Guglielmo Marconi invented wireless telegraphy in 1894 ships at sea could be contacted and eventually messages sent by their skippers were received regularly on land. Synoptic weather forecasts became possible on the basis of a vast weather map that reached across the Atlantic Ocean and that could therefore predict what sort of weather was on its way.

But, very sadly, Robert Fitzroy took no comfort from his achievements. He had suffered from the effects of long years of overwork and endured bouts of illness. Also, he was penniless, having spent his personal fortune on his meteorological work. Fitzroy suffered from depression, and one morning it overwhelmed him. On Sunday, 30 April 1865 he awoke and appeared to begin to get ready to go to church. Instead, this gifted and dedicated man walked into his dressing room, locked the door and cut his throat with a razor. It was a tragic end to a life that had given so much to others.

★   ★   ★

Where Fife Ness juts its chin into the North Sea, a three-kilometre-long jagged reef lurks under the surface. It ends with the North Carr rock, a ship killer that claimed sixteen vessels wrecked or stranded between 1800 and 1809. Having completed the miraculous Bell Rock, it was a challenge Robert Stevenson could not resist. Buoys had been torn off the North Carr repeatedly by strong tides, and the great engineer's recommendation was not a light-house but an ingeniously designed stone tower topped by a bell, creating an actual bell rock. It would be tolled loudly by a mechanism Stevenson called 'a tide machine'. Instead of keeping the sea out, he wanted to let it into the hollow tower and make it work for him. An aperture approximately 7.5 centimetres in diameter was to be cut into the bottom course of the jigsaw of dovetailed granite stones so that the waters of a rising tide could flow in and rise up. Their pressure would activate a series of levers linked to hammers, and they would ring the great bell, 1.5 metres in diameter and audible over enough of a distance to warn approaching shipping of the deadly presence of the North Carr rocks. When the tide ebbed, the levers would continue to work for some time, tolling the bell across the sea.

It was a brilliant idea. But it didn't work. Stevenson had only a toehold, too little rock to work with, an area just over five metres in diameter. Nevertheless, the crew who had worked on the Bell Rock did manage to estab-lish foundations. But not for long. Between 1813 and 1816 storms dislodged or scattered the granite stones, even though at one point seven courses had been laid. Eventually Stevenson had to admit defeat, and six cast-iron columns were raised instead of the tower and surmounted by a beacon ball. It has defied the North Sea's attempts to destroy it and can still be seen from the Fife shore. But it was not satisfactory, and ships continued to founder on the North Carr.

The Commissioners of the Northern Lighthouse Board

eventually, finally, more than sixty years later, came up with a solution. They decided to have a lightship built, a vessel instead of a lighthouse that could be permanently anchored off the deadly rocks as a constant warning of their presence. The most recent of the lightships was decommissioned in 1975 and replaced by an automatic beacon and a low light on Fife Ness. Almost a century old, the old ship is now moored in the Victoria Quay in Dundee.

★　　★　　★

It was a sparkling, rain-fresh morning when I drove through the farmlands of North Fife with George Rosie, not only a friend of many years and a former colleague but also the son of the *North Carr* lightship's longest serving skipper, another George Rosie.

The old ship was a sorry sight. Tied up in a corner of the quay, with a large and busy modern hotel on one side, blocks of new, high-end flats looking out over the Firth of Tay on another, and sharing the quay with Wild Shore, a water sports complex offering paddleboards and other paraphernalia that spoke of Californian beaches rather than Dundee, the *North Carr* lightship was a rusting relic of another era, covered in flaking red paint, its stories and the heroic constancy of its crews fading into the darkness of the past.

On board were two volunteers from Taymara, a maritime preservation trust that had bought the old ship for £1 and hoped to restore it to make sure its stories are not forgotten. But they were not optimistic, talking of the urgent need for a 'sugar-daddy', a wealthy philanthropist to foot what would be a seven-figure cost. The deck was scaly with rust, the twelve-metre tower and its lantern forlorn, the wooden decking damp and moss-fringed and the huge foghorn green with mould. But when our guides took us below deck, their enthusiasm kindled, and the lightship began to come alive once more. The radio room still had its equipment, complete with Bakelite telephone handsets and headsets attached to four units festooned with a bewildering array of dials and tuning knobs. The skipper, George's dad, had a saloon, separate quarters from his crew. There was a narrow box bed with high sides, a reminder of the ship pitching and rolling in heavy seas, and below it were six drawers with lovely old brass cupped handles. Every bit of space was used. In the private saloon was a black coal-fired stove with a chimney, and George remembered how warm it kept them on bitter winter nights. Several of the shelved cupboards were for books, reading being the crew of ten's main diversion when off duty.

Beyond the living quarters, down very steep ladders with shallow iron steps and handrails on both sides, were the engine rooms and fuel tanks. The *North Carr* lightship could not move under its own steam (it was towed everywhere) but it needed power for its light, the foghorn, the operation of the anchors and their winches and much else. Under the bow deck were coils of mighty chains that had been attached to the anchors that held the ship on station. Before we boarded I noticed a mighty anchor, four tonnes I was later told, lying on the quayside. Our tour of the old ship was not only an elegiac journey into the past, especially for George, but also a reminder of the complex technical operations that the skipper and his crew undertook every day and every night, tasks that had to be completed in a vessel that was constantly in motion, sometimes violently so. The *North Carr* was never off duty, except when it went for its refit every three years.

'My mother didn't like ships or the sea,' George told me once we had found a café and some coffee after leaving the ship and its guardians. 'When the *North Carr* was in harbour she would go aboard, but even a swinging rope made her seasick.' But there was no disguising the fact that it was a dangerous job. George told me that every evening there was a sigh of relief when 'on the trawler band [a radio frequency used by fishing boats] at 7 p.m. sharp, my dad did a daily bulletin on the sea conditions. We could get it at home in Granton [in North Edinburgh]. And he always ended it with "and goodnight to everyone at home". My mother was always pleased to hear that.'

In 1998 George wrote a long essay for an edition of the literary magazine *Granta* about the ship and his father's time as its skipper from 1946 to 1968, and he recalled an indelible, dangerous, tragic episode:

In the early hours of December 8th, 1959, my mother received a telephone call from the NLB [the Northern Lighthouse Board]. The North Carr had severed her anchor chain and was adrift in heavy seas off Fife Ness. The wind was from the south-east and it was pushing her towards the rocky shore. My mother was remarkably calm. I wanted to stay at home but she made me promise to attend my lectures. There was nothing we could do. Everything would be all right. Nothing would happen to the North Carr so long as my father was in command.

But when I telephoned her from college later that morning she was distraught, in tears. She had just learned that the Fife Ness coastguard had called out the Broughty Ferry lifeboat, the Mona, to assist my father's ship. In the howling darkness the lifeboat had foundered on the sandbanks at the mouth of the Tay. All eight men aboard had died. And the North Carr was still adrift, perilously close to the rock-bound shore of Fife.

The next two days were a nightmare. I remember wandering around Edinburgh in a daze while newspapers, radio and television bombarded us with information about the North Carr. The telephone never stopped ringing . . .

Meanwhile my father was battling to save his ship. I have a copy of the terse report he submitted to the NLB a few days after the event. His main anchor had parted at 02.02 on Tuesday 8th December, 1959. Immediately he put the port bower [auxiliary] anchor over the side with 90 fathoms of cable. This held for a few hours, then at 06.30 that too parted 'with the result that we were adrift again driving in a north-westerly direction.'

Fifteen minutes later, and 900 yards off the coast, he tried again. He got the starboard bower anchor over the side along with 240 fathoms of cable 'to help hold the ship and also to lighten her head and make it easier for her to ride the heavy seas that were running.' It worked. The starboard bower anchor and the fathoms of cable held.

Meanwhile the Pharos [the NLB service ship] and the Admiralty tug Earner were barrelling their way down the Firth of Forth. They arrived early in the afternoon and began a long and futile struggle to get a line aboard the North Carr . . .

By daybreak on Wednesday 9th December the wind and sea were worse than ever. More attempts were made to get a line aboard. They all failed. At 11.30 the Earner contacted the naval base and asked for helicopter support. An hour later two Sycamore helicopters from RAF Leuchars arrived above the North Carr. The mizzen mast was chopped down with axes, heaved over the side, and the first man was lifted off the watch room [roof] at 1300. My father was the last to be picked up at 1345.

The lightships have all been decommissioned now, and all of the lighthouses are automatic, unmanned and controlled from the headquarters of the NLB in Edinburgh's George Street. Above the lintel of the main door there is a working model of the Bell Rock. And when we left Victoria Quay and the *North Carr*, I noticed that in the lantern a small blue light had been left on.

4

Blood on the Ice

In the latter decades of the nineteenth century the Dundee whaling fleet sailed far to the north, deep into the Arctic Circle, as far as the Svalbard archipelago. The captains of these immensely strong, purpose-built ships aimed to get as close to the edge of the pack ice as possible and drop anchor. In the dazzling polar light, either the captain or a trusted and experienced man would then climb up the main mast to the crow's nest. With a telescope he scanned the sea for whales breaking the surface, watching for spouts of air and water as they breathed through their blowholes. When he saw one the lookout shouted directions through a speaking trumpet to the crews of the whaleboats. The ships themselves took no active part in hunting. The whales were pursued by small, double-ended rowing boats with between six and eight men on board. The boatsteerer worked the tiller to get behind the whale so that the harpooner had a good angle from which to strike. When he had plunged his barbed spear into the animal's flank, the lineman made sure that the rope attached to it could pay out freely and was not fatally tangled around the leg or the foot of a crew member.

That was the moment of greatest danger. When the whale felt itself pierced by the harpoon, it might thrash its tail, or dive, or both. Boats had been capsized when this happened and men drowned in the freezing Arctic waters. Whales instinctively swam away from the pain, towing the rowing boat behind them. This too was very dangerous, for the boat might be dragged through the sea for a long time, perhaps into fog, perhaps a great distance from the ship. Other boats tried to follow because they knew that sooner or later the wounded whale would be forced to the surface to breathe. At that moment the whaleboats would circle and move in for the kill, plunging in more harpoons. Exhausted, bleeding profusely, the whale would eventually float to the surface where it was killed by long lances that could be driven deep into its body.

When the boats towed their kill back to the ship, the crew worked quickly. The head was cut off, and the process known as flensing began. Blubber was what brought the ships north from Dundee, and it was cut away in squares and stowed in the hold in sealed containers or barrels. Rendered in huge vats, whale oil was very valuable, widely used mainly for lighting and lubrication. On board the ship the jaw was also cut out for baleen, whalebone, which also fetched high prices. Depending on the cycles of ladies' fashions, the lightweight but strong bone was often in great demand for the manufacture of corsets or stays. Once flensing was complete, the crew began hunting once more, not returning home until the hold was full.

Some Dundee ships specialised in sealing, going after seals on the pack ice, either shooting them or clubbing them to death. They too had blubber, and their flayed skins could be sold for a variety of uses. Sealing was less dangerous but more labour intensive and time-consuming than whaling. Females would give birth to their pups on the pack ice in early spring and crews would arrive some time later when they had grown and were worth killing. Timing was important, because once pups had been weaned the huge colonies of seals on the ice would disperse. Some bull seals resisted. In an attempt to protect their mates and their young, they attacked the hunters, sometimes pushing or dragging them into the sea. But the killing went on, carried out on an industrial scale, and the brilliant white of the pack ice was stained red with hundreds, thousands, of pools of blood. A single Dundee ship could return to the Tay with blubber and skins from 2,000 young seals and 600 mature animals.

Towards the end of the nineteenth century Dundee was the home port of the largest whaling fleet in Europe. Elsewhere, there was decline because the intensity of hunting had drastically reduced numbers in the Arctic. Dangerous voyages to the edge of the ice became uneconomical. What kept the Dundee boats at sea was jute. Grown in India and Bangladesh, it is a long natural fibre that can be spun into strong but coarse thread, and the jute became central to the economy of the city. In 1883 a staggering one million bales of the fibre were landed at Dundee's quays. And to make jute more easily workable, whale oil was needed, and lots of it.

The outbreak of the Crimean War in 1854 suddenly stimulated demand for the coarse fabric to make sandbags, covers for wagons and gun carriages, sacking, nosebags for horses and many other items urgently needed by the army. Jute mills were thrumming with business in Dundee, and at one point more than 50,000 were employed, three-quarters of them women. Their comparative manual dexterity was essential to keep the looms working, as with most textile production, and husbands often stayed at home to mind children and cook. They were disparagingly known as 'kettle-bilers'.

When whaling ships sailed into the Tay in the autumn, full of blubber and baleen, the population of Dundee knew that the success of the hunters could be a mixed blessing. The boiling yards were to be found along the Seagate, in the centre of the city, close to the quaysides for convenient handling. When the blubber was rendered into oil in huge vats the stink was eye-watering and persistent. And profitable. The jute mills rattled and clacked, and as the nineteenth century wore on whale oil would continue to lubricate the economy of late-Victorian Dundee. But it was a precarious relationship.

In the 1870s and 1880s fewer and fewer whales were caught in the Arctic and, despite steam replacing sail, enabling more than one voyage to the north each summer, it was clear that a radical change of tack was needed. In 1892 the Tay Whale Fishing Company fitted out four ships to make the immense voyage south to the Antarctic in search of fresh prey. When at last they sailed into the Weddell Sea the lookouts in the crow's nests saw very few whales, and the only attack they mounted was not successful. Even though the whaleboats managed to fire several harpoons into a large blue whale, it was strong enough to tow them all. When the ship itself managed to get a line from a harpoon aboard and used its steam engines, it could make no progress. After a fourteen-hour battle the whale escaped.

The four ships' captains decided to hunt seals instead, and in this they were much more successful. Because they had never seen human beings before and had no concept of the danger they presented, the Antarctic seals were passive, not making any attempt to escape or offering any resistance as the crews clubbed thousands of them to death. One ship killed 5,200 seals, and the blubber from them and many others paid for the cost of the expedition. Nevertheless, it had been a failure, not a long-term solution. The jute industry could no longer rely on whale oil, and in any case coal gas was increasingly being used for lighting. In 1847 a chemist, James Young, noticed a natural form of what came to be called petroleum seeping from the seams of a coal mine in Derbyshire. From it he distilled 'paraffin oil', so called because when it cooled it resembled paraffin wax. Its derivatives could be used for lubrication as well as lighting and heating, and the demand for whale oil began to shrivel.

The Dundee Antarctic Expedition of 1892 was not a complete failure, for the city's expertise in building ships strong enough to survive in the ice pack turned out to be useful and epoch-making. At the end of the nineteenth century, Antarctica was terra incognita, the last uncharted and unexplored wilderness on earth. Captain James Cook had sailed through iceberg-strewn seas to its ice-bound shores between 1772 and 1775. He was looking for *Terra Australis*, the Southern Land, a hypothetical continent that had first appeared on maps of the world in the fifteenth century. Its existence was based on an assumption that if there was land around the North Pole there should be a balancing territory in the south. Antarctic derives from the Latin *antarcticus*, which means 'opposite to the north'. When Captain Cook sailed in search of the southern continent, he found no land, only small islands at temperate latitudes, and after unwittingly circumnavigating the frozen shores of Antarctica, he sailed home.

More than a century later, knowledge had advanced only marginally, and in the late 1890s interest in exploration and fresh expeditions to the furthest south began to gather momentum. The president of the Royal Geographical Society, Sir Clements Markham, chaired a conference held in London in 1895. A resolution was passed declaring that 'the exploration of the Antarctic regions was the greatest piece of geographical knowledge still to be undertaken'. But Lord Salisbury's Conservative government failed to take an interest, and the Admiralty refused to provide the funds to fit out any expedition, preferring to concentrate on expanding the Grand Fleet and to developing the new dreadnought class of battleships.

The Royal Geographical Society was forced to seek private funding, and, after a series of frustrating delays, was successful in raising enough money to commission the world's first research ship, fitted out specifically for exploration. All sorts of scientific and geographical reasons were quoted as the principal motivations for exploring Antarctica, but in reality the principal impulse behind the proposed expedition was patriotic. The vast, sprawling

British Empire was at its greatest and most lucrative extent. In 1902 the viceroy of India, Lord Curzon, was to hold the Delhi Durbar, a huge event attended by all of the rulers, rajahs, maharajahs and princes of India's states and provinces. They came bejewelled and bedecked on their plodding elephants to pledge allegiance to King Edward VII, the new Emperor of India. He didn't even bother to turn up, sending his brother the Duke of Connaught instead. But as a demonstration of raw power, opulence and the staggering extent of the military and naval reach of imperial Britain, the spectacle of the Durbar was eloquent. Britannia did indeed rule the waves, and a quarter of the world's population were part of the largest empire in history. It was therefore her impulse and her role to add to her possessions, set her bounds wider and wider, by first exploring and understanding and then colonising the last great wilderness on earth.

A ship needed to be built, one that could not only make the very long voyage south but that could also survive in the ice. A ship made from wood. Despite contributing no funding, the Admiralty had opinions: 'it would be a matter of great regret that a ship to carry a British Antarctic Expedition should be built outside these islands. We have only a few wood-ship builders left, but they are quite capable of doing all that you want.' Dundee had a long tradition of building whaling ships, but by the turn of the twentieth century that had all but died out. Unlike almost every other large ship, the vessel needed for the Antarctic had to be built of wood, and the necessary skills with the saw, the adze and the plane had almost gone and been replaced by those of metalworkers and riveters. The problem was that a metal-hulled ship would have been very problematic for the work of surveying and mapping the great continent of ice. A magnetic observatory, essentially a very accurate large compass and other accoutrements, was needed for the expedition, and any iron or steel near it would play havoc with the accuracy of the instruments. An existing wood-constructed Dundee whaler could not be adapted without being completely rebuilt, as, although its hull would have been wooden, its planking and boards would all have been nailed together, and on masts, decks and elsewhere there were many steel or iron fittings. A new, custom-built wooden ship was needed, one that would be called *Discovery*, after an earlier vessel.

Once again, the Admiralty was prescriptive. Written at the end of 1899 by Admiral McClintock, here is a very good and precise description of what the new ship would be like:

The ship will be 172 feet long, 33 feet extreme beam [the widest part of the hull] and will be 1,570 tons displacement. She will be built of oak and elm, with an ice casing of green heart . . . Her bows will be sharp and overhanging . . . and they will be specially strengthened for forcing her way through the ice. The thickness of her sides amidships at the water line will be 25 inches. The stern and counters will be so shaped as to afford protection to the screw and rudder, both of which will be fitted so as to be raised quickly out of the water . . . [As well as an engine], she will be fitted with masts and sails and barque rigged [with 3 masts], so that fuel can be economized while making a voyage, and advantage can be taken of favourable winds, even when navigating in the [ice] pack. The magnetic observatory, 8 feet by 6 feet six inches, will be on the bridge before the mainmast, and no iron work will be permitted within 30 feet of it . . . The total complement of the vessel was not to exceed 48 to 50 souls.

Robert Falcon Scott was a lieutenant in the Royal Navy, and he was selected to lead the expedition. He took a very keen interest in the design of the *Discovery*, for he understood well how strong she needed to be when the great weight of the ice pressed hard against the hull. Wood could flex and was a good insulator, whereas metal plates, only a couple of centimetres thick, could buckle, popping their rivets, and were in any event liable to conduct the cold, freezing on the inside. Here is what Scott wrote about the construction of his ship:

The frames, which were placed very close together, were eleven inches thick and of solid English oak; inside the frames came the inner lining, a solid planking four inches thick; whilst the outside was covered with two layers of planking, respectively six and five inches thick, so that in most places, to bore a hole in the side would have to get through twenty-six inches of solid wood. The inner lining was of Riga fir, the frames of English oak, whilst the outer skin was of English elm or greenheart. The massive side structure was stiffened and strengthened by three tiers of beams running from side to side . . .

The tender from the Dundee Shipbuilders Company was accepted and the keel laid on 16 March 1900. Construction took only a year, and on 21 March 1901 the last wooden, three-masted ship to be built in Britain was launched into the waters of the Firth of Tay. It was also arguably the strongest ship ever constructed, and that is almost certainly the reason why it has survived. After having been moored in the Thames in central London for many decades (and having survived the Blitz) the *Discovery* returned home to Dundee in April 1986, to where she had begun life and set out on her many voyages.

Not far from the Victoria Dock and the sad, rusting hulk of the *North Carr* lightship the *Discovery* is shown off in all her splendour. I walked along the new promenade on the north shore of the Firth of Tay, where once there had been quays, shipyards and where the stink of the blubber boiling yards would have been eye-watering. It is another world now, a place of amenities and visitor attractions. On a morning of brilliant sun children played in a large sandpit while their parents sipped coffee from an upmarket vendor's van. And with its outshot prows almost leaning over the waters of the Tay, the new Victoria and Albert Museum in Dundee rose up and over the promenade. It is a stunning architectural achievement, ship-like in its outward shape, with its parallel lines more resembling a hull than walls. Shimmering under the landward overhang are geometric ponds, and a wide tunnel under the building leads walkers to Discovery Point and a real ship. It is a perfectly conceived counterpoint, and I immediately began to take photographs of the new building and the old ship, enjoying the cleverness, the holistic arrangement so carefully conceived and perfectly executed. On one façade of the V&A was an appropriate message: 'Be open to the joy you deserve'.

Set up in a narrow dry dock so that all its lines can be clearly seen, the *Discovery* looked sleek, surprisingly narrow and her bow sharp and forward-reaching. It was easy to see what Admiral McClintock meant when he envisaged the ship riding up over the ice sheet and coming down as its weight broke through. Beside the *Discovery* is a museum that tells its story. Before boarding the ship itself visitors are invited to understand how it came about, who its builders and its crew were and what happened on its voyages. These are all good stories, very well told in a mix of exhibits and short films, but what principally interested me was the shape of the ship itself and its atmosphere below decks.

Sleek on the outside, its lines a contrast with the chunky V&A behind it, the *Discovery* was tremendously solid inside. Once I'd carefully stepped over the 'ankle-breakers', the portholes let not into the sides of the ship because that would have weakened the hull, but into the deck, I went below, into the bowels of Captain Scott's ship. It was another world, a brilliantly designed, protective cocoon, and also a home for forty-eight souls. The designers knew that the crew would spend the darkness of an Antarctic winter on *Discovery* and it had to have everything that both a ship and a living space needed. The cabins for the officers were small, with the same narrow bunks I'd seen on the *North Carr* lightship, and the crew quarters had enough corners and nooks, and both offered some privacy, enabling what we now call personal space.

The great beams mentioned by Scott that acted as thwarts to stiffen the skeleton ribs of the hull timbers were enormous, looking like the squared-off trunks of whole trees. On one of them I read in white lettering 'certified to accommodate 12 seamen' in the bulkhead behind it. The wardroom seemed to be the heart of the ship. The dining and meeting room for the officers was beautifully wood-panelled and polished a rich toffee colour. Off it were the cabins of Captain Scott and his staff officers and scientists. There was a sick bay nearby, a laboratory and a darkroom.

Let into the massive 63.5-centimetre-thick hull were letter-box slots that allowed access to the space between the inner and outer skins of wood. Known as salt boxes, they used to be filled with coarse rock salt. If there was any leakage or seepage, the salt would absorb the moisture and thereby help to preserve the timber. When I put my arm into one of these slots and stretched my fingers, I could only just touch the outer skin of the hull. The sheer mass of the wooden ship was evident everywhere, no doubt something that gave the crew confidence and also, as a good insulator, a feeling of real warmth and security.

At the rear of the ship ('aft' sounds a little pretentious for the likes of me, a confirmed landlubber) was the engine, its many metal moving parts far enough from the magnetic laboratory to avoid contaminating readings. Built by Gourlay Brothers of Dundee at the vast cost of £10,322, a third of the cost of building the whole ship, it needed a great deal of coal to power it and was only used when the *Discovery* was close to land or the ice and when it needed to manoeuvre. At all other times the sails drove the ship through the waves, but because it was so heavy its maximum speed was only eight knots.

Up on the deck, part of which was cordoned off for restoration, was the ship's wheel. Set back so that the steersman could see the sails and from what compass direction the wind was billowing them, it was a classic design, and easy to imagine it being spun around. But it was the tall masts that impressed me most. Too tall to have been made from single trees, they must have been composites, but having been fitted together so seamlessly it was impossible to tell. So that they could safely flex as the wind caught the sails, each had to be able to do that without excessive stress. That in turn meant the straight lengths of trunk had to be planed smoothly and then soaked in long mast pits. These were filled with salt water, thought to be a better and more effective means of seasoning the wood than simply leaving it in the open air. The masts and the cross spars with their rigging seemed like objects of great beauty to my eye, like soaring, slender sculptures.

The *Discovery* set sail for the Antarctic on 6 August 1901, and for almost two years the crew and the officers undertook a great deal of pioneering work in surveying, mapping and discovering and recording previously unknown species of animals. There was an attempt to get to the South Pole that failed but managed to reach the furthest south any human being had travelled. In the winter of 1903–4, the ship became trapped in the ice but was not damaged. Two relief ships arrived but could not reach it. On 14 February 1904 the ice suddenly broke up, and the *Discovery* managed to make its way into open water and then back to Britain to eventual acclaim. Eight years later Captain Scott would once more attempt to reach the South Pole. He and his companions did reach it, but only after the Norwegian Roald Amundsen had beaten the British to it. They failed to make it back to their ship, the *Terra Nova*, a refitted Dundee whaler.

The *Discovery* continued in service, and in the 1920s was involved in estimating the number of whales left in the polar oceans. It is a striking example of how the wheel of history turns: a ship built with techniques honed in a city whose industry depended on killing whales completed its long service helping to ensure their preservation.

V

Cromarty

Yonder

Travelling northeast from Dundee and the shores of the Tay seems at first like a summer journey through lushness, fertility and bounty. The ripening barley ripples like yellow waves in a sea breeze and the leaves of the roadside trees are an intense, dense green after a wet and warm July. I love the fields of Angus and the Mearns: free-draining, undulating, often thorn-hedged and with wide, grass parks on the braes above them for hay and sileage and waiting for when the sheep come down off the hills to winter grazing. For me, fields are not only open spaces, places where cattle graze or crops grow; they are filled with memory, common monuments to the labour of countless generations who tilled and harvested them. I am the descendant of the people the first census of 1843 called farm servants, families of ploughmen, labourers and bondagers, women who did all the work not associated with horses. They have no other monuments beyond the walls of graveyards, only the fields where they worked and walked throughout their lives. The earth is grained into their hands. The grand estate mansions and farmhouses were built by the tiny minority who owned the land, and there their names are remembered. But it was my people who made the land come alive, who planted and reaped the barley, who scythed the hay and stooked it for the milker cows to munch in the winter byre. It was my people who weeded and shawed turnips in the late-autumn rain, sacking tied across their shoulders to keep out the worst of the wet. The fields and their fecundity are a far greater legacy than any pillared portico or imposing entrance gate and tree-lined carriage drive, for they fed the people, all the people. And when I see farmland in its summer splendour, I am always much moved, proud of those centuries of dogged day in, day out labour that made the land bountiful.

The farmhouses of Angus and the Mearns and the steadings clustered around them often look to the east and the south, to where the sun rises, to where the light first creeps over the horizon, to where it seems that the day and its weather will come from. For behind the fields and the grass parks the mountains rise in the west, the cloud-topped Grampian massif glowers over the landscape, and the farms turn their backs to it. Driving up through the Howe of the Mearns, formerly Kincardineshire, there is the sense of a narrowing edge. The mountains crowd closer, and to the east the North Sea and its shelving cliffs make the road seem like it runs along a windowsill. But before I reach Stonehaven and the coast, where the railway line and the main road will rub shoulders as they edge their way around the high ground, I turn away to a place where a great artist looked over yonder, looked out over the North Sea and saw it differently.

★   ★   ★

In 1945 Lillian Browse opened a gallery in London's Cork Street with her partners Henry Roland and Gustave Delbanco. The first woman to become a prominent and influential art dealer, she loved the work of Degas and Sickert but determinedly championed the work of contemporary British painters. When she came across Joan Eardley, Lillian did not hesitate to offer her a solo exhibition, a rare opportunity for a female artist. Opening in May 1963, it was an immediate success, bringing Eardley's work to a British and international audience. Her talent had been quickly recognised in Scotland, and in the previous two years the Scottish National Gallery of Modern Art, Aberdeen Art Gallery and the Glasgow Art Gallery had all bought her paintings, and the Scottish Arts Council had commissioned a film.

Two weeks before Lillian Browse was due to open the show Joan Eardley travelled to London to help with preparations. It was vital that all went well, for she knew that this could be a breakthrough moment. But at the same time she realised that she herself was not at all well. On 22 May she wrote to Lil Neilson, a young artist who had become a close friend:

I intend to go to the rounds of the [London] galleries. Though my bosom has been playing up quite a bit and making me feel a bit below par. I'll *have* to get something done I'm afraid, for it is definitely worse. God what a life. I hate it when bodies go wrong like this. I'm really quite frightened about this bosom. Though I suppose perhaps there's no need to be. But I'll need to see another doctor, I think.

By June it was clear that Eardley had an aggressive form of breast cancer that had spread and affected her sight as well as giving her a great deal of pain. She died on 16 August 1963, only forty-two years old and just at the moment when her immense gifts were being widely recognised. No one – before or since – saw the North Sea in the way Joan Eardley saw it, and no one has painted it so vividly, so vigorously and with such a sense of atmosphere, such elemental drama.

Having graduated from the Glasgow School of Art in 1947 with a postgraduate diploma, she began to work in the Townhead district of the city, renting and setting up a studio. Her portraits of local children in what was a very poor, overcrowded, inner-city slum were particularly powerful and memorable. But in 1950 she sought a radically different source of inspiration. Eardley travelled to Catterline, a tiny fishing village south of Stonehaven. Little more than four rows of single-storey white cottages perched on a clifftop above a crescent bay and a pier used by local inshore fishermen, it eventually became a more or less permanent home. In a BBC radio interview, Eardley offered something that sounds like a manifesto, certainly an explanation of where all that visceral power came from:

> Catterline has such a terrific clarity and terrific light, whereas Glasgow feels as though it has a sort of lid on top of it, but at the same time it's [Catterline] a little community and the place I chose to paint in Glasgow is also a little community in a certain district, a little back street, where everybody knew everybody else.

The same thing seems to be the case in the village where I live in the north-east. It's the sort of intimate thing I like, and I think you've got to know something before you paint it . . . I suppose I'm essentially a romantic, I believe in the sort of emotion that you get from what your eyes show you and what you feel about certain things. Well I don't really know what I'm painting, I'm just trying to paint.

Not only are painters drawn to the quality of the light, they also understand its subtleties and how geography influences its nature and its quality.

Francis Cadell and Samuel Peploe were painters associated with the school known as the Scottish Colourists, and they spent several summers in the 1920s and 30s in the Hebrides, mainly on Iona. Both were captivated by the intensity of the light, and Peploe often worked outdoors on the northern rocky coast with its dramatic views towards Staffa and Mull. He was out in all weathers, and his palette was dominated by cool greens and blues to reflect how he saw the sea and the clouds that raced in off the Atlantic and the play of light on them.

Without preliminary drawings, Francis Cadell painted directly onto his canvas, also in the open air, and his work is fresh and luminous, glowing with sunlight, the sea often a bright turquoise. There is a particular landscape that looks over the Sound of Iona to the Ross of Mull, and its warmth and vibrancy are astonishing, as though the paint has only just dried.

What Peploe and Cadell instinctively understood was that Hebridean light is different. Its crystal clarity, its rapid changes of mood, its subtlety have obvious causes: there is little or no air or light pollution and the minimal human activity in the Hebrides, compared to cities and towns, does not affect the light. The oceanic climate in the west also sees rapid and sometimes dramatic change. The unusual clarity is enhanced because light reflects upwards from water and that in turn makes the colours of the natural world seem even more vivid. Scotland lies between the 55th and 60th parallels north, the same latitude as St Petersburg, Alaska and Quebec. There are more than eighteen hours of daylight in June and only six in December. At these high latitudes sunlight enters the atmosphere at an acute angle, and that forces it to scatter and refract.

More than any other painter, Joan Eardley understood how different North Sea light is in Scotland. Colder, more muted, with greys and smoky blacks and blues, it is also little influenced by the land. Compared with the Inner Hebrides, where Peploe and Cadell painted, there is little or no reference to the shore, no islands to break up the light's mass and uniformity (although the North Sea's moods are as mercurial as the Atlantic's), only the horizontal of the horizon and the line of the sea coast. And as J.M.W. Turner saw at Margate, the skies were vast and constantly changing.

Strangely, Joan Eardley ignored the sea when she first came to stay and work in Catterline. Perhaps, coming from Glasgow, she felt she did not yet know it well enough to paint it. Instead, she chose the fields and the cottages on the clifftop as her subjects. Eardley once described the sea as 'impossible to paint', perhaps because it was in constant movement, the waves changing, rising and falling. In some compositions it seems as though she is carefully and consciously excluding the sea, even as a background, altering her point of view so that only the row of houses and the fields behind them are seen. Nevertheless, the early paintings are glorious. The richness of the yellows, greens and browns is intensified by the near-abstract technique. Eardley was a great admirer of American and European abstract expressionism and particularly the work of Jackson Pollock, and she also commented how much she disliked the paintings of J.M.W. Turner. There is a rare colour photograph of her painting outside in the fields, surrounded by white flowers and tall green grasses. Like Peploe and Cadell, at Catterline Eardley almost always worked out of doors in all weathers, often defying the elements. She once had to weigh down her easel with an anchor, and on some of her finished paintings there are several small, circular marks on the edges, the memory of G-clamps used to hold in place the wooden boards she worked on as the wind whistled around her.

By the mid-1950s Eardley had at last turned to the sea. For many years she had written almost daily letters to Audrey Walker, a photographer (who took many portraits of Joan) and violinist who lived in Glasgow with her husband. In 1955 she wrote about how quickly the work was going:

I painted all day today. One painting in the morning, one in the afternoon, and one at night. It's a great place for skies here . . . And clouds grow out of the sea. I think I am thinking a lot about clouds and sky in relation to painting.

Eardley worked down on the shore at the foot of the cliff, near the pier or the stony beach where nets were dried. In February 1958 she wrote again to Audrey Walker:

In between blizzards it has been so much just what I wanted for my painting – that stupidly I imagined I could rush out and in with my canvas. You know what a job it was setting up that canvas at the back of the house. Well I've had it three or four times to do and undo in the teeth of the gale . . . You really need to be tough for this game.

The game was made even more complicated and frustrating by Eardley's need to see the same weather conditions recur when she had been forced to abandon work for the day and wanted to complete the painting later. Unlike in Townhead, Eardley did not paint people from Catterline, fishermen or her neighbours. The work was elemental, passionately concerned only with the eternities of the land, the sky and the sea, the product of dogged persistence, an artist trying again and again to get it right, to make a true record of what she saw.

★   ★   ★

When I arrived in Catterline I walked first along a path between hedges, the gossamer strands of the night's spiders' webs on my face, to reach a cottage that stands apart. Known as the Watchie, it was the Watch House used by customs-and-excise men looking out for smugglers landing contraband. It has an excellent view of the bay and was the first place Joan Eardley stayed when she came to Catterline. Behind the white cottage are the fertile fields of the Mearns, and they stop only at the cliff edge. The paths that lead down to the shore and the pier are steep. It struck me that the village is abrupt, a place of edges. There is nothing gradual about how the land meets the sea and the vastness of the sky. Picturesque is not an adjective that could ever be attached to Catterline. Dramatic, certainly. Fields and fences run right to the cliff edge, tractors turn within metres of the steep drop.

Joan Eardley's ashes were scattered on the beach in 1963, and as I walked out on the pier and felt the cool of the sea wind I thought how short her career was, only fifteen years, and how much she achieved. But I would very much like to have seen how she painted in her fifties, her sixties, seventies, how her passion might have developed and perhaps changed its focus. What a terrible loss – perhaps one most keenly felt by Audrey Walker. After her own death in 1996 a tribute she wrote was made public, as were the many letters Joan wrote to her. Here are two passages from them:

I am thinking a lot about clouds and sky in relation to painting just now. That's what seems to dominate me this time – here . . . I seem to have little to say tonight. I think I'm tired. I wish you were here. I've had a good day – and perfection would be to have you here tonight. But that's a thing that I daren't let myself think about.

I just feel I love you so much – and there just ain't
words – to say it – not words that mean what I feel
inside of me – and there's nothing else that I really
want to say – nothing at all.

And here are some lines from Audrey's tribute:

If anyone ever has a mind to write, many years from
now, a book dealing with Joan the person, as well as
Eardley the Painter, I feel somehow they should have,
sort of germinating in some remote corner of their
mind, the conception of the whole Joan.

To me she was quite simply the winter sea to which
and for which I would give my life.

Reading these warming, gentle yet passionate words
of love, I can't help thinking that Joan's extraordinary
achievement as a painter – as Audrey clearly understood
– was intimately bound up with her emotional life. Her
father committed suicide in 1929 when Joan was eight,
and ten years later her mother brought the family to
Scotland at the outbreak of war. Throughout her adult
life she suffered from depression, and Joan and Audrey's
love for each other was a secret, although friends and
perhaps even Audrey's husband must have known.

Looking out over the sea from the pier at Catterline,
I was awestruck by the sense of infinity, that beyond the
horizon there was only more sea, that all the seas and
the oceans are linked and that it is possible to travel
ceaselessly on the water and under vast skies. The land

I love so much is fenced, mapped, sometimes intimately detailed, warming, solid and unmoving – while the sea and the sky are in constant motion as the winds blow, the tides rise and fall and the currents run. There is never stillness, not even when the weather is balmy and calm. In the extraordinary, restless vigour and dynamism of her painting, Joan sometimes captured that sense of infinity and constant movement as her own emotional restlessness spilled onto the canvas. Audrey was right. She was the winter sea.

2

German Bight

Late in the evening of Tuesday, 30 May 1916, the British Grand Fleet sailed out of its anchorage at Scapa Flow in Orkney and the Second Battle Squadron left Cromarty, setting a course eastwards into the Moray Firth. Shortly afterwards, at about 10.30 p.m., the Royal Navy's battle-cruiser fleet steamed under the Forth Rail Bridge and out into the North Sea.

Under the command of Admiral Sir John Jellicoe, 151 ships crewed by more than 60,000 sailors were going into battle. Having broken the codes used by the German High Seas Fleet, the Admiralty knew that they had left their bases at Wilhelmshaven in order to lure at least part of the Royal Navy's forces into engaging with them. What followed on 31 May was the greatest surface sea battle in history, an action involving 250 ships and 100,000 sailors, and it essentially decided the outcome of the First World War. The warships engaged off the western coast of Denmark, and the action became known as the Battle of Jutland and much of the fighting took place in the shipping forecast area of the North Sea once known as the German Bight.

The first shots were fired in the late afternoon when the Royal Navy's battle-cruiser fleet sighted part of the German High Seas Fleet. Basic battle tactics had changed little since Trafalgar a hundred years before. Ships fired broadsides at each other, picking out specific enemy ships as targets, but shooting across much greater distances. Visibility at 12.8 kilometres was variable with patches of fog and low cloud thickened by tremendous plumes of black smoke from the funnels of coal-fired ships moving at full speed, and also from the huge guns once the barrage had begun. When the British battle-cruiser started firing, not all of the German ships in their line had been correctly targeted. Commander Georg von Hase, the gunnery officer on the SMS *Derfflinger*, later wrote:

By some mistake we were being left out. I laughed grimly and now I began to engage our enemy with complete calm, as at gun practice, and with continually increasing accuracy.

At 16.16, von Hase trained his guns on the large battle cruiser, HMS *Queen Mary*, and the effect was spectacular, and utterly catastrophic:

Since 4.24pm every one of our salvos had straddled the enemy. When the salvo fired at 4.26 and 10 seconds fell, heavy explosions had already begun on the *Queen Mary*. First of all a vivid red flame shot up from her forepart. Then came an explosion forward which was followed by a much heavier explosion amidships, black debris of the ship flew into the air, and immediately afterwards the whole ship blew up with a terrific explosion. A gigantic cloud of smoke rose, the masts collapsed inwards, the smoke cloud hid everything and rose higher and higher. Finally, nothing but a thick, black cloud of smoke remained where the ship had been. At its base the smoke column only covered a small area, but it widened towards the summit and looked like a monstrous black pine.

The *Queen Mary* was destroyed by her own munitions. In order to damage the battle-cruiser's ability to fight, von Hase's shells tended to hit the gun turrets, but the 'flash', the explosion of the German shells, had ignited bags of cordite, the explosive and unstable propellant that gunners used to send the huge shells into the air. Speed of fire was important, and the Royal Navy gunners had got into the fatal habit of stacking silk bags of cordite close to the turret for quick access, and indeed leaving the anti-flash doors that led to the main magazines open. There were therefore too few impediments to the chain reaction of the German bombardment and the huge explosions that broke the *Queen Mary* in half and then blew her to smithereens. If the anti-flash doors had been closed and the cordite stored in brass casings, as they were on the German ships, this catastrophe would have been averted.

Midshipman John Lloyd-Owen, one of the pitifully few survivors of the death of the great battle-cruiser, remembered the moments before she sank:

After all the men had gone out of the turret I went up myself and found the ship lying on her side. She was broken amidships, her bows were sticking up in the air and the stern was also sticking out at an angle of about 45 degrees from the water. I was standing on the back of the turret which was practically level . . . I looked towards the stern and saw that it was red hot and that all the plates had been blown away, nothing but the framework remained. All around us men were falling off into the water. A few moments afterwards a tremendous explosion occurred in the fore part of the vessel which must have blown the bows to atoms. The stern part gave a tremendous lurch, throwing me off into the water. Just before entering the water another explosion occurred, apparently just above my head. I sank a considerable distance and on reaching the surface could see nothing of the ship, only a great deal of wreckage and oil fuel floating on the surface.

A staggering 1,266 men died as the *Queen Mary* blew herself apart and sank in minutes. Many men had been down in the bowels of the ship, some trapped in windowless steel chambers behind locked hatches and doors, thrown around in the black darkness as the electric lights cut out and the stricken cruiser lurched and rocked in her death throes, the dull thunder of the explosions drowning out the screams of those suffocating to death in their metal tombs. It was a hellish, unimaginable ordeal, but it may have been brief as the *Queen Mary* continued to break apart when it crashed onto the bed of the sea, fifty fathoms below the surface. In 2003 marine archaeologists found that the ship had split into three pieces.

Like John Lloyd-Owen, many sailors were tipped into the water or thrown off the bucking, breaking super-structure of the ship as explosions ripped through it and the hull fractured. Men in the sea close to the cruiser were killed by the shock waves of the explosions or by the mass of falling debris, steel plates and fittings, timbers and other heavy objects raining down from the sky and landing amongst them. The tremendous suction caused by the submersion of such a large object also dragged men under, while others died of shock and exhaustion. Petty Officer Ernest Francis was lucky, and ultimately determined to survive:

I struck away from the ship as hard as I could and must have covered nearly fifty yards when there was a big smash. Stopping and looking round the air seemed to be full of fragments and flying pieces, a large piece seemed to be right above my head and acting on an impulse I dipped under to avoid being struck and stayed under as long as I could and then came to the top again. Coming behind me I heard a rush of water which looked very much like a surf breaking on a beach and I realized it was the suction or backwash from the ship which had just gone. I hardly had time to fill my lungs with air when it was on me. I felt it was no use struggling against it, so I let myself go for a moment or two, then I struck out, but I felt it was a losing game and remarked to myself mentally, 'What's the use of you struggling – you're done!' and actually eased my efforts to reach the top, when a small voice seemed to say, 'Dig out!' I started afresh and something bumped against me. I grasped it and afterwards found it was a large hammock; it undoubtedly pulled me to the top, more dead than alive. I rested on it, but felt I was getting very weak and roused myself sufficiently to look around for something more substantial to support me. Floating right in front of me was what I believed to be the centre bulk of our pattern four target [a wood-mounted mechanism from a gun turret]. I managed to push myself on the hammock close to the timber and grasped a piece of rope hanging over the side. My next difficulty was to get on top and I was beginning to give up hope when the swell lifted me nearly on top and with a small amount of exertion I kept on.

While it was devastating, the relative accuracy of the gunnery of Commander von Hase was not determinant. It was raw numbers that mattered. The Royal Navy sailed 151 ships across the North Sea to fight the Battle of Jutland, while the German High Seas Fleet could muster only 99 vessels. More than that, the British had been the first to develop and build the new dreadnought class of battle-cruisers. They were equipped with bigger guns that could fire at longer ranges, and these huge ships could move faster through the water. Prior to the outbreak of the First World War, and indeed one of its contributing causes, was the accelerating naval arms race. The

Germans also built dreadnoughts, but not as many as the Royal Navy.

Consequently, Admiral Scheer's strategy had to be a nautical version of divide and conquer. Using part of his fleet, under the command of Admiral von Hipper, he wanted to lure part of the British fleet, certainly not all of it, into battle and defeat them decisively, evening up the odds as much as possible. The central difficulty was that the Admiralty, having broken their codes, was well aware of German plans. Nevertheless, unaware of this, von Hipper sailed north from Wilhelmshaven with part of the German High Seas Fleet, and in the late afternoon of 31 May 1916 he engaged with the Royal Navy's battle-cruiser squadron under the command of Admiral David Beatty. HMS *Queen Mary* was quickly lost as well as HMS *Indefatigable* and HMS *Invincible*, the latter two also blown to pieces as their magazines exploded. A chilling example of military cold-bloodedness came from Captain Alfred Chatfield on board Beatty's flagship, HMS *Lion*:

> The *Indefatigable* was a smaller and more weakly protected ship than those of the First Division [the dreadnoughts and other battle-cruisers] and was not really a serious tactical loss.

When the *Indefatigable* exploded and sank, 1,017 men lost their lives and only two survived.

German gunnery was more accurate in part because those operating their range-finders and aiming equipment were better trained. Mathematics and a version of trigonometry had to be understood and correctly calculated.

If ships were firing at a range of thirteen kilometres and a shell was in the air for twenty seconds, the enemy target's speed and course needed to be accurately determined. Versions of a slide rule were developed by each side to calculate and collate all of these values, something that was done while a ship shuddered as salvos were fired and vibrated as it travelled at full speed. Then this information needed to be communicated to the gunners through a mechanism known as a range clock. And then they fired. And mostly missed. And the British missed much more often than the Germans. In the opening twelve minutes of the engagement that saw the *Queen Mary* sink, all but one of the Royal Navy ships had been hit by German shells, and only four British shells had found their mark.

When Admiral Jellicoe's Grand Fleet arrived on the scene in the early evening of 31 May the two opposing fleets engaged directly as 250 ships exchanged fire, and the sea was lit by the flash of guns and hidden by billows of black smoke from funnels and direct hits. After a series of brilliant manoeuvres in fading light and with incomplete intelligence, Jellicoe almost trapped Scheer's fleet, getting ships between them and the safety of their base at Wilhelmshaven and its protective screen of minefields. Fourteen Royal Navy ships were sunk in the Battle of Jutland, with the loss of more than 6,000 men, while the Germans lost eleven and 2,551 killed. Under cover of darkness, Scheer's fleet managed to slip through the British encirclement and return safely to port. For the rest of the war the German navy stayed there.

As the battle unfolded the stakes could not have been

higher. Winston Churchill had been appointed First Lord of the Admiralty in 1911, and he wrote that Admiral Jellicoe's responsibilities were unique because he was 'the only man on either side who could lose the war in an afternoon'. With the Grand Fleet based at Scapa Flow in Orkney, the battle squadron at Cromarty, Admiral Beatty's battle-cruisers in the Firth of Forth and a squadron patrolling the eastern entrance to the English Channel, the Royal Navy had effectively blockaded the North Sea and forced the German fleet to remain at anchor in their bases. British strategy was simple. If the Germans had no access to the Atlantic, their war economy would come under increasing stress as vital supplies slowly shrivelled. In addition to what could be grown at home or in the Low Countries, the Baltic was their sole source of food and horsepower, an extremely important resource for the armies on the Western Front. Between 1914 and 1918 Denmark became a gigantic pig farm, and most of the Germans' horses came from Sweden, also a source of iron ore and other resources. To the Kaiser and his general staff the Battle of Jutland was known as the Battle of the Skagerrak, the narrow strait that linked the North Sea with the Baltic. They were alarmed at the possibility that the Royal Navy might use its superior numbers to gain control of the Baltic and quickly strangle the German war economy.

The British lost more ships and many more men at the Battle of Jutland than did their enemy, and these statistics have provoked a century-long debate about who won. But the historical reality is that whoever remains in control of the territory over which a battle was fought, be it land or sea, are the de facto victors. The outcome of Jutland was that the Germans could no longer hope to win the First World War, and as the German economy slowly choked and shrank it was only a matter of time before they lost.

In November 1918 the German High Seas Fleet at last sailed out of Wilhelmshaven. The terms of surrender compelled them to rendezvous with a Royal Navy escort eighty kilometres east of the Isle of May in the mouth of the Firth of Forth and then sail north in groups to Scapa Flow to what would become their prison.

More than six months later, on 21 June 1919, the great German battle-cruiser, *Friedrich der Grosse* suddenly listed to starboard and began to sink. It was the flagship of the High Seas Fleet, and forty minutes earlier Admiral Ludwig von Reuter had sent a coded-flag message to all seventy-four ships. It instructed their captains to sink their own ships, to scuttle them by opening seacocks, flood valves, smashing internal water pipes and loosening port-holes and leaving bulkhead doors open. All of this activity was invisible to the Royal Navy guard ships in Scapa Flow. After a short time ship after ship began to go down as their crews abandoned them. As they sank British sailors saw that each had run up the Imperial German Ensign on their mainmasts. It was a symbol of defiance. Of the seventy-four ships under von Reuter's command, fifty-two were sunk. And, while the remainder were towed into shallow water by the Royal Navy, the entire German Fleet was destroyed in little more than an hour.

At the same time the terms of the Treaty of Versailles were being negotiated, and the outcome greatly concerned the German admiral. The likely consequence would be that his fleet, which included several dreadnoughts – notably Commander von Hase's SMS *Derfflinger*, the destroyer of HMS *Queen Mary* – would be divided between Allied navies. That was something von Reuter could not countenance. There was also a possibility that Germany would not accept the terms of the treaty and that war might break out once more. In which case, Germany's own navy could be used against Germany. There was only one honourable, patriotic alternative.

So, in May 1919 the admiral made plans to scuttle the entire fleet in Scapa Flow, rendering it useless in the event that war resumed. While the high command of the Royal Navy suspected that something might be afoot, they did nothing to prevent it. The redistribution of seventy-four battleships to other navies might make them a little too powerful, threatening the dominance of the Royal Navy. Noon on 21 June was the time and date fixed for the signature of the Treaty of Versailles, exactly the same time as the *Friedrich der Grosse* listed to starboard and the German fleet began to destroy itself.

3

The Last of the Hunters

The title page of O.T. Olsen's *Piscatorial Atlas of the North Sea, English Channel and St George's Channel*, published in 1883, is like a fanfare followed by a clash of cymbals and a royal salute. His publisher, Taylor and Francis, did not hold back, and nor should they have, for the fifty pages of maps that follow are not only a magnificent achievement, a rare work that combines art and science but also important – and elegiac – historical documents. Here is the text of the title page:

THE PISCATORIAL ATLAS
of the
NORTH SEA, ENGLISH AND
ST GEORGE'S CHANNELS
by
O.T. Olsen F.L.S. F.R.G.S.
illustrating
The Fishing Ports, Boats, Gear, Species of Fish
(How, Where and When Caught)
And Other Information Concerning Fish and Fisheries.

Grimsby
O.T. Olsen, Fish Dock Road
London
Taylor and Francis, Red Lion Court, Fleet Street, EC.
1883.

This beautiful book is dedicated 'by Special Permission' to His Royal Highness, the Duke of Edinburgh, Prince Alfred, the second son of Queen Victoria. The introductory remarks set out clearly the painstaking working methods of Ole Theodor Olsen, a Norwegian who settled in Grimsby, at that time England's busiest fishing port. He had worked with Lieutenant Matthew Maury of the US Navy, acknowledged as the founder of oceanography. These are some of Olsen's 'Introductory Remarks':

Some eight or ten years ago, when engaged in studying the physical conditions of the North Sea, more particularly with reference to the nature of the bottom, depths, sounding, &c., for the purposes of navigation, I was led into daily consultation with the masters sailing from Grimsby and Hull. My previous career on board ship, where, among other duties, I devoted considerable attention to the preparation of a log for Lieutenant Maury, of the United States, in which physical conditions predominated, caused me thereafter to consider how I could apply like data for the benefit of our fishermen in the North Sea.

To be completed by sixteen masters of fishing boats each time they put to sea, Olsen's logs asked for details of navigation, the name of the fishing ground, the quantity and nature of the fish caught, whatever other remarks were appropriate and much else. He also asked that the captains should do something that must have been awkward and not a little messy.

Frank Buckland was a naturalist, keenly interested in the fauna of the North Sea and Olsen attached this note to his logs:

MR. BUCKLAND would feel obliged if specimens could be kindly forwarded to his address, —37, Albany Street, Regent's Park, London.

1st. Stomachs of Soles, Plaice, Turbots, Brills, Halibuts, Whiting, Haddocks, &c.

2nd. Hard and Soft Roes of Fish while Spawning.

3rd. Anything that looks like Eggs or Spawn of Fish or Marine Animals attached to Shells, Stones, &c.

4th. Samples from Deep Sea Oyster and Mussel Beds.

5th. Samples of Bottom of the Sea as brought up by the lead [net].

N. B. – All specimens should be labelled.

Exactly how and in what condition a very considerable quantity of fish guts arrived in Regent's Park is hard to imagine, even taking into account the famous speed and frequency of the Victorian postal system. For the London postmen the delivery probably couldn't have been fast enough. Nevertheless, the result of all of this research and its analysis produced fifty very beautiful and richly detailed maps of the fisheries of the North Sea.

There are four introductory maps detailing the movement of ebb and flood tides (clearly showing the collision off the Kentish coast and around the Thames Estuary), the depths of the sea, the composition of the seabed and the names of the fishing grounds. The following forty-six maps illustrate the distribution and abundance of each species of fish and shellfish with sidebars on its habits, when it is in season and also its quality. Some are familiar – like cod, haddock, herring and mackerel – others seem as though they have strayed into Olsen's maps from another culture and from other seas. Anchovies were caught in the Wash, the Thames Estuary and in the Firth of Forth. Some of the classic ingredients of bouillabaisse – grey mullet, bass and wrasse – shoaled in the southern North Sea. Whelks, crab, lobster and mussels could be found close to the eastern coasts, and shrimp boats fished the mouth of the Thames and off the Kentish coast. There was an oyster bed to the southeast of the Dogger Bank that was the size of Wales. Conger eel is described as 'wholesome, much used by the poorer class'. In the top right-hand corner of each map Olsen has drawn and painted fishing boats typical of various coastlines, such as a Brixham trawler, a Scotch herring lugger and a Tenby boat. All of them were sailing boats.

Herring is first on Olsen's list, and they could be found all around the coasts of Britain and the Low Countries.

In his sidebar to the first map he notes that this surface-swimming fish is 'very wholesome, nutritious and savoury'. He goes on:

> The Herring is a migratory fish, captured in different localities at different seasons. It is very prolific. Its graceful form and silvery brightness are as pleasing to the eye as the taste is grateful to the palate. It is also food for all [larger] fish.

The herring fishery was also a stimulus for tremendous economic growth. At the outset of the nineteenth century, Wick, on the North Sea shore of Caithness, was a small village at the mouth of the river of the same name. But within a matter of twenty to thirty years, it had become the busiest fishing port in Britain – because of the vast volume of herring caught. More than a thousand boats, many of them like the Scotch lugger painted by O.T. Olsen, sailed out into the North Sea and cast their nets. A new harbour and a new town, Pulteneytown, were designed and built under the supervision of Thomas Telford on the south side of the river, and by 1840 thousands worked not only as crew for the boats but in the curing and cooperage businesses in the booming town.

This remarkable surge in economic activity was based on a peculiar characteristic of the herring. They come together in schools (large shoals all travelling in the same direction) in huge numbers. Taking up almost five cubic kilometres of the sea, a single school can contain several million fish. There are so many that they make waves as they move along. Keeping an approximately uniform distance from each other, these vast numbers of herring swim as one at a constant speed, travelling between their spawning grounds where they feed, and their nursery grounds where their young grow to maturity. Quite why the herring do this in such vast numbers is unclear, but the schools, also known as draves in Scotland, made the fish easy to find and catch and in enormous quantities.

Around the coasts of Britain the various populations of herring mature at different times of year, something Olsen was careful to note, and that in turn led to the creation of a peculiarly peripatetic workforce. Of all flesh foods, fish goes off most quickly because it is very susceptible to tissue decomposition, the rapid development of rancidity and microbial spoilage. Once the boats had landed their catches, the herring had to be gutted, salted and sealed in barrels as quickly as possible. In May and June the fishing season began off the coasts of the Hebrides, and when the luggers and other boats tied up at the quaysides of Stornoway, Lochmaddy or Castlebay, brimming with the 'silver darlings', *na clann nighean an sgadain*, the herring lasses, took over. Working in teams of three, two gutting and one packing (usually the tallest so that she could reach down to the bottom of the barrel), they stood at the farlans, troughs into which the creels of herring were tipped straight from the boats. Out in all weathers, the lasses wore long oilskin aprons over a wide skirt, a cotton blouse and a woollen cardigan. It was wet and slippery work even on dry days, and they had on knee-length boots and shawls on their heads tied under the chin.

Before they started work the lasses wound clouts, or bandages, around their fingers to stop the wet fish from slipping as they cut them open with short, razor-sharp knives and flicked out the guts. The clouts also bound up the frequent cuts. Gloves were not an option, for speed was vital. Experienced women could stand at the farlan, which had a narrow shelf attached to the edge, and gut a fish in two seconds. Like the women who worked in the Dundee jute mills, it was female manual dexterity that was valued, to say nothing of stamina and a willingness to do demanding, repetitive work. The hours could be very long, since incoming catches had to be processed, salted and packed into the barrels within twenty-four hours at the very latest. Typically, the teams of lasses were on the quays at 5.30 a.m. and could go on into the late evening until the light failed. There were regular breaks for big, much-needed, calorie-rich meals. But the money could be good as they moved around the coast from the Hebrides to Wick and then further south, following the huge schools of herring to Peterhead and eventually down to Great Yarmouth and Lowestoft. Each lass could finish the season with between £17 and £20, but it was hard, hard work.

Steam power revolutionised the North Sea fishery. Just as the station at the Fish Quay at Tynemouth delivered the daily catch to a wide hinterland in Northumberland, Durham and Yorkshire, the expanding British rail network made fresh fish widely available before it had time to spoil. Wick station opened in 1874, and not only could goods wagons transport barrels of salt herring all over the country they could also get fresh fish catches quickly to market. Trains leaving Wick early in the morning, after landings from the herring fleet had been boxed, could be in Glasgow and Edinburgh before lunchtime, and at Billingsgate, the world's largest fish market in London, by late afternoon.

Ice made it all possible. In the 1850s the Norwegians began to export large quantities of natural ice to Britain. It was cut from the winter fjords, and a great deal came from Lake Oppegård, south of Oslo, close to the Oslofjord, the Skagerrak and the North Sea. Much Norwegian ice was imported through Grimsby, and no doubt O.T. Olsen enjoyed conversations with his fellow countrymen on the quaysides. The railway had arrived on the shores of the Humber early, in 1853, and large blocks of Norwegian ice – the larger the block the slower it melted – would be loaded onto trains for distribution all over Britain. These would be crushed into the small chips used to keep the contents of fish boxes cool. In 1900 the Grimsby Ice Factory was built, a huge building that still stands near the harbour. Steam powered the compressors that converted water into ice, and at its peak the factory was producing 1,200 tonnes a day, much of which was transported by train to other fishing ports. As demand increased and the North Sea fishery prospered in the early twentieth century, the factory expanded, the last extension built in the 1950s.

At Granton, on the shores of the Forth near Edinburgh, the first steam trawler, named the *Enterprize*, was built. Being dependent on the wind, sail-powered fishing smacks had limited effectiveness as trawlers because they were unable to drag large nets behind them when the herring draves arrived. Steam seemed to be the future, but the *Enterprize* was not a success. It was feared that the propellers could foul the net, and in an extreme case leave the trawler stranded out at sea with no ability to move forward. In 1881 O.T. Olsen no doubt followed the process of construction of a better designed steam trawler at Grimsby. The attraction was a balance of economics and outcomes. Because they were much more powerful than the sailing smacks, the new trawlers could catch three or four times more fish, and these boats were not prey to the vagaries of the weather. If there was no wind, the old fishing smacks could not put to sea, but a steam engine meant that crews could fish in all but the worst conditions. Balanced against these manifest advantages was the fact that coal cost money and the wind was free.

Change was very gradual, but in 1894 John Robert Scott of Granton, Edinburgh, designed a new net that made steam trawling both more attractive and potentially less dangerous. Bottom-trawling nets are kept on the sea floor by heavy weights, or a beam, and dragged along by the boat at a steady rate. They are efficient, but in scraping the bottom a great deal of by-catch, unwanted fish, oysters and other debris – like the moorlog broken open by Captain Pilgrim Lockwood – is caught up, and it all has to be sifted through and got rid of over the side. Scott came up with a version of what was known as an otter trawling net, and it largely replaced the beam. Two otter boards on either side of the net were attached to hawsers and they kept its mouth open, allowing it to be towed at the side of the boat and not from the stern. This made it very unlikely that the propellers would be fouled. Known as the Granton trawl, the net did not need to be dragged along the seabed and could catch fish in the mid-level depths and not collect so much unwanted and wasteful by-catch.

For much of the twentieth century fish from the North Sea and the North Atlantic was cheap and plentiful, distributed quickly all over Britain by the rail and road networks. The schools and the shoals belonged to no one – although there were disputes with the Dutch herring fleet in the eighteenth century and the Cod Wars with Iceland in the middle of the twentieth – and the killing of wild fish, the last great hunt, had much less impact than the slaughter of livestock. Meat was comparatively expensive because when a cow, a sow or a ewe went to the abattoir, that was also the end of its productive life. There would be no more calves, piglets or lambs. Not until the last quarter of the twentieth century and the first of the twenty-first would the reproductive cycle of sea fish become a cause for concern; from the advent of steam trawling in the later nineteenth century and for most of the twentieth fish were consumed all over Britain.

Salted and smoked (and none better smoked than an Arbroath smokie, a Finnan haddie [haddock] or a Craster kipper), fish were also preserved long before the advent of the railways and eaten in the most landlocked of communities. In the town of Langholm, deep in the eastern hill country of Dumfriesshire, the annual common riding festival (a now largely ceremonial checking of the bounds of the town's common land at the end of each summer) preserves a memory of ordinary people regularly dining on salt herring. For the 'crying of the fair' a man stands on the hind quarters of a horse, as the rider keeps it steady, declaiming the terms of the fair to a huge crowd in wonderful, archaic Scots. His declarations end with 'I'll away hame and hae a barley bannock and a saut [salted] herrin' tae my denner.'

As late as 1975 almost all of the fish, 89 per cent, landed at British ports was consumed by the British public, and not only when they visited the chip shop. Even small towns had a fishmonger as well as a butcher, because fish was cheap. The shops were serviced every day (except Mondays, for few fishermen would sail out on the Sabbath) by the rail network or, increasingly as the smaller stations were closed in the 1960s, by fleets of lorries and vans run by fish merchants. A wide variety lay on the marble slabs, and fishmongers were skilled at filleting fresh fish, and some of the more enterprising cured herring into kippers or haddocks into haddies. It was more expensive, because much of the catch was wild, but some also had smokehouses for salmon and trout. Stalls selling whelks and other crustaceans were not uncommon in the major cities, and especially in London and the southern coastal resorts. Dated 19 May 1975, there is a very jolly archive photograph of Tubby Isaac's east London seafood stall with its display of trays and bowls of whelks, crab claws, pots of shrimp and potted shrimp (in butter), jellied eels, brown shrimps, mussels, scallops, rollmop herrings and oysters.

Between 1975 and 2019 the proportion of fish and crustaceans landed on British quays and consumed in Britain crashed from 89 per cent to only 40 per cent. A major contributing factor was the rapid and widespread expansion of supermarkets. Over that period they not only radically altered shopping habits – as well as radically reordering society – they also changed our diet. The 'big five' – Tesco, ASDA, Morrison's, Sainsbury's and Waitrose – now account for more than 80 per cent of British grocery retailing, and to run such vast logistical oper- ations efficiently they need to reduce detail, rationalise their all-important supply chains and, above all, keep costs down. As they have with many other primary producers, their policies and operating methods have had a direct effect on the fishing industry. Only five species now account for 80 per cent of all the fish bought in Britain: cod, haddock, (mostly farmed) salmon, tuna and shrimps/ prawns. The relentless pressure of price competition and the lure of convenient one-stop shopping has also made a charity-shop desert of most high streets. Local grocers, butchers, bakers and, very sadly, fishmongers have gone out of business in their tens of thousands. These radical changes have not only had a clear impact on the variety of fish the British eat, as the skills of the fishmonger have disappeared into history, they have also shaped the tastes of many younger people. Herring, mackerel and other smaller species are often thought of as oily and too bony, and researchers have detected a 'yuck factor'. Many, it seems, feel queasy at the sight of an unfilleted fish with its head still attached, its glassy eye staring accusingly. We are increasingly wedded to processed food, whose appearance often has little detectable relationship with the animal it comes from. Fish fingers are often far pref- erable to an actual fish.

Partly because of the pursuit of certain species of fish, and perhaps also as a consequence of climate change, the North Sea stocks have fluctuated wildly in recent decades. In the 1970s the previously plentiful schools of herring virtually disappeared, and the population of cod seems to have collapsed since the turn of the twenty-first century. Scientists now fear that there are too few fish to reproduce, and the North Sea cod might become extinct. In 2008 the European Union put in place its Cod Recovery Plan, but decline appears not to have been halted. General overfishing has certainly contributed to these perilous statistics and the annual aggregate catch in the North Sea of all fish of three million tonnes in the 1980s had dropped to 2.3 million tonnes by 2022.

Consumer taste and retail habits have also been factors in a surprising inversion. In 2022 Britain exported 454,000 tonnes of seafood with a value of £1.7 billion. A great deal of salmon (much of it farmed), mackerel, scallops, langoustines, crab and prawns went to France, Spain, Holland, the USA and China. But in the same year we imported a staggering 1.2 million tonnes of seafood with a value of £3.6 billion and most of it was cod, haddock, shrimps and prawns, salmon and tuna. It was caught in Norway, Iceland, the Faroe Islands and, surprisingly, Vietnam and China. No doubt relative cost – perhaps like the garment industry and almost all other manu-factured goods, it seems – Far Eastern fish is so cheap that even the cost of bringing it halfway around the world, frozen or chilled, means that supermarkets still make more of a profit from it than they could from what is caught by British fishing boats. Nevertheless, this ratio does seem more than perverse, and when the mounting unease with food miles mounts, as it must, this will change.

Other paradoxes blur the picture and no doubt perplex politicians and policy-makers. In 2021 an apparently encouraging report reckoned that fish stocks in the North Sea were rising. In Scottish waters, what is known as the combined biomass, all species of fish, had risen spectacularly, from 800,000 tonnes in 2001 to two million tonnes in 2021. But it turned out that only three species accounted for the entire increase. The number of plaice had grown by a massive 800,000 tonnes in the twenty-year period, and hake and haddock by 200,000 tonnes each. By contrast, cod had declined by 12 per cent and coley by 31 per cent. The obvious problem in addressing this is that fishing nets do not discriminate. But if public taste was more catholic, ready to eat more hake and plaice, then that might go some way to righting a few of these imbalances. However, it is unlikely, given the overweening power of the supermarkets, that the skills of the fishmonger can help in curing the yuck factor or pushing back against the restricting, conservative tastes of the British consumer.

★   ★   ★

'Well, it might be daft,' said the young man. 'In fact it is daft.' Talking to me while expertly sliding the twin prongs of an electric hoist under a palette of twenty fish boxes, he smiled, adding, 'But it keeps me in a job.' I had driven up to Peterhead, Europe's largest fishing port, to watch an auction at the vast fish market, having checked on timings online. But I found that it had concluded about an hour beforehand. The market office was deserted, and no one seemed to be about. A cleaner let me through the barrier and showed me how to climb over a machine that washed and brushed fishy boots for those leaving.

'It's chancy,' the driver said, as he lifted up the palette. 'The boats sometimes get in earlier. Maybe the tide?' At the far end of the echoic auction hall a man in waterproof orange overalls was spraying a power hose over the cambered concrete floor. Drifts of ice, coloured sale tickets and chunks of damaged fish were being washed down towards the series of harbour entrance doors, openings hung with thick plastic strips. Beyond them was a long and narrow quay where the fishing boats tied up and unloaded their catch. It was spattered with bird shit, where the gulls had tried to snap up what they could. On the opposite side was another series of exits to where refrigerated lorries backed in to be loaded by drivers like the young man I was talking to. It was a simple, efficient and brutal piece of architecture. Fish arrived through one set of doors, were auctioned in the middle and left through the opposite set of doors. The process needed to be quick. Too quick for me.

But my conversation with the young driver was illuminating. When we talked about the amount of fish exported to Europe he shrugged, shook his head. He had twenty palettes to load, and all were bound for France. 'I'll drive this lot to Glasgow, and then they'll go on another wagon and maybe a trailer with catches from the islands [Hebrides]. Two drivers, so they can swap, keep going so they don't have to stop. All the road to Boulogne and the big market there. That's it. That's how it goes.'

Each palette carried a label, 'FR' for France, and details of the catch (cod, coley and whiting that morning) and when and where it had been caught. FAO27 represented not a North Sea fishery but an area of the north-west Atlantic. 'They're all whole fish, no fillets,' said the driver as he lifted the last of the palettes. 'That's because they [Europeans] like to use it all, make soup and all that.' I wished him a safe journey and left the market soon after he drove off, certain my pullover stank of fish.

I'd had just as long a journey up to Peterhead, driving through the fertile farmland of the Buchan, a northeast corner of Scotland I had never visited. It is very beautiful, lush, detailed, settled, the fields and farmhouses somehow bedded into the shape of the land. Buchan may be a rare example of a purely Pictish place name – for no one is sure what it means. But when I reached the outskirts of Peterhead, the contrast could not have been sharper. The chimneys of a huge power station rose up on one side, while on the other stood a vast, anonymous set of buildings that housed a converter station – which I later discovered brought together supplies of electricity produced in the north so that it could then be sent south through a subsea cable. There were various compounds for North Sea oil services, and in Peterhead Bay a wide harbour protected by long breakwaters. The inner harbour was unapologetically industrial, with large boats tied up at the quaysides, all with superstructures festooned with the scanners, dishes, antennae and masts associated with electronic equipment. In the past there might have been a spindly radio mast on the wheelhouse of a fishing boat so that the skipper could listen to the *Shipping Forecast*. When I parked, a huge herring gull immediately landed on the roof of my car, just to make the point.

Peterhead may not be pretty or picturesque, but it is productive. In 2021 its fishing fleet landed a large annual catch, 151,000 tonnes, that fetched a total of £172.8 million in the market's auctions. There are ninety-five boats registered at the port, crewed by 370 fishermen, the last hunters, the last to go out to hunt wild animals and risk their lives in peril on the sea. What they bring back in their white plastic boxes (sad to see the passing of the old orange wooden fish boxes) is nutritious, tasty, health-giving food. And yet we send 60 per cent of it to Europe, where they like whole fish and appear not to suffer from the yuck factor. And they keep the young man I spoke to in a job. It is a baffling, saddening trend, that the silvery bounty of the North Sea, our sea, and the North Atlantic, should be sent abroad, and at such cost, not only in cash but also to the environment. I long for the simplicities of the days of the herring lasses, the trains that brought the day's catch inland to towns like my hometown of Kelso, thirty kilometres from the North Sea. I can still summon the intensely savoury smell, the memory of my grannie frying fresh herring coated in oatmeal that she had bought that morning from Cowe and Burgon, the fishmonger who had folded the fish in greaseproof paper and wrapped it all in newspaper to contain the salty drips.

What O.T. Olsen might have made of all this is not hard to parse. His sidebar notes on his fifty beautiful maps, collectively a portrait of a North Sea fishery now long lost and gone, show that he loved to eat fish and had probably had had each and every one of these species on his plate at one time or another, relishing the variety. Lucky man.

4

Beyond the Forest

Pliny the Elder believed it was possible to know everything. In the decade leading up to his death in the eruption of Mount Vesuvius in 79 AD, he wrote his *Natural History*. In thirty-seven books, arranged in ten volumes, he breezily offered the reader 'a brief excursion under our direction amongst the whole of the works of nature . . . or in other words, life'. Subjects ranged from astronomy, geography, mathematics, anthropology, agriculture, art and sculpture to zoology and botany. Pliny also included what he knew of the strange peoples who lived on the edge of the world: the Cynocephali, the Dog Heads, the Sciapodae, whose single foot could act as a sunshade, or the Astomi, who had no mouths and lived on scents and smells. When he wrote of the lands far to the north Pliny was on much surer ground. The *Natural History* is dedicated to Titus, the son and successor of the Roman Emperor Vespasian, who had campaigned as a legionary commander in the invasion of southern Britain in 43 AD. The advance up what is now England and Scotland had been slow, and the imperial armies 'have not yet penetrated beyond the vicinity of the Caledonian Forest', wrote Pliny. This was a revealing comment from a scholar who had also been a soldier and the admiral of the imperial fleet. It seems that the *Silva Caledonia* was a place so well known in the Roman world as not to require any further explanation. And in his *Natural History*, Pliny does a lot of explaining. What did the Caledonian Forest mean to the Romans? Was it a limit, a boundary, or a problem?

It could have been a disaster for Gnaeus Julius Agricola, the governor of the province of Britannia, when he launched his invasion of Caledonia. In 83 AD, the IX Legion almost lost their eagle standard when they were overwhelmed in their camp by warriors of the Caledonian confederacy in a night assault. After reinforcements arrived in the nick of time to rescue the situation, the historian Tacitus wrote that 'had not marshes or forests covered the retreating enemy, that victory would have ended the war'. The legions dared not pursue the Caledonian warbands. In 9 AD, a huge Roman army commanded by Gaius Varus – the core of which was comprised of the XVII, the XVIII and the XIX legions – was ambushed in the Teutoburg Forest in southern Germany and slaughtered by hordes of so-called barbarians led by the general Arminius, the original Herman the German. The Romans were terrified of marching through the deep dark woods and always preferred to fight their battles in open field, where their iron discipline and bristling shield walls would wear down a charging enemy. Soon after the attack on the IX Legion, Agricola got his wish at Mons Graupius, a battle probably fought at the foot of the singular hill of Bennachie in the heart of fertile Aberdeenshire, and in the open. There the legions defeated the Caledonians, and again Tacitus described the action. What caught his eye, amidst the terrible slaughter, were the number of enemy warriors, presumably men of high status, who rode in chariots, their drivers showing immense skill and daring as their ponies galloped over the rough, tussocky ground.

In 150 AD Claudius Ptolemy, a geographer based far to the east, in Alexandria in Egypt, drew a map of what is now Scotland. Presumably from information gathered from military sources and perhaps merchants, he plotted the names and approximate territories of the kindreds who lived to the north and west of the Caledonian Forest. Some had animal names, probably their totems. The Lugi of Easter Ross were the Raven People, the Caereni of the northwest were the Sheep Folk and in Kintyre were the Epidii, the Horse Lords. Although written sources for the name lay in the future, we may think of these kindreds as the ancestors of the enigmatic, fascinating peoples known to history as the Picts.

Sixty years after Ptolemy drew his map the legions tramped north once more. Led by the ailing Emperor Septimius Severus and his sons, a huge army of more than 40,000 was careful to skirt the eastern edges of the Caledonian Forest; unable to draw the kindreds into a pitched battle, where they would certainly have been defeated, the Romans instead scoured the countryside and killed as many of the natives as they could find, women and children as well as men. This campaign of genocide was devastating, and Pictish society took generations to recover. And to exact a long, sustained and history-making vengeance.

Five kilometres north of Catterline stand two monuments just as dramatic as Joan Eardley's magnificent visions of the North Sea. They also rewrite the history of one of the earliest and most powerful North Sea kingdoms, the realm of the kings of the Picts. In 1832 a gang of youths, probably from the nearby town of Stonehaven, climbed the crumbling sea stack known as Dunnicaer, and on the summit they came across a series of small stones carved with curious designs. One was recognisable as a fish, perhaps a salmon, but the others were geometric, more abstract, a set of circles, some zigzagging lines and a crescent. Unimpressed by their discovery, the youths amused themselves by hurling the carved stones into the turbulent sea below the stack, no doubt with some whooping and shouting. The stack was apparently – and on that day, appropriately – known locally as Dinnycare. But by 1857 six of the stones had been recovered and drawings of them included in the *Sculptured Stones of Scotland* by John Stuart. This valuable rescue and record was published by the Spalding Club, a group of antiquaries from Aberdeen.

The symbols were recognised as characteristic of one of the most persistent and widespread survivals of Pictish culture. Found all over the lowlands of the north and north-east of Scotland, with concentrations in Aberdeenshire and the Moray coastlands, symbol stones are mysterious memorials in the landscape to a society that seemed to fade entirely after the ninth century, the last major ethnic group to disappear from Britain and Ireland. No one can utter a sentence in Pictish, even though as late as the eighth century Bede of Jarrow noted it as one of the four major languages of Britain (five if you counted Latin, but that was spoken mainly to God), but apart from a scatter of place and personal names, no whisper of the Pictish language survives. All that speaks of their culture is the enigmatic alphabet of the symbols carved on their stones.

Some of the carvings are recognisable. A menagerie of animals, like the fish from Dunnicaer, are regularly represented, and they may reflect the use of totem names by some of the kindreds mapped by Ptolemy in 150 AD. There are wolves or hounds, bulls, deer, eagles, geese, horses, boars and serpents, and they may be seen as emblematic. The more abstract geometry of the stones is much more difficult to decode. Some seem to be representations of high-status objects such as mirrors, combs and jewellery, but two recurring motifs might be understood in the context of prehistoric religious rituals. In the first millennium BC, valuable metal objects were sacrificed to gods, perhaps the gods of the underworld, when they were thrown into sacred lakes or other watery places. Weapons were often given up, but before swords or spears splashed into the water they were slighted, bent or even broken. Two very common motifs on symbol stones are known as Z-rods and V-rods, and they look very much like damaged spears or arrows. Often combined with a double disc – what might be a diagrammatic representation of a chariot, such as those that caught Tacitus' eye at the battle of Mons Graupius – these combined designs may be commemorative, what was carved on a stone to mark the death of a warrior-king or a magnate of some kind. There were both a double-disc and Z- and V-rods carved on the stones hurled into the sea by the youths who climbed up Dunnicaer in 1832 and did such damage.

In 2015 a very different group of people scrambled up the sea stack. Archaeologists from Aberdeen University discovered that a short stretch of timber-laced stone ramparts had survived. By using radio-carbon dating techniques, they radically rewrote the conventional story of the Picts. The wall that had contained the characteristic symbol stones was built some time in the later second century AD, showing that the origins of Pictish culture were much older than had been previously believed. The fortress on Dunnicaer had probably been occupied when Ptolemy drew his map in Alexandria around 150 AD and had named the kindred of that part of the North Sea coastlands as the Taexali. No scholar has been able to parse what it means, unlike some of the other names such as the Lugi and the Epidii. Perhaps it is a rare Pictish word, a description whose meaning remains stubbornly obscure. The fort was probably manned, and was perhaps a safe redoubt, during the genocidal invasion of the Romans in 210 under the Emperor Septimius Severus and his sons. Dunnicaer was built in a pagan Scotland, long before the coming of Christianity, therefore the cultural context for the creation and for the meaning of the symbol stones was also pagan, but since the beliefs held by the natives of Britain before the coming of the missionaries are also obscure, they do not provide a key to the code.

The Taexali, whatever it means, was an endonym, what the people called themselves. Picti is an exonym, a name conferred by outsiders. The context of the record of its earliest surviving use is in a panegyric in 297–8 for the Emperor Constantius I:

> But at that time Britain was not prepared with ships for any kind of naval contest . . . In addition to this, the nation of the Britons was still at that time unciv-ilized and used to fighting only with the Picts and the Hibernians [the Irish], both still half-naked enemies; and so they submitted to Roman arms so easily that the only thing that [Julius] Caesar ought to have boasted of was that he had navigated the Ocean.

Leaving aside the author's ingratiating attempt to inflate the reputation of the Emperor Constantius I by downplaying Julius Caesar's role in the conquest of Britain, it is the use of the term Picti that is significant. It means the Painted People or, more precisely, the Tattooed People. When the Romans first crossed the Channel, which they called the Ocean, in 55 and 54 BC before landing at Pegwell Bay (and managed to retreat without mishap), they knew the main island as Britannia. The name derives from Priteni, a Greek word that meant the land of the Painted People, the Tattooed People, which suggests that body decoration was widespread in Britain in the later decades of the last century BC, but that it had died out in mainland Europe. After the Claudian invasion of 43 AD, when most of the main island became a province and was absorbed into the Roman Empire, the British living in the south stopped tattooing their bodies – although from my visit to Butlin's, it is a cultural habit clearly making a comeback. By 297–8 the writer of the panegyric for Constantius used the name Picti because the people in the far north had persisted with body decoration. It is very likely that the lexicon of animal carvings, in particular, found its way under the skin of the peoples of the various kindreds. And it was not only the Romans who noted this particular cultural characteristic and used it to label the people of the region: the Gaelic speakers of Ireland, who had also begun to settle on the eastern shore of the North Channel, in Argyll, called the Picts the Cruithni, the Painted People.

By the dawn of the fourth century, the sneering tone of the panegyric had changed to fear, perhaps even respect. A metal turricula – a dice tower used to throw dice after they had been inserted at the top and then made to tumble out at the bottom to avoid the suspicion of a cheating hand – was discovered near Cologne, in the Roman province of Germania. On the side of the little tower was an eloquent inscription: PICTOS VICTOS HOSTIS DELETA LUDITE SECURI. It translates as '[Now that] the Picts are defeated, the enemy annihilated, let us play without a care'. Clearly the warriors of the north, despite their old-fashioned habit of body decoration, had acquired a fearsome reputation, and not only in Britain but across the Western Empire. In 305 Constantius I led an expedition against the Picts, presumably provoked by their raids in the province to the south, and claimed a victory, calling himself Britannicus Maximius II. He was accompanied by his son and heir, later to be acclaimed at York as Constantine I. After his father's death in 306 the new emperor renewed the attacks on the Picts, strengthening the network of forts in the north and ordering the repair of the roads that linked them.

It was most likely the sea roads that mattered more to the kings in the north. Instead of attempting to breach Hadrian's Wall, Pictish captains navigated their way around it, launching raids from promontory forts like Dunnicaer. When they excavated the site the Aberdeen University archaeologists realised that the fury of the North Sea had much reduced the size of the fortress. Now a sea stack, it had once been a promontory linked to the shore by a narrow but easily defended spit of land. This had been badly eroded by the pounding of storms, and at some point at the end of the fourth century the fort was moved to Dunnottar, another, larger promontory around a kilometre to the south. Now the site of a spectacular medieval castle, it has relatively sheltered bays on either side where ships could be dragged up the beaches to be safe above the high-tide line. When Dunnicaer was excavated, evidence of contact with Rome, perhaps peaceful as well as military, was found when the archaeologists turned up sherds of Roman pottery and glass, the latter probably imported from France. The successor fort at Dunottar became an important focus, and it was besieged twice in the late sixth century, a rare appearance of a Pictish stronghold in the written historical record.

Before coastal erosion forced its abandonment, Dunnicaer was almost certainly a base for raiding the wealthy province to the south in 340 or 341, breaking what appears to have been a treaty. There were also destructive overland attacks. In 342 the Emperor Constans arrived in Britain with detachments of the field army and immediately moved north to Hadrian's Wall. Perhaps in concert with allies from Gaelic-speaking Argyll and Ireland, warriors who were confusingly known as the Scotti, Pictish warbands had burned the outpost forts north of the Wall at High Rochester, Risingham and Bewcastle. What happened next is unclear, but it was not a defeat for the Picts. A treaty, and perhaps subsidies, were accepted by the northern kings, and for almost twenty years there was peace on the frontier. And also a balance of relative power. The Emperor Constans ruled over the Western Empire (while his brother held the East), which included the provinces not only of Britain but also Gaul (modern France), Italy, Spain, North Africa and part of the Balkans. But he was a realist and recognised that in the north of Britain, at the outer limits of his dominion, the best, most prudent, course of action was to negotiate a treaty with the Pictish kingdoms. Because they were powerful, well organised and probably well led – emphatically not an ululating, tattooed rabble but an efficient and even feared fighting machine that could bring the emperor of Rome to the negotiating table. In 2020 a sense of the scale of Pictish political and military power came to light in a series of dramatic discoveries.

Another team of intrepid archaeologists from Aberdeen University began to excavate the hillfort on Tap o' Noth, on the northern edge of the Grampian massif. It overlooks the coastal plain, the rich farmland of western Aberdeenshire. A citadel on the summit, surrounded by massive cairn-like deposits of stones, was thought to be from the Iron Age, or the late Bronze Age. But when radio-carbon dating tests, aerial surveys by drones and ground surveys by Lidar, the non-invasive analysis system, were carried out and analysed the results were epoch-changing in all senses.

The fort turned out to be vast, seven hectares enclosed by a wide, looping perimeter, and it contained at least 800 hut platforms, sufficient accommodation for more than 4,000 people. Scotland had to wait until the twelfth century for settlements of a similar size. Nothing approaching this scale has been found anywhere in post-Roman Britain. The ditches around Cadbury Castle in the south of England enclose three hectares, and the dramatic fort at Tintagel, off the Cornish coast, is two hectares.

An archaeologist I spoke to recently commented that Tap o' Noth 'makes Tintagel look like a pillbox'. The Aberdeen University archaeologists had discovered by far the greatest citadel of Dark Ages Britain. Not only is the fort huge, it does not date from the Iron Age or the Bronze Age as was originally believed. Carbon dating confirmed that Tap o' Noth is in fact Pictish. Work began on its huts and the defensive perimeter in the third century AD, in the decades following the genocide of the Severan invasion of 210, and continued on into the sixth century.

On the summit of the hill, 579 metres above sea level, sits the massively built citadel, rectangular in shape and apparently without an entrance. There is a depression inside that may have been a well or a cistern. Circling around the citadel is an outer fortification, a very long and looping wall, perhaps more than three kilometres around and rising to a height of six metres. It has ten entrances, but only five may be ancient. Tap o' Noth is spectacular, visible from a very wide area of northeastern Scotland. And those in the summit citadel could clearly see the Moray Firth fifty kilometres to the north and the Sutherland mountains beyond the far shore. To the east the flat blue horizon of the North Sea can be made out. This populous fort is the ultimate expression of what archaeologists call 'a statement in the landscape', and more than a statement, it was an assertion of great power.

Building on this scale clearly required the labour of many hands, and a great deal of organisation. Pictish society in the third century AD was, of course, principally concerned with food production, and the fertile, free-draining fields of Aberdeenshire could have supported a substantial population. But there must have been surpluses to enable periods when farmers became builders, hauling stone up the slopes to construct the immense walls of Tap o' Noth and carrying up timber for the frames of the roundhouses raised on the 800 platforms. Even though the creation of the fort almost certainly took place over several generations, it was nevertheless a project that required sustained, probably annual, commitment. And it was a project that needed leadership, an elite powerful enough to compel all that work, a series of directing minds who made decisions. Were they pre-Christian priests, were they kings, or were they both? There is little or no hard evidence to confirm or deny, only the massive ramparts of Tap o' Noth stand as an unequivocal witness to their great power, a well-organised power not seen across the rest of Britain on such a scale.

But at the foot of the hill there may be faint whispers

of answers to some of the questions around it. In the
fields of Barflat Farm, just to the south of the village of
Rhynie, the farmer hit a boulder as he began his winter
ploughing. It was a huge boulder, about two metres long,
and it had a remarkable carving on it. A bearded man
carries an axe-hammer, the shaft resting on his shoulder.
He wears a belted tunic and what seems to be a headdress
that looks faintly ceremonial. His axe-hammer is of a
type that has been linked to pagan animal sacrifice. The
stone was unearthed near the Craw Stane, another tall
monolith that has the outlines of two animals carved on
one side, a fish that might be a salmon and what is known
as the Pictish Beast. Deriving from the shape of a dolphin,
it is a mythic animal that appears on many other symbol
stones found around the shores of the North Sea. Six
other symbol stones have been found nearby.

In 2011 a team of archaeologists began work near the
findspot of the figure, who quickly became known as
Rhynie Man, and the location of the Craw Stane, thought
never to have moved from its original placing. They
uncovered what they called a high-status site, a stockade
surrounding large buildings. The earliest phase dated to
400 AD, and it is thought that both the Craw Stane and
Rhynie Man may have stood as monumental doorwards
at the gate of the stockade. Moulds for the manufacture
of decorative pins and brooches turned up as well as
items from as far away as modern Turkey, then part of
the Eastern Roman Empire, and also from Gaul France.
Fragments of Roman amphorae, wine carriers, were
found. Perhaps the name of the village itself, Rhynie, is
also eloquent. It probably derives from the Celtic root

rig or *righ*, and it may mean the 'Place of Kings'.

Rhynie may also have been the place where the Barbarian Conspiracy was planned. Perhaps in the autumn of 366, before winter storms made sea travel hazardous, the representatives of the kings of the Scotti, of a people known as the Atecotti (almost certainly from the Hebrides), of the kings of the Franks and Saxons of the western coasts of Europe, met in the palace of the kings of the Picts. In the shadow of the vast citadel on Tap o' Noth and its mighty walls, they talked of war and the invasion of the wealthy province of Britannia. Some more conservative historians find the idea of sustained, synchronised long-distance communication and sensible forward planning difficult to imagine amongst kindreds who left no written record, who find it difficult to shake off the connotations of being labelled as barbarians. But that would be a serious misapprehension. Long-range diplomacy had been undertaken for centuries down the North Sea coast of Britain, and on one occasion, documented in Latin, such links were recorded. When the Emperor Claudius came to Britain after the successful invasion in 43 AD, essentially to take the credit, he held court at Colchester. There, eleven British kings came to formally submit to the Master of the World. One was the Pictish King of Orkney, and to fit with the tight imperial timetable, there is convincing evidence that Roman diplomats sailed north to negotiate and help organise the necessary voyage. The notion of what amounted to an international war conference at Rhynie in 366 is by no means unlikely.

The following spring the province of Britannia suffered

as never before. In a concerted and apparently synchronised series of incursions coming from several directions,
the Picts and the Atecotti from the north, the Scotti from
the west and the Franks and the Saxons from the southeast all attacked. A prearranged plan was put into action,
and what became known as the Barbarian Conspiracy
played out. Without warning, Britannia's defences were
swept aside. In the north the *areani*, the border scouts
who patrolled beyond Hadrian's Wall, had been bribed
to raise no alarm and probably to provide military intelligence too. War bands penetrated deep into the province.
Nectaridus was killed, the commander of the forts of
the Saxon Shore, a string of defences stretching from
Portchester on the Channel coast to Kent and on up the
North Sea littoral to Brancaster in Norfolk. In what was
probably a planned action, the allies turned on the Dux
Britanniarum, the province's leading general, a man called
Fullofaudes, and either neutralised or killed him.

For two years the Picts and their fellow conspirators
roamed across the province, gaining complete control in
the north and west and locking up the garrisons of the
southeastern towns behind their walls. Their purpose
was not takeover but systematic looting and the taking
of as many captives as possible to be sold into slavery. In
369 the Roman commander, Theodosius, arrived with
four regiments of the field army to restore order, but by
that time lasting damage had been done. Within forty
years Rome would withdraw as Britannia began to
become Britain and the province began slowly to collapse.

Mere barbarians, half-naked and painted, the Picts had
contributed significantly to the fall of a mighty empire

and also avenged the genocide perpetrated two centuries before. To close an unlikely circle, these kings in the north, whose language has disappeared, whose symbol stones remain defiantly enigmatic, ruling from the magnificent citadel on Tap o' Noth, had an influence in the story of Pegwell Bay. When Hengist and Horsa, mythic forerunners of real Angles, Saxons and Jutes, landed there in 449, they had been invited by the British potentate Vortigern to help him deal with the raiding of the Picts and the Scots.

The most detailed, most accurate plan of a Pictish fort was drawn in 1793 by William Roy, a remarkable man who compiled the first ever reliable map of the Highlands of Scotland. Fascinated by antiquities, especially Roman remains, and the Antonine Wall in particular, he drew the large promontory fort at Burghead on the coast of the Moray Firth. Sitting on a wide headland with beaches on either side where boats could be safely dragged up above the high-tide line, it was a very well defended citadel enclosed by high ramparts on its three seaward sides and a series of ditches and banks on the landward approach. Below them lay the lanes, houses and garden plots of a small village. Roy arrived with his surveying equipment, paper and pens just in time. Between 1805 and 1809 the local landlord had Burghead completely redeveloped. The old village was swept away and much of the Pictish fort obliterated. In their place a rectilinear street plan was laid out and a new harbour built on the western side of the headland.

On his map of 150 AD Ptolemy noted a place he called Pinnata Castra, the Winged Fort, approximately where

Burghead is located. He also labelled Dunnet Head, on the southern shore of the Pentland Firth, as Tarvedunum, perhaps translatable as the Bull Fort. Working in Alexandria, presumably from written sources and a long way from Scotland, Ptolemy may have made mistakes. Six Pictish carvings of bulls have been found at Burghead, totem animals who may have given the fort a more appropriate name.

A road sign on the A96 simply notes 'Pictish Fort, turn right', but when I arrived at the outskirts of Burghead there were no supplementary directions. I simply kept going up the arrow-straight central street to the higher ground at the end, presumably the headland and the remains of the fort. There was nowhere to park and, more urgently, nowhere to pee. I'd been driving a long time. Having avoided ignominy and arrest, I walked over to the visitor centre (admission by donation) past a group of young people vigorously filling in a trench. Opposite the centre was a high mound of sandy soil protected by a mesh barrier. More people were digging in what seemed like a deep hole, and an older lady from the centre told me the group were from Aberdeen University. I'd stumbled on the same leadership team who had investigated Dunnicaer and made the extraordinary discoveries at Tap o' Noth.

When I approached the group filling in the trench, on the assumption that their work for the day was almost done, I asked if they had had any luck. 'A ring,' said a young man. 'We found a Pictish ring, quite rare, last week, the second one that's come up here.' He had indeed been part of the team who had dug Tap o' Noth. 'There might well be more house platforms on the hill, maybe a thousand,' he said. We then fell to discussing what the function of such a citadel might be, and when I argued that such a long perimeter would be difficult to defend and, further, that the significance of Tap o' Noth might be religious rather than military, he disagreed. 'No, there were thousands of people up there who could repel an assault that had the disadvantage of attacking uphill.' OK, but what about water and food? Besiegers might simply wait, throwing a secure cordon around the ramparts rather than risking an assault? We moved on to a discussion of the bull sculptures at Burghead and the Pictish symbol stones in general. 'Maybe AI will find the answer?' he smiled. 'And that's only half a joke.' I unpacked my own interpretation of the Z-rods and V-rods, and the young archaeologist nodded, saying that hadn't occurred to him. But the Pictish Beast was probably not a dolphin. 'I spoke to an older historian who said that it looked more like a charging ram. When the animal lowers its head to butt another ram, that's how what seem to be horns might look.' That hadn't occurred to me.

What I enjoyed and found immensely cheering was the young man's openness and willingness to talk to a passing stranger, to share his professional knowledge. Academics are not always so willing to discuss their work with lay people or, if they do, their conversation tends to take the form of an informal lecture. But together, on that blustery headland, for about twenty minutes we were attempting to understand history, to peer into the darkness of the past, to make something of the enigma of the Picts.

VI

Fair Isle

Across the Sea of Orcs

When he sat down in the sunlit, Mediterranean warmth of Alexandria to draw his map of Britain, Ptolemy may have shivered when he calculated the latitude of the land that became known as Scotland. Neither he nor his fellow Greek geographers believed that it was possible for human beings to survive in latitudes further north than sixty-three degrees – it was simply too cold – and so instead of drawing Britain on an approximate south to north axis, he bent it. Not just a little but through a ninety-degree angle. About where the Cheviot Hills now mark the English border, he bent Scotland to the east so that the rain-soaked, fur-clad, chittering savages could be kept south of sixty-three degrees. Consequently the Northern Isles became the Eastern Isles as Britain appeared to bow to Europe, an attitude that would have horrified many of the voters in a recent referendum.

Despite this extreme distortion Ptolemy got the name of one of the two archipelagos that make up the Northern Isles right when he labelled them the Orcades. It is another animal totem name, the Boar Islands. They are separated from the mainland by a totemic stretch of water, the place where the Atlantic Ocean meets the North Sea. It was once known as the Sea of Orcs, and such was the maritime prowess of the Orcadians, the sea roads between the Hebrides, the islands of the Atlantic shore, were also sometimes referred to as the Seas of the Orcs. Infinitely less than a historical fact, those ancient names are little more than feathers blowing in the wind. But they are suggestive. The ninth-century *History of the Britons*, a colourful mixture of fable and fact attributed to a Welsh monk named Nennius, stated at least one truth when it noted that 'the Britons originally filled the whole island with their peoples from the English Channel to the Sea of the Orcs'. When the Vikings sailed into history in the 790s they came up with a new name, one that has stuck, even though part of it is inaccurately translated. Their longships ploughed through the waves of what they came to know as Petlandsfjørð, the Pentland Fjord, the stretch of water below the islands of the Picts and above the lands of the mainland Picts. The Pictland Firth or the Pentland Firth is not a firth, the Scots term for an inlet of the sea, but a strait, and a dangerous strait.

Having driven the length of the A9, from its original beginnings in Edinburgh to the terminus at Thurso, I parked in good time at the pier at Scrabster to catch the midday ferry across the Sea of Orcs. It was a fine but blowy day, the wind whipping white horses across the water, and I decided to forgo the shelter of the passenger lounge and sit out on the open deck. On the ferry's hull I'd noticed a huge, cartoonish painting of a Viking. With his arm outstretched he pointed the way to the Boar Islands, his beard blowing in the breeze, his stern gaze resolute under the obligatory horned helmet (which no Viking ever wore; it was the invention of Carl Emil Doepler, the costume designer for the 1876 performance of Wagner's *Der Ring des Nibelungen*). The crossing takes ninety minutes, but the waters of the Pentland Firth can be treacherous, and perhaps the *Ride of the Valkyries* might have been an appropriate soundtrack.

The tidal races are amongst the fastest and most powerful in the world, reaching speeds of thirty to fifty kilometres per hour when the Atlantic surges through the narrow straits between Orkney and the mainland cliffs of Caithness. Constriction is what causes the tide to race, the ocean's rising tide funnelling through a narrow strait, and it causes swirling eddies, waves, hazardous currents and even whirlpools to form. These are found at overfalls, areas where the surface of the sea roils as it passes over shallows or underwater ridges. North of the uninhabited island of Stroma – appropriately from the Old Norse Straumey, the Island in the Current – there is a whirlpool known as the Swelkie. It also derives from Old Norse. Svalga meant the Swallower.

The tide tables for Scrabster had told me that high water was due at 12.44, half an hour before departure. With the mighty Atlantic having surged eastwards before turning south down the coast of Britain, the crossing might have been calm, but the wind was gusting strongly from the west. I suspected the skipper might have pointed the finger of the Viking on his hull well to the west of our destination, Stromness on Orkney, in an ancient practice known as aiming off to compensate for the effect of the wind and the strong current. On the voyage, once we reached open water, I saw no orcs, none that had strayed from the pages of J.R.R. Tolkien's *Lord of the Rings*, but I did see orcas, black-and-white killer whales. Two of them leaped clean out of the water as their pod seemed to track the course of the ferry. It was a spectacular, thrilling, magnificent sight, a fitting overture to the magnificence I had come to Orkney to see.

When we sailed past the Old Man of Hoy, with the sun lighting it and the red sandstone cliffs behind, the sea stack seemed to stand sentinel, guarding Orkney's shores, glowering at those who dared to sail the Sea of Orcs. It looked very like a gigantic version of one of the moai, the mysterious, frowning megaliths carved by the people of Easter Island and set up in a rank along their shoreline. After we docked at Stromness I decided to walk to my destination, to the place I'd travelled the length of Britain to see for myself, a place where the human spirit began to flourish, where epic ideas were first translated into action, where traces of the metaphysical were left in the landscape, where metaphors assumed physical form, where civilisation began in Britain.

The Stones of Stenness stand at a place of transition, between two worlds and at the centre of a natural amphitheatre formed by a ring of low hills. Near the middle of Orkney Mainland, the freshwater Loch of Harray drains into the salt sea Loch of Stenness, and just to the south of that link rise four majestic standing stones, all that remains of an elliptical circle of twelve. Three are around five metres high, almost three times the height of a man, and they formed part of the earliest surviving henge monument in Britain, the forerunner of all the others, including spectacular Stonehenge. The culture of the circles, of a ditch and bank, and thereafter a ring of stone posts, began in Orkney and spread southwards. It was the first, the earliest culture – mysterious in its practices, its basis now impossible to retrieve from the darkness of the past – to take hold all over Britain, from the furthest north to the furthest south. And its beginnings were between the fresh and salt waters of the twin lochs.

It was a bright late afternoon when I reached Stenness, and mercifully there were few people there and no tour buses had yet parked. The great stones stood stark against the open sky, defying interpretation, their ancient surfaces plain and a little mottled by age and exposure. In the centre of the elliptical circle are the remains of a hearth, somewhere ceremonies involving fire took place. Did they take place at night to enhance the drama? It is unlikely that all who came to Stenness saw the flames or took part in whatever rituals they lit, for the central idea of the circle and the rock-cut ditch that surrounds it was surely exclusion of some sort. The great stones almost certainly marked off a different space, a place not part of the temporal world that surrounded them but of the spiritual, a holy of holies, and inner sanctum sanctorum. The raising of the stones must have required the labour of many, but only a privileged few could have occupied the circle at any given time. To that basic extent these places were temples of some kind, but what precisely was worshipped or celebrated is now impossible to know, beyond a few basic observations.

To the north of the Stones of Stenness, very close to

the edge of the road that leads across a narrow isthmus between the two lochs, stands the tallest of them all. The Watch Stone rises to 5.5 metres, and like the Old Man of Hoy it appears to live up to its name, the guardian of a portal into the deep past, a place that turns on its head the prehistory of Britain, somewhere that lay hidden for more than 4,000 years.

The Ring of Brodgar was always visible, a rare henge monument in that the ditch and bank were perfectly circular, with the original sixty stones set up inside it. The stone circle was raised some time between 2500 BC and 2000 BC, at least half a millennium after Stenness and at about the same time as Stonehenge. Twenty-seven stones still stand, and they appear to have been brought, with great effort, from different parts of the archipelago. There is a faint sense of representation, and several of the Orkney islands seem to have some particular identity in prehistory.

In 1999 the Ring of Brodgar, the Stones of Stenness, the chambered cairn at Maeshowe, the houses at Skara Brae and several other prehistoric monuments were designated as part of a UNESCO World Heritage Site. This in turn mandated a thorough survey of the area around the two lochs with Lidar, as was later used to such good effect on Tap o' Noth. Its findings set in train a series of events, discoveries that were to rewrite history and confound assumptions, even prejudices.

Between the stones at Stenness and Brodgar, the road runs past an area of higher ground, a hummock rather than a hillock, a feature long thought to have been geological. It turned out to have been manmade, a massive burial mound that covered over a series of features that the Lidar identified as the shadows of something that was also manmade. A test trench was dug. And then in 2003 the farmer ploughed the mounded field at the isthmus and turned up a large rectangular stone. It had been decorated. Along one edge ran a series of notches, and archaeologists at first thought the plough had skinned the lid off a kist, a stone-lined prehistoric burial. But when excavation began a team from Glasgow University found what looked like the foundations of a substantial building. Between 2004 and 2007 more foundations of large buildings were uncovered. They had been made by skilled masons using Orkney flagstone. Deposits of this sedimentary rock can be found all over the archipelago, and masons found it easy to split the strata into rectilinear shapes of varying thickness. Orkney had few trees, and the use of flagstone for building was a necessity – and also the happy reason why so much of its prehistory has survived on the islands.

In 2012 the dig was extended in the area that became known as the Ness of Brodgar. Something remarkable came to light, part of a unique and highly sophisticated complex of large buildings. These were and remain unparalleled in northern Europe. The masons began working at a very early date on the Ness, some time around 3500 BC, well before the pyramids were raised in Egypt. The only contemporary parallels were the brick temples of Sumer, the first cities of the Harappa culture of India and the beginnings of the first Golden Age in China. The 2012 excavation unearthed perhaps only 10 per cent of what lies under the hummock at the Ness.

Archaeologists believe that at least fourteen substantial buildings were contained behind two massive flanking walls, perhaps 4.75 to 5.5 metres thick and at least two metres high. Built in drystone (the invention of mortar being far in the future), the structures are rectilinear with rounded corners, and their low walls were supported by interior buttresses. Using thinly split sandstone slates, the buildings were roofed, a new technique invented on Orkney.

The function of these innovative structures is mysterious but might be defined negatively. Unlike the much later barrows, they are not large tombs, for no significant deposits of human remains have been found. Most appear to have been dwellings. Except for one. Known as Structure 10 or the Temple, a massive building was uncovered. Twenty-five metres in length and twenty metres wide, it is by some distance the largest prehistoric building yet to be found in Britain. It seems to have been decorated. In the Temple, there was a paint shop, a place where pigments were ground from minerals or possibly ochre. Mixed with fixatives, like egg-white, the coloured powder became paint, hues of yellow, red and orange. Excavators have turned up stones that had been painted, and the exteriors of buildings may have appeared chequered with rectilinear patterns of colours mixed with plain stones. In a landscape of natural greens, greys and browns, such decoration would have been very striking, a way of making these grand buildings even grander, different, outstanding.

While the rituals that took place inside the flanking stone circles at Brodgar and Stenness must remain essentially unknowable, and the functions of the complex of buildings at the Ness at best conjectural, there can be little doubt that the latter were central, the focus of an elaborate ceremonial landscape. One thing is certain, these structures speak of power, of organisation and, like the citadel on Tap o' Noth, of directing minds. I believe that the Ness of Brodgar was a royal compound, a place where the ruler of Orkney held court, dispensed justice or issued decrees. Business was probably done in the largest building, the Temple, where people could gather to hear what was said or witness what was done. The other thirteen buildings may have been occupied by the ruler's retinue, his courtiers, his band of warriors, perhaps his priests. Those who came from all over the archipelago to witness the rituals, gathering around the stone circles, probably at the equinoxes, also came to the Ness to affirm loyalties and render tribute of some sort.

This is conjecture, of course, but it is not without some foundation. In 1958 Ronald Simison found a large, chambered tomb on his farm at South Ronaldsay. It came into use some time around 3150 BC, and for 800 years, during the heyday of the Ness, the dead were laid to rest there. Known as the Tomb of the Eagles, because the bones and talons of sea eagles (perhaps a totem animal for the island) were found there, it was also the repository of the disarticulated bones of 324 individuals. Almost half of them showed clear evidence of serious physical violence, having been hit so hard on the head with stone maces or other weapons as to cause depressed fractures that were serious but not fatal. Dating from the same time as the Ness and the monuments around it were being built, these injuries more than imply coercion. They also imply a ruthless social hierarchy. Those in power were clearly compelling many people to do as they were told and to contribute their labour and materials to grand projects.

However all that may be, there is no doubt that the discovery of the Ness of Brodgar represented a signal moment, one that demanded a new interpretation of the prehistory of Britain. Perhaps the spectacular scale of Stonehenge has been deceptive, encouraging the lazy notion that henge culture began there and spread across the rest of what is now the British Isles. And because the south of England has long been the political and economic powerhouse of the nation, it was difficult to imagine how somewhere thought to be as peripheral as Orkney could be central. But in fact that was precisely the case. Henges were first raised there, and all of the artefacts associated with them – such as a type of grooved pottery and carved stone balls – were first made on the archipelago. Most importantly, whatever the belief was that informed the rituals of these huge and enduringly impressive monuments, it was exported south, all the way down the length of Britain, the first unified culture to flourish across the British Isles. And its associated beliefs and artefacts almost certainly travelled south down the coastal waters of the North Sea.

In the summer of 2024 two related events offered themselves as both a coda and a fascinating, tantalising new discovery. In August of that year, after twenty years of patient, painstaking excavation, Nick Card, the director of the Ness of Brodgar project, announced that digging would cease and the site would be carefully filled in to protect and conserve the fragile stones of the buildings. Because the flagstone was all quarried it is likely to erode and degrade quickly if left exposed to the winter winds, rain and snow of the Northern Isles. The next phase will involve cataloguing all of the finds, including more than a thousand pieces of Neolithic art, more than has been found across the whole of the rest of Britain. More research and analysis will help develop what Card calls 'a coherent narrative of the site'. In an interview with the BBC, he added, 'Now we must never underestimate our Neolithic ancestors and what they were capable of.'

This considered judgement could not have been more appropriate when another announcement was made in August 2024. Tony Clarke, a young PhD student based at Curtin University in Perth, Western Australia, published a paper in the scientific journal *Nature* that made a remarkable and entirely credible claim. The stones of Stonehenge have long been classified in two categories. The huge sarsens that make up the outer circle and part of the inside were dragged to the site twenty-three kilometres overland from Marlborough, and the smaller bluestones set up beside them came from the Preseli Mountains in west Wales. Clarke analysed the geological character of one stone that appeared to be different from the others. Largely hidden under two collapsed sarsens, what was known as the Altar Stone lay in the middle of Stonehenge, and indeed may have been the focus of the whole monument. Clarke's research revealed that the six-tonne block had travelled a very long way from where it had been quarried and shaped. The Altar Stone had come from deposits of the Old Red Sandstone of the

Orcadian Basin and had either been shipped or dragged overland for almost 800 kilometres to be installed in the middle of Stonehenge. Nick Card was surely right when he insisted that we should not underestimate our prehistoric ancestors.

The deposits of sandstone in the Orcadian Basin extend far to the south of the archipelago and can be found across Caithness and on the eastern and northern shores of the Moray Firth. There is also, very suggestively, a significant outcrop of the same stone, what might be seen as sacred stone, around Rhynie in Aberdeenshire. How the Altar Stone was transported south is not a mystery. It came either by land or sea. But from exactly where? Professor Richard Bevins of Aberystwyth University has analysed the geological makeup of the Stones of Stenness and the Ring of Brodgar and concluded that Orkney itself was not the beginning of the journey. It seemed much more likely that the Altar Stone was quarried from mainland deposits of the Old Red Sandstone in the wider Orcadian Basin. If it had originated on Orkney then it would have been much more likely that most of the 800-kilometre journey south would have been made by sea for the simple reason that it had first to cross the turbulent waters of the Pentland Firth. From there it would have been a much simpler matter to continue the voyage down the North Sea coast.

Acknowledging that her views could only be speculative, Heather Sebire, a senior curator for English Heritage based at Stonehenge, said, 'My gut feeling is that it [the Altar Stone] came overland and it possibly took a long time, and was not necessarily in one fell swoop. Getting places as quickly as possible is a modern concept – we're always in a hurry. Their mindset was probably very different. You can think of it as a pilgrimage . . . it could have taken years.' Other experts have written of how large stones could have been pulled along on rollers set out in front of them like railway sleepers. One has pointed out that these can be difficult to control, especially on sloping areas, and a strongly built sledge might have been a better proposition (the invention of wheeled carts lay far in the future). A coastal route has been plotted that followed the shores of the Moray Firth and then turned around the Buchan to aim for the Tay before cutting across Fife to reach the Forth and the coast. It may have turned inland at Durham to be dragged down the spine of England to its destination at Stonehenge.

Such a journey, a pilgrimage, from the origins of henge culture and its ceremonies and beliefs to perhaps its most spectacular expression, reinforces the sense of a unified cult down the length of Britain. Along a landward route local communities could take part in the pilgrimage, perhaps also lending their resources and even their muscle to the journey. Possibly the journey was conceived in relays, like the progress of the Olympic torch to the stadium where the flame waited to be lit. If Heather Sebire is right, the pilgrimage could have taken years, with the Altar Stone temporarily erected in focal places so that many could come to see it and worship or perform other acts of reverence. Perhaps this was done somewhat in the same way that saintly relics are brought out of churches and paraded through crowds on feast days. To that extent the progress of the stone through Britain might be seen as unifying. It must certainly have been coordinated and overseen by controlling minds of some kind.

Was the Altar Stone brought or sent? Archaeologists believe that it arrived at Stonehenge between *c.* 2620 BC and *c.* 2480 BC, and the Ness of Brodgar was still occupied at that period, although perhaps in decline. It is very likely, however, that its influence spread beyond the islands. A sense of this can be gleaned from what happened when the site was abandoned.

Not long after the latest date for the arrival of the Altar Stone at Stonehenge a great slaughter took place on Orkney. Perhaps the most compelling evidence for the Ness of Brodgar as a royal compound was the manner of its destruction. Some time around 2200 BC the Temple was closed. The reasons for this are obscure, but there is evidence of what happened at that important moment. Archaeologists have discovered a mass of cattle bones, particularly on the paved walkway around the Temple. It appears that an enormous feast that may have fed thousands was mounted as the life of the Ness came to an end. Approximately 400 head of cattle were slaughtered, cooked and eaten, their bones split so that the succulent marrow could also be consumed. And this huge number of cows, in an act of conspicuous consumption, all came from one herd, the herd of the most powerful and wealthy individual on Orkney, surely from the royal herd.

How many people could feast on 400 cows? Perhaps 5,000 or 6,000? If the numbers are even remotely accurate, then they must represent the whole population of the archipelago and perhaps also people from beyond its shores, from the Orcadian Basin. Or, alternatively, the feast may have gone on for several days and fed fewer. Whatever the historical truth, this was an enormous event and an example of conspicuous consumption, a statement of power on the part of leaders.

Was the passage of the Altar Stone from the Orcadian Basin to Stonehenge therefore emblematic of a power shift, the movement of the centre of henge culture from its origins to its greatest expression? Whatever the political reality, this remarkable incident shows how dynamic and connected prehistoric communities were.

2

Local Heroes

It was a mist-shrouded morning, dampness hanging in the still, silent air, visibility so poor that bulky, looming grey shapes only became buildings when the car head-lights played on them. I was driving so slowly that I could make out the dense patterns of silvery cobwebs on the cow parsley by the roadside. It was forty or more years since I'd made my way down this B road, but its contours were printed on my memory. Even though it was muffled under the blanket of fog, perhaps a sea haar, I knew that once the road began to turn to the right there would follow a steep descent into another world, into a version of Brigadoon.

As a young TV reporter I had not much enjoyed the macho world of the newsroom, its clouds of blue cigarette smoke and the culture of the long lunches. Documentaries were what interested me, and through a mixture of bad management, an eye for a good story and the fact that the ITV companies' monopoly of adver-tising revenue meant that financial controls were not as tight as they might be, I had been allowed to help make a successful little half-hour film. It chronicled the adventures of a US-style marching band, all high-stepping majorettes twirling flags and boys playing trumpets and drums, at the national championships in Glasgow. Despite their origins in the grim housing schemes and their chronic lack of funds, they triumphed and the film had an authentic charm. It led to other things, not least several trips to Brigadoon.

Bill Forsyth had written and directed a lovely film called *Gregory's Girl*, and that had led to other things for him. His new script, *Local Hero*, had been picked up by the Oscar-winning producer David Puttnam. Set in the highlands of Scotland, it was to be filmed in locations that fell, just, inside STV's transmission area – or rather, most of it did. That gave us an entrée into making a documentary film about the making of the feature film. Unable to find a suitable highland village on the Atlantic coast to stand for the fictional Ferness, Bill Forsyth's Brigadoon, the producers decided to shoot at Pennan, an old fishing village on the Moray Firth coast of the North Sea, and through the magical processes of ingenious set design and clever editing, Pennan would appear to have the stunning beach at Camusdarrach, near Mallaig, just around the next headland.

When I made my way down the steep descent into the old fishing village there occurred another magical moment. The mist did not lift, but instead it seemed that I had driven through the cloud and under it, for Pennan was bathed in warm morning sunshine, as though the lights had been switched on on the set of *Brigadoon*. The red phone box was still there, a crucial location in the plot (*Local Hero* was made in 1982, before the advent of mobile phones) as an American oil company tries to buy the entire village of Ferness and its bay so that they can pipe North Sea oil onshore and make fortunes.

$\star$ $\star$ $\star$

Brendan McKeown did not trust telephones of any sort. Far too much was at stake to risk a conversation being overheard or even recorded. Amoco's oil drilling superintendent communicated with his exploration headquarters in Great Yarmouth by radio and in a code based on the names of American high-school football teams. McKeown had received a message from the *Sea Quest* rig that was exploring the bed of the North Sea about 240 kilometres east of Aberdeen. 'There was something there, but the people on board wouldn't bring it to the surface until I got there,' he later recalled. Having commandeered a helicopter from Aberdeen Airport, McKeown landed on the *Sea Quest* and immediately began to investigate.

After he was absolutely certain about what had come up from below the seabed, McKeown put the helicopter on stand-by and radioed Mitch Watt, the Texan in charge of the exploration programme, but only with a message that he had something to show him, no details. Amoco's rivals – Total, Shell and BP – had been drilling in the same area of the North Sea for some time, and not all of those who worked on the rig at that time were to be trusted. In any case, *Sea Quest* was owned by BP. McKeown remembered:

I suspected from the information that was available on the logs that we would see good oil. The most significant thing was to see if the pressure and the flow would stabilize over a period of time. As soon as the valves opened, we knew we had a winner . . .

None of us were prepared for oil. We thought we might find some gas or at the most, watery oil traces, so I didn't have any stainless steel containers. I had to clean out an empty pickle jar from the mess hall to collect the sample.

It was what we call sweet oil with not a trace of hydrogen sulphide. Mitch then poured it into an ashtray on his desk and set it alight and it burned well. But unfortunately the heat caused the ashtray to crack and the bloody stuff spilled all over the floor.

The mess on the floor turned out to be the stuff of history. Amoco had discovered the Montrose oil field, named after the Scottish harbour town. As an experienced geologist who knew that there had been sporadic finds around the margins of the North Sea, it became quickly clear to McKeown that under the waves there was a great deal of oil. A year after Mitch Watt's ashtray cracked, BP discovered 'a giant oil field' 175 kilometres northeast of Aberdeen. Because it lay near the Long Forties Bank, where the sea is shallow (the bed only forty fathoms down), and which in turn had given its name to an area of the *Shipping Forecast*, it became known as the Forties Field. At its peak, the field produced a staggering 500,000 barrels of oil a day. In 1971 the Brent Oil Field was found, and it lay almost 195 kilometres northeast of Shetland.

Estimates fluctuated wildly at first, but it was obvious that the licences granted by the British government to oil companies would become very lucrative, despite the challenges of drilling in such a hostile environment as the North Sea.

Watching all of these developments from his office in Lerwick was a man who could have changed the course of Britain's history with his vision and single-minded drive. Ian Clark was the county treasurer of the country's smallest local authority, what was then known as Zetland County Council. When it was amalgamated with Lerwick Town Council to become Shetland Islands Council, Clark was appointed chief executive. Clearly understanding the far-reaching implications of what was happening out in the North Sea – and it was happening quickly – he realised what needed to be done. 'Shetland would have to acquire special powers from Parliament if the feared free-for-all with the oil business was to be avoided,' he later wrote. Urgent discussions took place between councillors and the local MP, the redoubtable Jo Grimond, then leader of the Liberal Party. In 1973 he introduced a private member's bill to the House of Commons designed to allow what became Shetland Islands Council to negotiate directly with the oil companies over the key issue of onshore facilities. Edward Heath's Conservative government was anxious to see revenues begin to flow from North Sea oil, especially in light of difficulties with the miners' unions, and they did not oppose what Grimond proposed. The bill quickly became an act, and discussions began. Apparently the oil companies later said that the Libyan dictator Colonel Gaddafi was easier to deal with than Ian Clark, and the whole process was given added piquancy by the 1973 oil crisis, when the Middle Eastern producers who led the OPEC consortium reduced supply and tripled prices.

The oil had to be brought onshore as soon as was feasible, and geographically there was no other choice than Shetland for tankers and, later, pipelines. The Islands Council became a port authority. Most important, Shetland Islands Council agreed to fund and facilitate the construction of the huge oil terminal at Sullom Voe as well as other infrastructure such as the necessary improvements at Sumburgh Airport. Ownership of these as well as the tugboat fleet that piloted supertankers in and out of the voe allowed the council to charge for the use of all that had been built at their expense. In one year these revenues could amount to £56 million. This made Shetland Islands Council the second richest in Britain, behind the City of London. All sorts of welcome facilities were built for community use, including a large sports and leisure centre in Lerwick and eight swimming pools with centres attached in the rest of the archipelago. Investment funds were also made available for the indigenous industries of fishing, fish processing, knitwear and for crofting. The Shetland economy boomed.

In 1982, between breaks in filming at Pennan caused by poor weather, Bill Forsyth told me that he had been inspired by Ian Clark's story when he sat down to write the script of *Local Hero*. The fictional Texan company, Knox Oil and Gas, run by Burt Lancaster's character, wished to buy the village of Ferness and its beautiful bay, and the leader of the local community was an accountant, like

Ian Clark, played by Denis Lawson. In the event the deal did not go through, but all ended happily even though no one got rich. And the film was a tremendous success.

The impact of North Sea oil on Aberdeen, the eastern Highlands and the Northern Isles was electric, powered, it must be said, by the entrepreneurial inventiveness of the companies despite tremendous and sometimes fatal difficulties (the North Sea could be a dangerous place to drill for oil, and in 1988 the *Piper Alpha* rig exploded, killing 167 men) and their conviction that a great deal of money could be made. Many thousands of new jobs were created. At Nigg Bay in Easter Ross, not far from Invergordon, the construction of oil rig platforms began. The local economy quickly expanded, with more than 5,000 employed at the yards, and more found work in oil-related businesses. Houses and schools were built as communities expanded dramatically. Around the coasts of the Highlands and Islands more construction sites were set up at Kishorn in Wester Ross, Arnish near Stornoway and at Ardersier, close to Inverness. The changes were very positive. In 1961 the number of people in work in the region was 97,000, but by 1991 it had jumped to 134,000, a 40 per cent increase.

Oil also changed the political map. 'It's Scotland's oil' was a potent slogan coined by the Scottish National Party, and it had the effect of making independence look both possible and desirable. If Scotland did not secede from the union, the SNP argued in the campaign before the first general election of 1974, then Scots would see little material benefit. After the votes were counted seven nationalists had been elected out of Scotland's seventy-one seats, and the party attracted 22 per cent of the popular vote. Eight months later, when Labour called a second election in order to secure an overall majority, the SNP gained eleven seats and 30 per cent of the vote. North Sea oil had transformed them from a fringe group into a powerful political force, and while production has declined, the notion of oil sustaining an independent Scottish economy still hovers in the background.

In 1975 Ian Clark was appointed chief executive of the British National Oil Corporation, based in Glasgow. Harold Wilson's Labour government was attempting to adapt the Shetland model on a national scale, and Clark and his team began to take stakes in oil companies developing the North Sea oil fields and also to invest overseas. Because Shetland Islands Council had invested its own oil revenues, the council had behind it a fund of between £400 million and £500 million. Wilson wanted to see the creation of a state oil company, the equivalent of Statoil in Norway. Set up in 1972, Statoil now has 23,000 employees and a staggering $1.71 trillion in assets, making it the world's largest sovereign wealth fund. If the company were to be dissolved each Norwegian would receive $307,000.

In 1979 the Conservative Party, led by Margaret Thatcher, decided to privatise, to sell off the British National Oil Corporation, beginning with its exploration and production functions. Eventually everything was sold to BP in 1988. The revenues from these lucrative sales enabled the Thatcher governments to cut personal taxes while maintaining a relatively high standard of social services. But it was a short-term political gain that obliterated any hope of future prosperity. These actions also deprived Britain of the enduring benefits of the North Sea's greatest bounty, an accidental geological gift that could have secured the nation's future, funded the National Health Service properly and backed the economy with a near impregnable sovereign fund. It was a defining, tragic miscalculation, the effects of which are still playing out forty years later as governments grapple with the problems of an underfunded NHS, crumbling infrastructure, falling educational standards and a host of other difficulties. The North Sea's oil could have enriched and nurtured a very different Britain.

Envoi: Stories of the Sea

The dogs stirred when I came downstairs, lifting their heads for a moment before settling again as I ignored them and went into the kitchen to make coffee. They knew it was too early, not their time. When I pressed the ignition and my car's headlights suddenly penetrated the silent, starlit darkness, I regretted the brutal breaking of the spell of the early dark. It is a magical, liminal time, the brink of day, the hour before the edging light, when the night world turns to meet the morning sun. How much more gentle, better, would it have been to walk or saddle one of the horses to make my last journey down to the sea, the North Sea. But sixty-five kilometres was far too far to contemplate anything but the car.

The night before I'd listened to the *Shipping Forecast*, been reassured that the day would not be wild, and Admiral Fitzroy's Met Office had promised sun, rising at 6.42 a.m. Driving east to the coast there is a right-handed corner where the road leaves woodland on either side and opens up to look over the Tweed Valley. That early morning the dark heads of the Cheviots to the south and the Lammermuirs to the north defined a cloudless, clear horizon, the sky indigo blue, and they drew the eye to the vanishing point, to where the great river winds its looping, lazy meander towards its destination, the estuary at Berwick-upon-Tweed and the little seaside resort at Spittal, where the story of the North Sea began for me a lifetime ago.

By the time I'd parked behind the Pavilion Family Fun Centre, what used to be the slightly more raffish Johnny's Amusement Arcade, the sky had brightened; blue grey had given way to yellow tinged with scarlet on the gossamer drifts of the horizon clouds. Walking south along the promenade well wrapped up against the backing southeasterly, decreasing 4 or 5 for a time, I saw that the tide was coming in. Pushed by the brisk sea wind, whitecaps foamed and spent themselves on the smooth sloping sand, and the hypnotic shush of the waves lulled me when I sat down on a bench dedicated to the memory of Tom Middlemass 'who loved this view'. Perhaps Old Tom was looking over my shoulder, perhaps uncounted generations behind him were waiting for the sunrise. But there was no one, not another soul in sight, not even any sound of activity, only the ceaseless sea.

When the rim of the fiery yellow disc at last peeped over the horizon the sun seemed to rise in moments, moving upwards as I stared at it. Its light first caught the stripy, red-and-white light on the end of Berwick Pier, then the top of a tall chimney at the harbour, and the first rays made the overhead rail gantries on the main line to London glint. Moments later the morning peace was broken when I heard the rumble of an early train travelling south to King's Cross and the whoosh when it had gathered speed.

I'd come back to where my dad's idea of a swimming lesson was to throw me into the North Sea, to where Spittal Trip had introduced me to candy floss, the seaside and girls, to the penny arcades and the donkey rides. It was the end, the last day of an 800-kilometre journey along the edge of Britain, a place I'd come to believe was not peripheral but central to our sense of ourselves in this scatter of islands on the northwest edge of Europe. Much of our history – a lot of it to Pegwell Bay in Kent, it seemed – had come to us across the North Sea, and on its shores much of our identity was compiled, and continues to be compiled. I'd found the fenlands strange and fascinating, and the survival of Anglo-Saxonism in modern British politics a revelation – once I had understood something of its context and beginnings. And most important was the experience of having been in the Fens, having caught a sense of its *genius loci*, its very powerful and particular spirit of place.

Contrasts appeared at every turn of the journey. Florrie Forde, fish and chips, Billy Butlin and seaside fun of all sorts formed one side of the story, and on the obverse was the fatal storm surge of 1953, the sheer malice of the sea and the magnificent response of the mighty Thames Barrier. And, although I'd crossed the border only a few kilometres north of where I sat on the promenade, there had been a developing sense of a common North Sea culture, from Kent to Shetland. Perhaps that was most evident where the story turned to the nature of the sea itself, its fishermen and sailors, its ships, lighthouses and harbours. And the long, sustained – even heroic – effort to predict its weather.

By the time the sun's perfect disc had somehow levitated, its bottom rim clear of the horizon, and the light had returned to the land, I decided to walk and warm up. At the northern end of the prom, prom, prom, where no bands played tiddly-om-pom-pom, I listened for music of a different sort. Looking over the Tweed Estuary to Berwick's forbidding walls, I realised that the shush of the waves, the whistle – sometimes the roar – of the wind, the harsh squawk of the gulls and the chug of small boats were the background music of the sea, the accompaniment to a very distinct chorus of history, the music of things as they happened. Change seemed to be insistent, constant, like the sea itself. As the North Sea had gnawed at the East Anglian coast, smashed ships against the Bell Rock or given up its spouting, black bounty in the shape of the dangerous, sometimes fatal, business of oil extraction, it also nourished us all. More than the catches auctioned at Peterhead it enriched our culture, deep-dying it with the identities and epic stories that sailed across the North Sea to make us British. All of us.

I'd arrived at journey's end not at the end – perhaps I'd returned to the beginning – but, whichever way, I'd arrived at the middle of it all, halfway down or halfway up my 1,300-kilometre journey. And as I walked along the banks of the Tweed Estuary I realised something simple. The sea still scared me. It would never be my element, and its power is elemental, immense but not closed or forbidding. Like Joan Eardley and J.M.W. Turner I'd become fascinated, returning to the coast again and again. The North Sea was no longer a grey blank, somewhere to be crossed. Its dynamic richness had brought colour as well as a simple revelation. After the best part of a year travelling up and down its shores I'd come to believe that the North Sea made us who we are.

Acknowledgements

I would like to thank Simon Thorogood and also his former colleagues at Canongate for all their belief, kindness and skill in making this book possible. My steadfast, supportive agent, David Godwin, has a house on the North Sea coast and from the first he understood what this book was attempting. Andy Lovell has designed all of the lovely, lyrical covers for my books with Canongate and this one catches the mood of the sea brilliantly. On a long and often broken journey over a year, I met many people whose willingness to share their experience of living and working by the North Sea was warming and enriching. Often we met near the shore or on a promenade, and after a time I began to notice that as they talked, we did not look at each other but instead out over the waves and their shushing rhythms. Over 800 miles, I often stopped to stare and to wonder.